Afternoon Tea in Heaven

conversations with the spirit world
as experienced by Nanette Adams

tokoloshe books

tokoloshe books

First Published 2002 by Tokoloshe Books
an imprint of STE Publishers
PO Box 93446
Yeoville 2143

First printed 2002

Printed and bound in South Africa by Jakaranda Printers
Tel:

ISBN Number: 1-919855-04-1

Editor: Pippa Dyer
Consulting editor: Cathy Eden
Illustrations: Andrew Lindsay
Book and Cover Design: Thabo Matlejoane

Set in 11pt on 12pt Perpetua and Scala Sans

Dedications

To my children Michéle and Michael who were there from the beginning to share this extraordinary experience with me.

Contents

Chapters

Section 3 Convents, Monasteries & the Church

Section 4 Philosophies of Life

Acknowledgements

Mazoé Bosman (Tara)

My heartfelt thanks to Michéle for insisting that I should meet Mazoë Bosman, without whom this book would never have existed.

In 1966 as the wife of the British Consul, Charles Adams, a chance meeting led me to meet Zoë, the ancient soul whose abilities as a psychic medium are used in this book. Thereafter, a special chapter in my life began. One that was to culminate in the fruition of *Afternoon Tea in Heaven*.

Besides our group who were sitters in the circle at the séance sessions, I owe my acknowledgements and gratitude to the people who assisted me in getting this book out of my soul and onto the shelves!

To my friends, Ken MacKenzie for his most helpful interest and encouragement, and Rosemary Howell who first put the transcriptions onto computer, some of them still in longhand. Rosemary generously laid aside her own work on the I Ching to do this for me, a big thank you.

To Michael for the long hours carefully considering which pages from the five hundred page mountain of manuscripts should be used, I was too attached to be the one to do it. To Michéle, thank you again for another propitious introduction, this time to Pippa and Reedwaan who dared to take the plunge with me into the unknown. It has been a pleasure working with Pippa who used much midnight oil devising the unusual editing and co-ordination of the manuscript. Thank you also to Cathy Eden for taking a deep interest in the book and assisting us with her sharp editing eye to bring it to fruition.

Finally but not least, to the team at STE who translated the vision onto paper and made something special out of material that was not all that familiar to them. In particular thank you to Thabo, a young designer for her layout and imaginative cover design.

To everyone who comes into contact with this book, I would like to say that I have noticed that when we meet evolved souls half way, they in turn touch our lives in surprising and wonderful ways.

I hope that *Afternoon Tea in Heaven* will be an enriching experience to all who touch it.

1

Living in the Spirit World

Chapter 1: Crossing Over

Nanette Adams
"How it all began"

This book is not mine. It belongs to many personalities, known and unknown, famous and infamous, who have long since left the earth plane but had the earnest desire to make contact through a physical medium. Their reasons were many and varied. Some wished for their own peace of mind to clear away misconceptions about their previous lives. Others, rather like travellers who have gone on ahead of us to a new country, simply wished to share their newly found knowledge and experiences. They hoped to bring comfort and a happy assurance of the activity, beauty and interest that exists in that other dimension where they now live.

It was during the summer of 1966 at Narrow Waters, my beautiful home at Bishops Court in Cape Town, that my daughter Michéle spent the afternoon with two student friends. They were the grandchildren of Mrs Mazoë Bosman. One of them suggested they all drop in on gran. It was quite late when my daughter joyously returned home to an anxiously cross mum.

"I will tell you all about our evening in the morning," she said. I had a feeling it would be wise to possess my soul in patience until then.

At breakfast next day, in the garden with the warm sun filtering through the oak trees, Michéle recounted her meeting with the amazing elderly lady and her spiritual experiences.

On being introduced to my daughter, Zoë immediately began to describe my mother, Ella Tait, and the unusual bracelets she always wore. She also spoke of my son, Michael, whose health was causing some concern. This was all true! The group then settled in for some of gran's stories on 'spirits and things'.

"Mum, you really must meet her – she wants to meet you – will you phone her?"

Of course I did phone her and was delighted to hear her merry voice. I learned that she was recuperating from an operation and arranged to bring her to my house and meet Ella. During this time, I often assisted Zoë by taking meals to her house or driving her to places. Very often we would discuss philosophies and share psychic experiences. One day, during a lull in the conversation, we noticed Zoë being taken very gently into a deep trance by a spirit being who proceeded to introduce herself as Angela. We found her quite delightful and the three of us chatted away as easily as old friends – which apparently we were, lifetimes ago!

One of the things that Angela remarked on was the garden and the many beautiful trees in it, the view of the mountain and the peaceful vibrations of the home. My husband, Charles Adams, and I had recently moved into Bishops Court when he commenced his tour of duty as British Consul to the Cape of Good Hope.

Angela suggested that we start a group or circle, for which she would be the 'Doorkeeper' and 'Mistress of Ceremonies', which indeed she was for the next twelve years.

This experience was to bring together sixteen strangers who would blend harmoniously into a group, desired by the guiding spirits who wished to communicate with us through the precious mediumship of Zoë Bosman, or Tara as Angela later told us that she was called in spirit.

Although there were odd visitors from time to time, the main participants of the group that you will meet in this story were these remarkable people:

Ella and Rennie Tait, my parents who were both retired from the British Theatre world and whose inspiration showed me a different way of life.

Michéle and Michael Maxwell, my children who were young students of about nine and fourteen years old when this story began

Nora Rowlands who was a tree conservationist whom Tara and I met one day when we were browsing in I.D. Booksellers. Tara was commenting on one of the spiritual books when we suddenly heard a voice say, "Carry on, I'm listening too". We turned around and there was Nora! An elderly woman with gleaming eyes. We were soon to discover that she was an indefatigable seeker of knowledge. Needless to say she became an enthusiastic member of our group.

Charles Orfang who was an elderly gentleman and commercial artist from Scandinavia. He was a friend of Tara's, a charming man with white hair and a beard. He became a stoical member of the group and died at the ripe age of ninety-nine!

Guy Baron was a South African businessman interested in the esoteric. He would come to Tara for advice and she invited him into the group. He would particularly enjoy getting in touch with his guides.

Annabel Rampley was an Italian who was with the Diplomatic Corps. She met a South African in Italy during the war, married, had children and did exceedingly well at the IP Consultancy New Foundation.

Brian Buckley was Annabel's son of about twenty at the time. He was studying Civil Engineering.

William Richardson was the writer of Indian travel stories, a disabled man of approximately fourty. Tara would often go to his flat to give sessions.

Betty Schelp was the wife of an American consul living in Cape Town.

Joan Goodwin was a spiritual researcher who was involved with the Aquarian Foundation.

Beau Rowlands became an ornithologist and writer.

Helen and Walter de Bruyn were both esoteric researchers from Holland who joined us infrequently.

During the time of the sittings we had many spirit visitors whose discourses and conversations were tape-recorded, some of them now transcribed into this book.

Zoe's trance condition would last an hour, sometimes a little longer. All that time she was quite unconscious of the men and women using her body and vocal chords.

After every recorded meeting during the first two months, my tape recorder had to be repaired by an increasingly perplexed electrician. Eventually Angela explained how Michael Faraday, the famous 19th Century electronic scientist, had kindly come and adjusted the machine to take the high electrical field that accompanied many of the communicators. We had no further trouble after that.

We learnt that Angela's last incarnation was as the famous Victorian poetess, Christina Rossetti, sister of the pre-Raphaelite painter and poet Dante Gabriel Rossetti. She explained that by using a different name in spirit, the vibrations of the previous earth life can be more easily severed, thus freeing the soul of any sad or painful lingerings connected with that life. It is, however, a personal choice.

Although some of our visitors emphatically refused to give names, some were clearly recognisable. In other cases, Angela would give their earth names later.

From earliest childhood Tara had manifested great psychic powers and a faith in God that sustained her through a life of much physical pain, several life-threatening illnesses and the death of three of her six children. (One died at birth, one of diphtheria and the third one, Michael, died of meningitis.)

Tara was born at Aliwal North in South Africa in October 1900. After her marriage to Dr Koos Bosman, she helped him in his clinic in the outlying district at Keis Kammahoek until they moved to Cape Town where he became port health doctor until his retirement.

Although a busy doctor's wife and mother, she always had time for people from all cultures and walks of life who came to her door. People would continually be seeking and receiving wise advice in times of trouble. Tara would give consolation with proof of survival after the death of a loved one, sometimes through a spirit artist who would use her hand to draw the portrait of the person who had passed on.

She could not turn anyone away even if she herself felt unwell. But her private time was the very early hours of the morning, for three to five hours, which she strictly reserved for prayer and the deep meditation practice called Sabikalpa Samadhi, an evolved yoga practice known as 'The breathless deathless sleep'.[1] This practice took her far from her earth body to commune in spirit with her teachers and the ascended masters who, it is said, direct their wisdom and power towards the help and upliftment of mankind.

Although Tara was concerned with the serious matters to do with earth, she also, on her flights of the soul experienced a joy and ecstasy that was almost beyond words. She diarised as much as she could.

A spiritual mentor, the Master Babaji[2], taught her how to dematerialise and re-

---

1. See the book *The Science of Self Realisation* A.C. Bhaktivedanta Swami Prabhupada.
2. Babaji was a teacher – a master from India – a high soul who taught in the groups in America. He is well known in spiritual teaching groups around the world, such as the Aquarian Foundation.

materialise the atoms and molecules of her body, making her invisible to the human eye.[3]

The first time she attempted this, Tara was sitting in her meditation chair, a little later than usual, when she saw one of her daughters open the door and look around the room at the chair in which she was sitting. She watched her daughter go out again and then heard her call, "Where is Mom?" The domestic was heard to reply, "She is in her room praying." During this time Tara quickly and literally pulled herself together so that when her daughter returned to check the room again, Tara was still sitting in her chair, but now completely visible!

They then went out on a normal shopping expedition and after a while Tara thought she should explain what had occurred earlier. Her daughter's laconic reply was simply, "Mom, nothing you do ever surprises me!"

Things of the spirit are not always serious. I recall an afternoon when Tara came to tea. We were chatting lightly. Tara took one bite of her scone then continued talking whilst putting out her hand to take another bite, only to find that the scone had disappeared from her plate. She looked at me questioningly. No, I had not touched it, I had not moved from my chair. We searched high and low for that scone and neither of my dogs were in the room at the time! She decided it must be one of her young friends in spirit who was most likely to enjoy playing such a trick. We laughed and left it at that.

Two days later I had a phone call from Tara asking me to go to her immediately as there was something she wanted to show me.

I went straight to her room where she had been sitting alone by the window reading all the morning, and there in the centre of the room, on the floor, was a neat little pile of crumbs ... scone crumbs!

On another occasion, during a sitting, a spirit guide brought a young American sailor from a recently sunken vessel. According to Angela, several of the boys were in a frantic state of mind, being engaged to be married next home leave. They were deeply dismayed, even angry at finding themselves in spirit. Some of the sailors had not yet fully realised where they were. They were still confused and needed a particular kind of help. So they were brought to our meeting to watch the proceedings.

One of them was placed in Tara's body so that he could speak with us. Angela assured us afterwards that they would soon be all right. In fact she confirmed this a month or so later.

After closing the meeting we were having tea when I noticed to my horror, a very dark, wet patch on the carpet. It looked like a footprint and it was not my carpet in this rented consular house!

The room in which we held our weekly séance had a wall-to-wall, fairly deep piled white carpet with an indented self-coloured pattern.

Well, the five of us, including Tara, were on our knees, feeling, smelling and tasting this footprint, which had appeared during the séance and quite flattened the carpet to that shape! On investigation we found that it was sodden, wet, oily to the touch and salty to the taste. We all took turns in rubbing it dry, trying to get the pile back to normal, but to no avail.

---

3. *These practices are explained more fully in a book called,* Autobiography of a Yogi *by Yogananda.*

It was later explained to us that the conditions under which the sailors died were still within the mind which brought about this manifestation. To my eternal sorrow we never thought to photograph it.

That evening my husband suddenly asked, "What on earth is that footprint in the carpet over there?" I had some trouble trying to explain, as he was not, shall we say, quite fully aware of what actually happened at a Tuesday afternoon tea party!

Knowing my husband's disinterest in God and spirit communication, I simply left it unsaid. However, it wasn't long before the cat leapt out of the bag! This bit of Consular office news came to me eventually from Charles Orfang, in his marvellously understated manner.

It was after one of my ladies' luncheons to which I had invited Tara that the conversation turned to things spiritual. She fascinated everyone with her occult reminiscences, mentioning too, how we met. She commented on our weekly séances at my house, which of course was in constant use for delightful but most conservative official entertaining. One of the ladies, on her return home that day, related my extramural activities to her husband, one of the Britannic Majesty's vice-consuls, who thereupon, so it is said, rolled upon the floor in helpless mirth!

Only to a very few would Tara reveal her inner life, preferring always to be regarded as a very ordinary woman. She was a motherly figure, the epitome of kindness, seldom alone, for people loved to be near her, attracted by her warmth, her wide knowledge and delightful sense of humour.

This was the person who lent her body and vocal cords to approximately one hundred men and women that they might contact earth once more to bring you their message.

Tara's health was failing. The cause was not known to us, she never spoke about it, but the sittings ended, sadly, in 1979 when she died.

But here begins our story with an introduction by Angela, as the 'Doorkeeper'.

Angela as Christina Rossetti (1830–1894)
"The land of the Lotus Eaters"

Christina Rossetti was born in London. Although suffering from ill health, she still managed to publish her earliest works at twenty years old, in the first issue of *The Germ* under the pseudonym Ellen Alleyne. *Goblin Market* was her best known collection of poetry. Other works included: *The Prince's Progress; Time Flies; The Face of the Deep: A Devotional Commentary on the Apocalypse* and *Memory Serves*. She was a devout Catholic.

I am not going to philosophise now, I come for light relief you know! I am a guide of Tara. Do you know what Tara means in the Hindu language? It is Princess of Light.

I was a poetess, a very minor one who lived on the earth in the Victorian age. I did achieve a little fame, not too much but quite enough. Am I vain glorious?

I thought very deeply of life after death and had inquired with great ardour and fervour into what it would be like when I eventually passed into spirit.

My own life on the earth was not at all a happy one, although I'm not complaining for I had chosen it before birth and knew full well what it would mean. It was crammed full of vicissitudes, trials and tribulations, heartaches and frustrations. Goodness me, I'm going on like a dictionary! I must correct my eloquence a little, mustn't I?

I freely admit my yearning heart was happy when I finally left my body and found myself in spirit.

Well, being a poetess I had visualised this perfect heaven. You see a poet translates earthly beauty into visions, so a great cloud cluster will become a castle in the sky, will it not? We seem to have an inner registering. I have discussed this matter with the other poets with whom I am in daily contact. I call it 'music of the spheres'.

Yes, well, it gives me the greatest joy to tell you all that the anticipation can fall ridiculously short of the realisation. I was much-blessed inasmuch as I avoided, through my guide who fetched me, the halls of disorder, and 'the mists'.[4] I have no knowledge of passing though them and I found myself, when I opened my eyes, in the third plane, what is euphemistically called here the 'Summerland' where all the families come. There are great and wonderful reunions. I have called it, 'The land of the lotus eaters.'

We can follow what we wish to do, whatever our frustrations on the earth plane.

---

4. *The Mists, see 'The Prelate' on page 27.*

In more beautiful words, God shall wipe away all tears from their faces. This is what happens. For those who have sorrow and grief (and which of us do not have sorrow and grief on the earth), it is a haven of peace, beauty, and harmony.

After a while the soul settles down into this glorious routine and is occasionally inclined to become a little lazy. That is a peculiar word, but do not worry, the time comes inevitably when you have a mental nudge! You can return to the earth or you can atone and work off your karma in the lower astral, helping all the poor souls there to progress to the light. Oh, the work is limitless and the joy is limitless.

I have died a second death and have passed on into the fourth plane[5]. I had thought there could be nothing more wonderful or beautiful than this but was permitted to glimpse over the horizon into the next state and it is an illusion. An illusion that points the way to finding reality. It is the school to which the soul descends to pass through the kindergarten stage, upwards.

I was a school teacher for a short time on the earth, my dear friends, therefore as I am constantly referring back to my period, which my brother[6] refers to as a school marm. So I use the word kindergarten and take you right up to university.

We are infants of the spirit world surrounding the earth planet. I don't like to ask too many questions because I show my ignorance so vastly. Others in joy say to me, "You are too ignorant to be a guide on the earth plane, come back!"

Ask Tara to take you there in sleep state, for then you will get a glimpse of what awaits you on the Summerland plane.

I must go now.

---

5. See 'the Prelate' page 27.
6. Pre-Raphealite poet and painter Dante Gabriel Rossetti (1828–1882).

The Unconquerable – a British racing driver
"Why don't these parsons tell us what's going to happen when we die?"

The light … it's so bright!

I thought I could come in here and have a few words but … just a minute, I have to adjust to this light. How many are there of you here? Four? Nanette and you, Charles and you're Ella – Cinderella! And you're Guy.

This is very strange to me. I have to gather the reins. It's like driving a four-in-hand here! Yes, it's very strange indeed.

I was told I could come to acclimatise myself in this other unknown world where I am at the moment. I'm in that ghastly position known as half way. I'm neither here nor there and I'm neither there nor here! It's all most damnably confusing.

Why don't these parsons tell us what's going to happen when we die? I remember when my little brother Brian died, the parson came and my mother … forgive me for a moment because this is getting me untangled from the earth … my mother saying to this dog collar, "Why did God do this to me? My beautiful child." And he said (you know their dreadful voices), "Who are we to question God?"

My mother was overcome with grief about the death of this child, which seemed to her to be so damnably unfair, as he was a child of her middle age, you know, a Benjamin.

She wept and wept and said, "Can you tell me where my Brian has gone and will I see him again?"

The fellow said to her, "I do not know. You must have faith."

My poor distraught mother said, "In what? You give me nothing to have faith in!"

Then my father left the bedroom and went to his brother (I've never forgotten his words) and said to him, "For God's sake, Hugh, go into that room and kick that confounded fellow out, he's driving my wife mad."

And that's my experience of parsons. They know nothing, pretending to know all. Well, they should be taught how there is this world … oh yes, there is this world which I am discovering.

When I was at Cambridge there was a fellow who was always talking about the spirit world. I used to say to him, "Poppycock! There ain't no such animal!" Now I know what he meant. Why didn't I listen to him then? The gate would have been opened for me and I would have found my way instead of groping like a mumbling idiot in the mists.

I was an ordinary run-of-the-mill bloke on the earth … in the earth, on the earth, it sounds so funny. We don't say that when we are there, do we? We talk about 'this world of ours' not this funny rather pedantic expression 'on the earth'. For if you're on the earth or in the earth, what does it matter?

I had a death that is quite a common way of dying today. I was killed in a motor smash. I was a racing driver, one of those hell-for-leather fellows. Never counted the cost, never thought my ticket would come up. Well, I had this crash. I knew nothing of it, and it was over instantly. Do I bore you? If I bore you, send me away for you have it in your power to say we've had enough of you! But you are helping me in a way that these spirit guides cannot because I'm in this in between state and can use this lady's body quite easily.

You see it is not so long ago that I ended up in that flaming wreck. The shock of that holocaust ejected me from my body very much the same way that a parachutist jumps from a plane. I was flung out of my body from the force. Well, now comes to me the strangest part of it all, which confounded me so. I knew nothing of an afterlife beyond Spooky's talk at Cambridge. From the day that Brian died no clergyman was permitted to come to my mother and church became out of bounds to us.

Now I stood there. Yes, I stood on my two feet and make no mistake it seemed to me I was still in my racing togs, my helmet and all the paraphernalia. I noticed a smell of smoke, you understand, it was all so real. I had smelt it before when there had been crashes and I thought, 'some poor devil's had his chips' and I strode over quickly to see who it was, see if I could lend a hand. I looked down and … my God, I had the shock of my life when I saw it was myself! Well, that was only a glimpse because the flames didn't leave much to be recognised.

Now I ask you kindly people, can you imagine my dilemma? There I stood, a solid human being it seemed to me, fully accoutred in my racing outfit and there was my burning body. Talk about a man having delirium tremens. I thought I had gone mad.

I realised that the car that was burning was my own and I thought I had escaped unharmed. I looked down at my hands in their gloves and moved my feet. I felt my head, it was solid, all solid. There was no pain so I thought I had got a crack, unknown to me, through my helmet and my brains were addled. I thought, "Ye Gods! This is the end of me now? I'm a lunatic!"

Two years ago … yes, you read about me in the paper … 'The unconquerable' they called me. 'Flirted with death' is what they said. But death caught up with me in the end.

Well, I went up to my mechanics in the pit. Pitifully, I touched each one on the shoulder and murmured, "Turn around, for God's sake and look at me. Turn round!" I started to sob, I cried like a kid. The one who had laughed at death, the one who had no fear, the one who had survived two other crashes.

But this was different. Why didn't they talk to me? Why didn't they turn round and say something?

Now comes the most terrifying part of this whole drama of mine, when I put my gloved hands on their shoulders, can you imagine my horror when my fingers seemed to sink through their flesh? Then I really thought I was mad.

I wandered away, so I thought, from the place. I wandered like that Jew who wandered. For two thousand years it seemed to me, I cannot tell you where I was because it was a phantasmagoria, a nightmare. I have been told since that guides were trying to get through to me.

I enclosed myself in a cloud of horror and a cloud of fear and it was like a cocoon. Nothing and nobody could reach me because you mustn't forget I was convinced I was mad. There was nothing to tell me I wasn't mad. I only noticed after a while that I no longer had my gloves and I no longer had my crash helmet.

Do not think that help is not present. Oh yes, the lifelines are there waiting to be held out to those who are confused. It is our training on the earth that is so at fault!

At long last, I lifted my hands in supplication and cried out from the depths of my despairing heart, "God help me, God help me" and instantly the cocoon burst and fell away from me and there was a light … it seemed to me to be a light. As I gazed at the first gleam of light I had seen in my darkness I saw it take the shape of a man. In those eyes looking at me, it was only a yard or two away from me, I saw pity. I hurled myself at this man who had taken me out of my madness and I heard him say, "Gently brother, gently please", because I was suffocating him in my embrace. Here was a human being, a man, helping me. I patted his back and I thought 'thank God' when my fingers didn't go right through his flesh. I was sane at last, I was sane!

"Tell me, when did they take me out of the lunatic asylum? When? When?"

He said, "My friend, you were never in a lunatic asylum."

Do you know what I said to him? "Then where the hell have I been?"

He replied, "You have been in hell, that's where you have been."

I looked around me and I said, "Where are the fires of hell?"

He said, "They are the fires that burnt in your own brain because you didn't know. You had closed your heart and your mind to the truth of God."

Well, now I am now coming out of the darkness with his tutelage. He is with me. But as a finale I have to contact flesh again to part from it, so that I can go forward in confidence now that I am in my spirit body, which, I may inform you, is a facsimile of the me ... the I ... the bloke, whatever you like to call me, that I was on earth.

Now this will be my bowing out of the vibration of the world in which I am entrapped because otherwise I cannot, after being in the darkness for nearly two years, emerge into the great light ...

Did you hear me saying, "The light, the light"? I felt it on my eyeballs, I felt the light was too strong because here where all these great spirits come, the light is almost appallingly bright to me. Now I am going into light, not that light, I couldn't bear it, but I come with a double intent and that is to tell you that you have been so kind to me, I was so afraid I would bore you to death.

All: Certainly not.

The Unconquerable: Secondly, gratitude to this woman whose body I have been allowed to use. I have but one aim and object, as they say in the courtroom when they take the oath, "The truth and nothing but the truth, may God help me."

I am going to become a crusader for truth. I am going to fill myself like one of those geese they force feed with the truth of the spirit world, of the life I know is waiting for me. I'm going to take post-graduate courses until I know the *a b c* of it all! Then I am going to lurk in the shades and in the mists and as I see these poor people come, they too will hear me saying, "Gently please", as I embrace them.

Now I have to go. I am not going to give you my name, it doesn't signify a damn anyway, but I am feeling so released.

Sitter: Perhaps your first name?

The Unconquerable: No, I must forget it, but I will come back when I am clear of everything of the earth. I came to cleanse myself. Now you have released me and I am like the bride who smells orange blossom.

Sitter: Take our love with you.

Many sessions down the line Angela came in one day with this message.

Angela with a message from the racing driver

I have a message from the racing driver! He wanted me to tell you that he has graduated now with full honours in his new world! Yes, he will do great work over here.

You see Guy, I don't know whether you understand these people who are in the mists. It is impossible for them to see those guides who go down to help them at the beginning and later on, even much later on, because their eyes are not accustomed to light, being in the mists and darkness. And the guides, even such humble ones as myself, have a light, a vibrationary light.

Marian on her starlit path remembers the experience of death
"Rest in peace, I am far too happy, that's the last thing I want to do"

I was cremated. It's the best way, without a shadow of doubt. No little worms crawling around. Oh, don't ever be buried. Cremation is much cleaner you know.

Ella: I've always thought that.

Marian: I wasn't very old you know, only thirty-two. How old would I be now? Yes. Thirty-seven, that's right. I died through an illness in my heart and quite glad to go really.

I just came to put my little oar in. It's awfully nice to be here talking to you. I could never take part in anything strenuous even though I had this awful longing to have a child but wasn't able to have a baby and that has to be experienced to be understood. We only discovered that after we were married … that my heart …

We knew then that my time was limited. There was nothing to be done, no surgical help. But I knew and had great faith that nothing is ever lost. In my hours of pain when I was alone and couldn't sleep, it was strange that if I took it all philosophically and did not rail against things, how the avenues of life opened up one by one. Deep within, the soul knows the time has come. Would you like to know how I died?

Charles Orfang: Yes, of course, tell us.

Marian: I am told I have five minutes more. I hope I can encompass this all in five minutes. I'll try anyway. I was always one of those fast speakers, I always felt I had so little time left I simply had to bundle on to the next word. My husband used to say I was quick fire!

I had to sleep in a special bed that was high and I can remember my husband had to use a handle to turn the top part up to raise the bed. The bedroom door was open between his room and mine so I could call out to him. I wouldn't have him sleeping there with me.

Don't think I am setting myself up as a martyr because that's not the case at all. I would 'l   oved to have him sleep with me, the comfort in the morning. But I was restless all through the night. My window was wide open too, because I read an old fashioned poem once about 'throwing the window wide and letting the soul escape'. I realise now what a fallacy it all was. Oh, three minutes left!

I was lying on my bed very late one night and I had an attack. Struggling for breath … it seemed very bright, brighter than usual, it wasn't quite moonlight but it was luminous and I seemed to turn my head on the pillow and very far away I heard music and I thought, 'I wonder who is playing the wireless so late at night?'

Then I realised there was a different quality about the sound of this music coming to me and the moonlight became more and more luminous and the music became sweeter and sweeter. I had no idea that I was dead.

Ella: What a lovely way to go.

Marian: You see, it's all so natural. I knew it would come so I never fought it at all. I just accepted it. I looked at the moonlight and it seemed to me that it was a sort of pathway coming through the window and I thought wouldn't it be nice to walk that pathway of light.

So you see … I just slipped out of bed. You must remember I wasn't quite sure I was dead because I felt exactly … me! But the breathlessness had gone and the pain had gone. So I just stepped out into the pathway, the window was gone. It just wasn't there any more and there was this radiant pathway. It seemed to lead right up to the stars, which I could see quite plainly. I felt so free.

For a moment I did feel fear when I remembered I was dead, but then I had been dying for so long and the pathway was so beautiful.

Yet it was lonely for me. I think most of us feel that after death, when the spirit body separates from the body of which it has been counterpart for so long, it feels a little lonely. I always had the feeling right from school days that when you died you had angels around you. I haven't seen a single angel yet! But the moment that lonely feeling came over me, at my side appeared two radiant figures. One of them was my sister Rosalie. She died when I was nine. The other was my grandmother whom I had never known. Isn't it strange how the mind works? I said, "Oh, poor mummy. Oh, poor mummy. Two of us gone!" My grandmother, who must have been a brisk woman on the earth, got hold of my arm and said, "Listen darling, don't talk nonsense. Come along, you are coming home now."

That's all I remember. I just remember putting my feet on the pathway and then there was nothing.

The Prelate
"Not even the creator can return the soul to the body once the cord has been severed"

A high ecclesiastical dignitary, a bishop perhaps, known only to us as the Prelate.

I will lift the corner of the veil for a moment, for I do not want your curiosity to get the better of you that you lose the thread of my discourse. Therefore let me say I was a well known prelate of the church.

No, don't conjecture. I get it from each one of you. You are all wrong.

I speak of the spiritual body, the facsimile of the body. Should one of you die, I shall not go into the electrons, neutrons and molecules, but as you withdraw from your physical body and wait poised above it, it is visible to the clairvoyant eye on the earth.

When the silver cord is detached, severed, never ever to return again, not even the creator, the great one, can return the soul to the body. Therefore, I give the lie here and now, to the exaggerated story that Jesus died.

Not even he could avoid death, my friends. By death we mean the severance of the cord of life. Well, had that happened to Jesus not even he could have come back to his body. Remember that, for the truth is coming to the earth plane in the not too distant future. Forearmed by your knowledge, when it comes, you will be able to accept it.

To continue, you drift away from your body in a kind of mist, a beautiful half dreaming state in which you seem to be sinking, rising … sinking, rising. But it is a beautiful state, believe me, it is the anaesthetic provided by God to do away with any shock of parting from the body.

I do not include here, my friends, 'sudden death'. I speak of the ordinary passing of the spiritual body.

The facsimile of the physical body bears the simulacra of every organ in the body. In the foetus, the cells, spiritual and physical, were reproduced together, therefore you take with you the simulacra of every cell you had in the physical body. You are not going to use them. No, no, life changes from the moment the silver cord is severed, but do remember, you have gone through life with the knowledge in your mind of all these organs of your body. Sometimes completely wrong, believe me, but you know the organs are there. Therefore if you found yourself in your spirit or astral body minus your organs, you would feel rather queer, would you not? You would feel empty and think 'I'm empty, what's the matter with me?' Well, you are not empty, so we'll pass the matter by.

Now you have gone and your sleep-state will vary according to your disposition and peculiarity of temperament. There are those who come out of the sleep-state immediately because they wish to. This is the secret of it my friends, they wish it. They have done with the earth life before they passed from it, so they are prepared. They wish for the great dawn of their spirit life, for the great aurora, so their sleep-state is not as prolonged, perhaps, as it is with those timid souls who say, "What will

I see? What will happen to me?"

It is like a bird that has been in a cage for a long time. If you open the door, do you think the bird flies out at once? Not the average bird. He peers around for quite a long time. He has his freedom but has forgotten what freedom is like. It is a new venture for him out in the open and out into the beyond.

Well, that is the human soul venturing out of the human cage.

God opens the door by severing the cord and the soul should soar like a bird testing a remembered freedom. For remember, you have always been a soul and always will be a soul, given by God. It is only from God that souls are born.

The Akashic Records

For the soul who welcomes the new dawn, before his mental vision will pass his entire Akashic record, written on the ether surrounding him. His own vibration, his every deed and every thought, be it good, bad or indifferent. All that has followed him in his pathway through the earth, his training school. That is why we come to say, "Oh, be careful how you live upon the earth plane." Guard every thought, guard every word and every deed, for you and you alone are the judge of how and why you have lived upon the earth plane. There is no great judge sitting on an awful throne. No. You and you alone are the judge.

Now you are faced with your Akashic records. There you see your life portrayed as it reels past you. Your entire life and let me tell you, you will sit appalled at some of the things you thought, said and did! You'll sit entranced at other things you thought were of no importance at all and you will see what wonderful action and re-action to little deeds you brought about. Well, according to your make up, physically, spiritually and psychically, you benefit or you don't.

Then you are left alone in whatever plane you have been destined to come, by the way that you have lived on the earth. Not from the point of view of importance on the earth, titles mean nothing, fame means nothing, unless it has been for good deeds. Remember, bow your knee to no man on this earth, only to God, or if you have to bow, bow your knee to the God within that prompted that man or woman to become great, that is all.

Do you think I did not feel contempt for those that prostrated themselves at my feet? It was to my office. What is office in the eye of God? Nothing. It does not exist in spirit. Ceremonial does not exist, burnt offering sacrifice does not exist. It is how you are, what you are as God in your body. Now you let that God take supremacy over the arrogant earth self and live, think and act as God would have you.

The planes

You come to the plane, which you have earned for yourself by your thought processes on the earth. There you will find friends that have been waiting for you, your loved ones, even friends from the long ago past who have come down to greet the wanderer back into the fold. Well, time will pass and you will have no realisation of the passage of time. When I speak of planes, I speak of a condition of light and beauty to which you go.

The third plane – Summerland or Family Land

You will come to what is euphemistically known as the Summerland or Family Land. The Summerland is a place of existence identical to the earth plane where we can, if we wish, stay five to six hundred years. The Summerland is where you meet those bound to you by blood and by love, but blood does not always bring love. No, there are many bound by ties of blood who, alas, hate each other on the earth plane. You do not have to meet them. Why should you? You meet those to whom you are drawn by the great 'as it is above, so it is below' love. And they will be waiting for you.

You will be in a transport of joy, for there you will see the etherealisation of the planet, mother earth. You will see it as it came from the dream of God, as it emerged from the mind of the creator and became reality.

When you come there, all is bliss. The bliss is divine, but let me tell you, this is but a shadow of what is to be!

In time you will grow weary of this life. This is the soul saying, 'onward' and the moment that urge goes out of the soul, the elder brothers are there to answer. Oh, they have been watching, unknown to you, for they are on the plane above, to which as yet, you have no access. The light would be too bright for the eye newly arrived from the earth, be it fifty years or a hundred. They will come to you and make themselves visible and they will say, "Well, my friend, what is it you wish to do?"

Now, which one of us on the earth has not had a secret dream? A dream of being a great poet, great artist, great gardener, great anything. But circumstances or time fought against the fulfilment of your unexpressed dream and you passed into spirit with this 'but a dream'. Remember?

Now comes your time to fulfil your dream from the mind of God, so you say, "I would love to be a gardener", and immediately you are wafted away.

Oh yes, you do not walk now in the slow heavy way of the earth on your two tired feet. You are wafted to an assembly of great masters of the past and you are taken to hall after hall, where they sit.

Young aspiring students like you are going to learn from the fingertips just what made these men the great masters that they are. There they are, in their great love, not going onwards, remaining there giving you a taste of heaven they knew upon the earth plane. That which they expressed through their ten fingers or paintbrushes.

Well, there you may practise your art for as long as you like. Remember you are in the Summerland. You are not on the great planes, the causal or mental planes, no, you are not even within glimpsing sight of them yet, but you are at peace with your dream. The dream that you have nurtured in your heart. Your soul God within.

Now you are free, complete, fulfilled and inevitably the time will come when you master your dream and stand master of your art as they are.

The fourth plane – The 'second death' or transference into the spirit plane

Now you may wish to collect your own band around you. You may wish to express your joy of fulfilment to those who come up from the earth plane, tired and dispirited, 'let me do for them what you have done for me'. But on the other hand, you may aspire to go onward. So you say diffidently, "I would like to go onward". Then my friends, comes what is known as the second death.

You must remember that while you are in the Summerland you are still in your astral body, inextricably holding the earth in your mind. Now if you wish to pass into the fourth plane, the first of the mental planes, you have to shake earth forever, so you pass into the same pleasant state, voluntarily.

With the same pleasant falling and rising of consciousness as when you parted from the body, you cast off the astral body. The great plan works up, as it is above so it is below, rather in the same way that you cast off the physical body of your mother and you emerge in all your beauty.

Now you are vibrating at such a speed, you feel uncomfortable on this Summerplane despite its beauty and its radiance. Although the soul coming from the earth plane feels no discomfort now, you are passing to the fourth plane and you come under the tutelage of the elder brothers who now start on your mind.

It is here that the vista beyond the earth plane is shown to you. Oh, very slowly is the new pupil released on this upward path. For remember this birth into pure spirit is very recent. Think of yourself as a babe in pure spirit.

The landscape is growing more beautiful, fairy-like, less solid than the Summerland appeared. Nevertheless, solid enough for its purpose. You can now, if you wish, work with the power of thought. You have been working with your hands on the Summerland but you are now working with God's instrument … the thinking mind, the reasoning power, the intellect and you are now taught to create.

You can and you must take my word for it, that this is the truth. For I am here to speak truth, what else?

You can create your own landscape. Do I hear a startled exclamation? It is true! For you are now master of the ether and you are taught to bring the molecules into creation.

You can create your ideal home, where you wish to live in this wondrous place, this mental plane. It is the beginning of the upward path of the soul on its way back to the source from which it came.

You must forgive me, but when I look upon the beauty and wonderment that is the source, I grow faint with emotion, I can't help it. I come from the fourth plane, I make no bones about it, why should I? I shall not pose as a martyr, or somebody acting in a sacrificial manner, no, it is a joy for me to come. But it is difficult, for although I am only on the fourth plane, there are three planes above me. While I am on the mental plane, I have to decrease my vibrations a great deal to come down to the Summerland. I cannot tarry there too long, for I feel like a diver on the deep sea-bed, weighted with lead. I feel sluggish and if I break off the threads of my discourse for a moment, well, I lose it. It floats out into the ether and I have to reach out and bring it back so that I can carry on without interruption of what I came to tell you.

Are you enjoying this? Taking it in?

[An enthusiastic response from the group]

Now I am on the fourth plane, here I am introduced to the glory of God.

Now it is here that you feel 'I must go on'. The soul yearning to be nearer to the source, the greater the urge, oh my friends, the greater this urge upwards and onwards.

You say to your loving tutors, by this time it is no longer pupil-teacher, it is brothers, you say, "I wish to go on".

Now comes to you the choice, would you like to go down as a pedagogue, a teacher to those infant souls? Oh, my friends, the struggle is great for you to incarnate as the great ones have and bring back with you the light of God and borne it as a torch aloft for mankind to proceed upon the upward path and not remain merged in the dirt and mire of earth.

Reincarnation is entirely by choice. Your own choice. Do not think that anybody will look on you askance when you decide, "No, I'm finished with the earth, I've had enough". You can say, "I wish to go onward to God" or you can say, "I must go back".

The knowledge is hidden within. Each man, his own way back to God.

If your way to God is finished with the earth, you will then pass into what is known as the Causal plane.

The fifth plane – Causal plane

Causal is the beginning of everything that ever was, that ever is, that ever shall be, from everlasting to everlasting. There the book of life is opened wide for you to read.

Now eons and eons will pass while the soul, rising … soaring … expanding its way to the Godhead, becomes Godlike in itself.

The light is so great, so blinding that even we of the fourth plane cannot venture there, we would be too uncomfortable. We would shrink, we're not ready for it. So I cannot tell you too much about that, do you understand? I can only tell you by hearsay.

Then you come to the sixth plane, which is very short-lived.

The sixth plane – The Great Christ sphere

You are here resident but a short time. Now I touch upon the very hinterland of God and my head must bow, for it is from here, from the very vicinity of the source that the great Christ spirits have elected to leave it all behind and take upon themselves an earth body again.

I name you but four – Jesus, Buddha, Krishna and Mohammed who was as great a light to his followers as Jesus was to his.

Remember in the dynasty of God, to each his own. Hold that in your mind.

The seventh plane – Galactic space

From there they go out into Galactic Space into the vast universe ever expanding, my friends, no horizons, only glory from everlasting to everlasting.

They can bring no word to us. They have finished with the little planet. Abolished universal cognisance. Now to be entrusted with the task of creating their own solar systems to fill the vacuum that precedes the expanding universe.

They cannot be held too long, these greatly evolved spirits. What happens to them? I cannot tell you.

Can you describe God? No.

Chapter 2: Life in Spirit

Angela talks about eating and drinking in the spirit world
"Afternoon tea in heaven"

Nanette: Angela, would you tell us about the aspect of food and eating in the spirit world?

Angela: When you come over to this side you come with all your usual ways of thought, likes and dislikes. This includes food and anything that appeals to the palate. You take that thought over with you. Your mind goes with you, so when you find yourself in a body that's exactly like the body you have just shed, which is just like an overcoat, you just 'wiggle' it off, that's all.

We have beautiful fruit trees growing here laden with fruit and anything you wish to eat you may have. No, we don't eat meat here, it would be too heavy for our spiritual bodies anyway. It's the things that grow, like fruit, mostly. But if you were partial to cake or bread and butter for instance and you thought about it strongly enough, you could have it because it is all produced by thought.

I know this is incomprehensible to the average being on the earth plane but it is a fact. A dispensation of a wise and wonderful God that his children should not come over to his side to long for something without having the fulfilment of that longing. Many of us on the earth plane long and long and long for things and never have fulfilment. Even in those darker planes, those who yearn for what we used to call 'strong drink', well, they learn after a while how to materialise this drink and they quaff it. But it has no sensation such as they were accustomed to, they could drink the ocean dry and it would not give them whatever they feel when they get drunk.

There are those who remain in the same mental state as when on earth. They are quite content to live the same way here. A suburban life if you want that. Even the vicar stands and greets them at the church! Hymn boards still go up. Do you know, there are little communities of Quakers still in their 17th century clothes? Happily living their way of life, quite unchanged from the way they were three hundred years ago.

It might quite surprise you, but there are many dear ladies brought up in the English tradition who loved their afternoon teas for a long time after they had come over. They found their heaven. They are perfectly content. No-one chivvies them and if they wish to have their afternoon teas and a little chit-chat, well bless them, they can have it.

I know a dear, sweet lady who was very well known in England before she came over, she even has her domestic to serve her tea! And there they sit, you could swear they were back in the drawing room in England! But of course the time will come when the urge to progress is there because the soul itself yearns always for one thing and one thing only, to go back to God.

So there we have it.

There is a word I've heard Tara use, euphoria. Well then, let's just be happy and have our afternoon teas and little afternoon walks. Croquet here too!

Those who are in the Summerland are quite content to carry on this glorified earth life while they wait for their loved ones to come over from the earth plane.

Three hundred years ago when I was a woman on the earth plane I had a china bowl with a lid in which I used to place rose petals and musk and orice root[7] and spices. Then the lid would be put on the little china bowl and after a period of time one could lift the lid and inhale the fragrance.

Well, the lid will be lifted soon after the brew has been mixed on the earth plane and all will be embued with the fragrance of the bowl.

7. *A violet scented root*

Angela chats about other aspects of living in the spirit world

Time

We cannot compute time here. There are no clocks or setting sun. Time is a tide in which there is no abiding. Nothing lasts forever.

Sounds

If you took a drum, covered very taut, spread with sand, and breathed the letter *a* into the sand, it would take the shape of whatever letter you thought of.

Lovemaking

The merging of the etheric bodies is far more ecstatic than the merging of earth bodies.

Hell

There is no hell, only the hell of remorse in the mind of each soul.

Out of body experience

When you are asleep, you come over to spirit at night and there is a great welcoming committee for all of you. Yes, yes, of course you do, but you don't remember anything. Well, Tara doesn't. She remembers very little. A fluttering little bat-like wing will come through but before she can grasp it, it's gone. Gone because you cannot be aware of two lives at the same time. You have chosen a life for yourself on the earth plane. It is not God's plan for you to remember the life you live at night.

Shock deaths and suicide cases

New arrivals such as these are taken to places of rest set in beautiful gardens. There are rooms and verandas where chaise longues are wheeled by the workers who dress as nurses so as to give the utmost confidence to those who do not realise they have passed into spirit. They are put into a sleep for a month or longer so that the shock can pass from the spirit body and the earth memory.

Five young boys were killed in a car accident, in Cape Town in 1960. The driver had been drinking heavily but we have them all in our care. They were not ready to come over and were resentful. They were well aware that the driver was unable to drive safely, but they took a chance. It was their own free will. You see?

The broad map of life is laid out, the track is there, but we have our free will. The knowledge is within. We must listen to the wisdom within.

There seems to be an almost suicidal wave of self destruction all over the world at the moment. It is quite frightening. Don't forget that we get people's thoughts and drift, the flotsam and jetsam that comes to us, of people's minds saying, 'I wish I were dead, I wish I could die, I'm sick and tired of it all'. Most distressing, they take their own lives too!

This is a terrible thing to do because you find yourself exactly in the same condition on the other side. Nothing is accomplished by a premature death. The moment they are out, I wish you could see how they try to get back into their own bodies and we see them frantically scrambling, trying to get back. They realise that nothing has been helped because there is no elevation of the mental process.

Angela informed us of an episode concerning the mother of one of my daughter's school friends who threw herself off the balcony of her Sea Point flat. The last thing she heard was the seagulls and the first thing she heard when she died was the call of the seagulls.

The plight of the suicide is pitiful when they find they have killed off their organic matter but the spirit body is very much alive, for it is the identical twin of the earth body as it was formed at the same time. They find they have a heart that beats, a pulse and lungs that breathe and they are as solid to themselves as those around them.

Man is a complex being. There are bodies within bodies inside your garment of skin. He can cope because each one falls into place and there's that one grappling desperately to overcome the other body. One of the most mischievous of them all is the emotional, the one that is busy with the likes and dislikes, hates, jealousy, anger and revenge. It is dreadfully powerful, but man can cope with all if he leads a normal, sensible life. Man's spiritual body should be the most beautiful and glowing, but sometimes from our side it looks quite shrunken and shrivelled.

Twin Souls

Angela informed us that twin souls, male and female, were created at the same time, for each other, for ever. Deep in the soul of every human being is the knowledge that somewhere their other half exists. There is always a searching for this perfect love and loneliness in the heart brings longing to be united again. Soulmates can come together at the same time on earth, but not in every life. They each have their own karma to work out, which parts them for a while. Angela once remarked, "Those people at the end of their life-cycles seldom have ecstatically happy marriages, especially if their soulmate is waiting for them in spirit. With a little smile she added, "It might just cause complications!"

Angela on a rescue mission of mercy and compassion

A child dies

I had to retreat for ten days, but yesterday we had to perform a very necessary task of mercy and compassion. I was eavesdropping as usual the other day when Tara was present and they were talking about a child who had just been killed. One of the women present was the mother and she said, "Isn't it tragic to think that death awaits just around the corner." This child had only just left her side and in a moment, all her hopes … her love … then nothing but a little quiet body.

I had to respond because I, being mistress of ceremonies in connection with Tara and the first to use her, had to come and initiate this child into being able to give speech because it was impossible for any of us to break through to him.

It was in response to a call from his grandmother who is very high in spirit. In her day she was a famous medium in England who gave much help to thousands of people, so that when she came over to our side, she rose immediately to the fourth plane. Being a very old soul and having been in her time, during various incarnations, what you might call a 'sybil'. Yes, she was of the sibylline group, used as a priestess, prophetess and she had ascended too high. But the agonised call for help came from her daughter, the mother of the boy who had been killed. So the grandmamma being unable to come down into the mists, sent us down. A call for help. We had to concede.

I was hauled out of my retreat because I was the only one who could really place the child in Tara's body and let him speak.

He didn't know where he was, poor child. The mother, had not followed in her mother's ways and had forgotten a great deal, so this little boy had a somewhat garbled version of life after death. His main feeling was the pain which he was still feeling, holding in his mind the last moments when the car crashed and he knew he was going to die. He couldn't remember half of what his mother had told him and he didn't know where he was.

Such a sad story. But all is well now.

Nora: Was that Julian?

Angela: Don't know his name, but he was killed in a car accident and I can tell you that it was not far from Tara's sister's home.

Nora: Maybe it was little Julian S.

Angela: Oh, yes? Is that the name? How tragic.

For us, of course, there is no tragedy because to be born into our world, the only real world, that is joy. But we do feel for those on earth when they suffer the pangs of agonising grief when a loved one is taken suddenly or over a period of time. Do not think we are heartless. Oh, no. We understand only too well. Yet, after a short while being over here, we would wage a bet, if I could do such a thing with any of you, that were you to walk amongst us here and ask, "Would any of you like to go back to the earth?" everyone would say, "No, never!"

Hannah: Would you come back, Angela?

Angela: Would I come back? I have been over here … let me see, about a hundred years. No, not at this moment. I have absolutely no inclination to reincarnate. I enjoy my work here, but it is open for me to give it up at any moment without a blemish to myself. I could withdraw from this now and never speak again and that would not sully my spiritual progression.

William: And if you were forced to do it?

Angela: I would want to say no! And if I said to you, I dare you Willie, you wouldn't know what to say.

William: We have a date in two hundred years time!

Angela: Yes, then we can have a good laugh because when I first came through Tara, oh, goodness me! I couldn't even lift a finger! Do you know, Willie, I would love to take you by the hand, say in another two hundred years time and go coasting around the planet looking for a medium like Tara. I would like to pop you into that instrument and say, now give voice. You have no idea how you would boggle at the thought of it.

William: I can imagine.

Angela speaks of children in spirit
"There are millions who volunteer to look after young children"

For the small children that pass over and who retain their memory of toys and so on, we give it all to them on our side. They find it difficult to get their young minds to understand that they have left the earth, so we take them to surroundings that are very, very earth like. They must get used to the transition.

There are millions who volunteer to look after young children. We have nurseries and so on, rocking horses for them to ride … animals to play with … but the time comes when they *must* understand that they are no longer of the earth.

At this time we bring them down to play with earth children. Now they can see the spiritual form of the earth children much more clearly than their physical form, because you must remember a child's mind is as pure as dawn. It has no confusing ideas of physical or spiritual.

Being spirit, they see very clearly with their spirit eyes and spirit bodies so they play with these children. You get many young children who still retain their memory of the heavenly place they have left to come down. So you find children of the earth playing happily with them with no quarrelling! They play so happily with their spirit friends that at first they don't realise that they themselves are not earth children any more. But gradually, so that there is no trauma or shock to the psyche of the little child, the realisation is born within that they don't really belong. Do you see?

That is how it is, all very beautifully done.

Joyce with her dog Goodnight

Do you remember at Nanette's home when we first started and I gave you a vivid description of little Joyce and her dog called Goodnight? This child had longed to have a puppy of her own and so one was found for her by none other than Azu. One night (we give them a semblance of night so that they can sleep) as Joyce was being tucked up into bed, someone placed the little puppy in her arms and said "goodnight". The delighted child thought this was the name of the puppy, so now this unfortunate little puppy runs through the halls of spirit answering to the name of Goodnight!

Night-time

We approximate night as close as possible so that the children won't be frightened and they have their little beds or cots. Joyce must rest because you know her mother was grieving so greatly for her child after she died that she couldn't feel her presence. The child was so distressed that the mother took no notice of her when she tugged at her skirt, so she was brought here. The nurses look after the children and follow a routine until the mind can adjust itself to the fact that it is living another life. The children get used to it very quickly because a child's memory is very short. Children don't mind when they pass over. They grow up and if they want to they can take up an earth life again. They can visit the halls of the Akashic Records and can decide on the best family, best country for them, and so on. There are charts and advisors. Oh, we are very well organised over here! You didn't imagine things happened by accident, did you? It is all a vast organisation!

As on the earth plane, you would do that too, if you were suddenly left with thousands or orphan children of all ages and nationalities. You have to arrange something for them. Well, we are in exactly the same position, because daily many come to us … children from stillborn babies onwards. We do not regard them as children if they come at the ages of fifteen to sixteen years. They have passed out of the child stage and can accommodate themselves quite quickly because there is so much to do and to find out, but it is the little ones that need the help.

Nanette: I believe there are special groups who care for the lost and homeless children.

Angela: Oh, yes there are legions of angels who work with the children. We know there are wonderful charitable people and institutions that care for children who are left destitute and orphaned but there are not enough of them to cater for all these children. So many die unknown to anyone.

In the olden days of early Rome and Greece when children were not wanted, they were simply put out as they were born and they died. Well, much the same thing happens now. Very often on the coasts of this world, there is many a little body taken out at night and dropped. Well, I won't dwell on that.

On the other side, however, there are special planes that cater for children and infants and half grown up children and there they are educated and loved. Loved far more probably than they ever would have been on earth because many a mother lives under great stress and has moments of irritability and feels her nerves getting stretched sometimes to breaking point, the very object of her love becoming the object of her anger and impatience. But not so with God. There are hordes and hordes of women who never had children on the earth, or may have left children behind. They take these little ones to their hearts with a love that is divine, so that no child and no baby is ever alone. No child lingers in the lower astral plane because the child is too pure. "Suffer the little children to come unto me for such is the Kingdom of Heaven."[8]

You know, never grieve for them once they have passed over.

8. *Luke 18 verse 16.*

Angela informs us of animals in spirit
"The psychic power of animals, never minimise that"

When a wild beast is being destroyed it knows its end is near and it stands at bay, showing its most vicious side due to the fear of being annihilated. Do you think that fear is not latent in every part of creation? When man discovered fear, it was passed on. Do not forget the animal is built of flesh and blood like man and he picks up the radiation of good and likewise of evil and fear. When man discovered death[9], he developed a fear so intense that it was, in those early days, passed on to the animals.

You know, I was eavesdropping a little while ago on a discussion on the psychic power of animals. Never minimise that. Never. You can see it in your domestic animals. You can see it in the animals in their wild state. An animal will be browsing in rapture and freedom one moment and there comes a tremor within and it knows there is an enemy at bay. Now if that animal did not fear annihilation, it would remain browsing, would it not? But in a flash it is gone ... danger!

The animal on its own evolutionary plain has no idea what death means, because they are not on the evolutionary ladder of the human being. They will, in time, and now I am looking ahead into the vast vistas of time, gradually be eliminated entirely from the earth plane, with few exceptions. No longer will they be bred to feed man. In other words, all your domestic animals, like the cows, sheep, lambs, even the free-bounding wild animals that are killed to provide man with sustenance, the day is coming when this will no longer happen on earth. Gradually the animal evolutionary group will pass away from this earth to the newer planet now coming into being[10] and there evolve into a new, almost human being.

Well, all mankind will arrive at that stage. Tara herself knows. She cannot kill even the tiresome fly. She spares all life, it's in her. Let's leave it at that.

There are so many stories of dogs showing extraordinary intelligence, life saving, guarding, warning, even comforting us when they sense our sadness or distress. Already there must be dogs well on their way from the group soul of canines through their love-contact with human beings. The humour and compassion of the dolphins, what is their history? The many human beings they have saved from drowning by supporting them and guiding them to safety. Some animals are more evolved than others. Elephants are very sensitive to their dead. It might seem that Angela's comments are quite far fetched, but there is a shift in the canine kingdom. Perhaps the next hundred years will show further developments.

9. See Chloris page 140
10. See 'Astronomy' Section 6.

Angela chats about clothes
"You can wear any style or fashion that you are inclined to"

I heard Nanette asking about clothes.

Well, for instance, I cannot wear the garment that I wear in my own plane or domicile because it weaves together with the vibration of that plane. Now, as I descend into the courser vibration, that finely woven garment disintegrates and I should find myself rather cold with the little winds! So being ever practical, I don a garment of a courser weave which is not going to disappear when I arrive. The other is a wonderful feel. I love it.

Naturally the higher we rise in spirit to the greater and shining planes, the quicker the vibration and the more flame-like. Then the body is no longer an astral body. We shed the astral and the garments become exceptionally beautiful. But it's strange, you know, that not one is like the other. Now you would think with all the trillions and trillions of souls in spirit there would be a similarity, but again my practical side reminds me that no person has the same fingerprint, therefore nobody has the same soul-print. Whatever lovely part of our soul we have perfected, we wear the appropriate garment. With our moods, believe me, the colour changes on the garments, so there is always a constant interweaving of these colours.

You can wear any style or fashion that you are inclined to. For instance, if you were particularly drawn to Regency clothes, you could certainly clothe yourself in garments beyond the beauty of any dressmaker on earth. Or, if you wanted to be like Queen Victoria, you could wear your bustle and little parasol, all very pretty and definitely Victorian and so on.

I must tell you that sometimes we have to put a hand up to hide a smile at some of the outfits that come out when they realise that they have the power of thought to build themselves a creation! I speak now of those who were vain upon the earth and lived entirely for the outward appearance. They are taught to think and I must say some of the guides are very mischievous because they encourage them to think in detail and I mean absolute detail as you would on earth, only the method differs. Well, they start off thinking they have the perfect specimen for today's fashion but half way through ... the thought principle cannot be held too long by the newly arrived person and things go a little wobbly! So you might get three or four distinct periods! You've heard of stories getting garbled, but believe me, a costume can get garbled too!

So you see, we have to be very kindly. I used to wear lacy fichus round my neck and I was addicted to wearing soft white scarves. We all have our little foibles and fancies!

Mercia
"A miracle happened"

I am a very humble worker, very thrilled that at last I am allowed to become one. We also have to go through a sort of graduation ceremony before we become a worker in the field of spirit.

All my hair is my own, you know.

Nanette: What kind of hairstyle have you given yourself?

Mercia: Would you like to know, for quite a long while I dressed like one of the Gibson girls.[11] I don't know whether you know the Gibson Girl type, it is most graceful and I used to admire them so. Not having that willowy figure or that magnificent pompadour of hair, I wore a false piece to achieve it! I don't know what I thought I saw myself as …. I don't know. Probably thought I looked like one of them!

I still wear a modified version of that fashion. It was my favourite garb, very feminine and I lower my eyes modestly and say I was completely feminine. No yearnings for anything that smacked of the male. In fact, I almost exaggerated my femininity. That was a trick too. It is a very colourful style, very frilly, for that's how I liked myself, frilly … frilly furbelows!

But when I look down and see how modest the colour of my gown is against the acquaintance from the other sphere who comes down to us, I am filled with complete terror at the thought of how far I have to go before it will be my turn to be garbed like that.

We had a visitor about … I can't tell you the exact time, because we don't understand that any more, but we had been prepared for his coming. One I call a courier appeared and like the town crier he went around telling us that this great one was coming down and that we must prepare ourselves.

We put on our best bib and tucker to meet this very distinguished guest. Well, this was the first time.

My first name was Mercia and I was like a schoolgirl, so excited I could feel my heart beat. We have hearts, naturally, and it was palpitating in my eagerness. We had been told of his wondrous beauty and I, with my brain still partly earthly, visualised an earthly beauty, a Sir Galahad. This is all I thought of on the earth plane and I suppose it followed me here. We shed it I suppose as time goes on but it still gives me pleasure, believe it or not. It does bolster one up when one sees a flash of admiration in the masculine eye and it happens here my dear friends … oh it does indeed! On this plane of course it does!

Well the great day came and we were assembled in an orderly group, but you could hear the buzz of excitement like being in a beehive when the queen bee is born. It just rippled and rippled all around in all those ranks of men and women and young people waiting for him to come. I managed to circumvent myself from being almost in the front row. Yes, I did. And I sat there, waiting with … oh, the most heavenly impatience! Not impatience as you know it on the earth, but an impatience so

11. *Performers at the Gaeity Theatre, London.*

glorious ... You know that you know it's going to happen and it's part of the anticipation.

Then a hush finally came and a voice said to us ... "Bē seated please." I sat tall. Then in the sky ... oh yes, in the sky ... a gorgeous blue light and a hush filled all of us seated there. I beheld this gorgeous man and prayed he would see me. I was lonely you see. Then this wonderful glow came closer to us rapidly and there was I, still sitting tall, craning my neck. It used to be called swan-like. Thinking back, it must have been ostrich-like! Then he came. When I say 'he came' and 'a new star is born', the star came.

I could never describe the coming of this being. I, who had been preparing to give him ... shall I put it vulgarly 'the glad eye', found my eyes closing before the glory of that face. When I opened my eyes he had started speaking.

You know on earth one can rarely say, that person has a beautiful voice. It is difficult to say why the voice is beautiful, it lingers in the memory. I'm not speaking of a singing voice, I'm talking of an ordinary speaking voice. It's a great rarity.

Well, this voice was ... how can I describe it ... like the sound of the sea ... chiming of a great bell, violins in the moonlight. I don't know, I'm ignorant. I don't know what he said ... not one word. I just sat ... like someone who is stage-struck!

Oh, how can I tell you of that beauty and those glorious eyes ... and he was one of the lesser lords, not one of the great beings of the whole universe! But he is a lord in his own right. What their appearance must be like after seeing this one, I'm sure I'd never survive it.

I was shaken to the depths of my being ... and you know ... I called from the depths of my being, 'Oh dear me, to think I could dream of attracting your attention to me'. Then the tears came and do you know ... a miracle happened ...

He stopped talking and turned and looked at me ... and from those glorious eyes ... there went out love. Not the love I had been looking for but a love so sublime I thought I was disintegrating and they would just find my little modest garment on the ground! Then he said, "My dear Mercia, you have my love, no need to seek it."

I could have died with shame and exaltation! You know I had dreamed and heard of adoration. This was a new experience and I knew what adoration meant in that moment.

Now if I can feel that for one of the lesser ones, what do you think I'd feel if I met my maker face to face. That is a very unlikely thing to happen but it could ... couldn't it? It could happen to me ... Well I must flash away now.

Ella: That was so interesting!

Mercia: It's all waiting for you, Ella. Goodbye Charles, did you like me?

Ella: Don't be lonely any more.

Mercia: No, I have Barry with me now. I didn't know him till I came here. He too was lonely. The thread goes out and you are united with another lonely one. Although it isn't your soul mate, the affinity is there in the way you think and feel in general. So for a while you find a companion and travel the road together until one or the other yearns for something else. The partings are always amicable and although you might never meet him again, you flash him a thought of gratitude for the one who took your loneliness away.

Someone is tugging at my skirts. I must away now.

All right, I'm coming!

Angela is awarded a new jewel
"A mode of identification"

I have a beautiful new jewel. You see, we devote our time, energies and hearts to try to bring light to the inhabitants of the earth. For so many of us come down to the dark places where there is very much more agony and sorrowing and grief than there ever is on the earth plane. A lot of us devote our time entirely to doing that and we seek no reward. Ever.

But the time will arrive when we will be summoned to our elders and there is our reward. We receive a jewel of some sort and colour. You see, why that is done is because others who are awarded similar jewels in colour, or whatever class of stone, don't all know each other. When I tell you how vast it all is, how could we all contact each other? It is quite impossible.

There can and does arise an occasion when our paths cross and then we see this particular jewel flash, either from the shoulder or the girdle or around the head and so we know that that soul is engaged on the same vibration of help that we are. Rather like a badge or brooch, which says you belong to this club or other. You know what I mean?

Therefore, one might go to a foreign country and wear it in the vague hope of perhaps contacting someone of the same organisation and your mode of identification is that badge. You see? That is what our jewels are. A mode of identification. So immediately there is an affinity between the wearers of similar jewellery.

I wear it on my left shoulder. What has just been given to me is a sapphire.

As Tara has told you, the sapphire denotes mercy, compassion and love of your fellow beings. The emerald is a standard of wisdom and the diamond is a symbol of devotion to duty and man's relationship with his God. Then the supreme one of all, the ruby. Only great beings wear the ruby. No need for me to tell you the Master Jesus is one, Buddha another, Babaji another.

The Lords

The great beings that they call, the Lords, are those who have never taken on the physical body and they do not need jewels. They have their own ways of communicating with each other.

But I am not allowed to dwell on that subject. You may have somebody spiritually more advanced than I who will come and tell you about that.

I told you a long time ago you'd be surprised at the revelations made in this room, but you didn't realise all it was going to be. All your patience and devotion and steadfastness rewarded.

Well, you see you can never really be the same people again after contact with these innermost vibrations of these wonderful beings. You will find your attitude of life changing. You will find you are more tolerant of other people. Also something which is good for you, a slow but sure withdrawal from the pinpricks of life and from the people who deal them out to you.

These people, you know, or should know by now, have no significance in your lives at all. The folk who plague and pester you, just look at them calmly and try and send them a thought of love, as Jesus did to Pontius Pilate. You might have the same effect on them as he had on his brotherhood. For remember, we are all children of the one source and I, in my own withdrawal, have had many great revelations made to me too.

I too, am on the ascension and will remain on the planet earth while Tara's feet still tread the earth.

But naturally when Tara finally makes up her mind to come to us, then I, too, will no longer come down. Then that mission is over.

2

The Creatives

Chapter 3: Actors, Writers, Playwrights, Poets and Musicians

George Robey (1869–1954), English comedian
"Eyebrows, baggy pants and all"

Born in Herne Hill, London, he made a name for himself in musical shows such as the *Bing Boys* and later emerged as a Shakespearean actor. Dubbed the Prime Minister of Mirth, he was famous for his robust humour, bowler hat, long black collarless frockcoat, hooked stick and thick, painted eyebrows. He made famous the song, 'If you were the only girl in the world' and was knighted in 1954.

I have been listening and I heard the remark that it is difficult for one of the members of this circle to hear what is being said. I would like that member to stand up in class and put up his hand. Not as a request to leave the room, but merely to tell me whether he hears me clearly or not.

Rennie: Yes, I can hear you clearly.

G Robey: That is good. That is good.
   Well, now comes the big surprise for you, my friend in the corner, I greet you as an old thespian![1] Yes, from a brother thespian! Now I'll tickle up your brain as I would tickle up the ivories and send you away with an ant nibbling away at the grey cells. I can hear you say, 'Now who the hell was that?'
   Well, I only want to say thank you to all of you seated here that I can at last feel and enjoy the experience of holding forth and having people listening to me. I stride

1. *Fellow actor.*

the boards again, Rennie. The lights are there beneath my feet and I look out on a sea of faces, all looking at me. What a fine fellow I was in my own mind!

Take it from me, you come into spirit to learn what a poor mountebank you are. Not you, Rennie. No, not you ... me! But it was good fun while it lasted and I loved every moment of it. Yes I did. I am going to emote and hold forth to you Rennie. I am brought here to see if my delivery is good.

[All the group assure him!]

You know me, Rennie. Yes you knew me! I'll let the cat out of the bag one of these days, old boy, don't worry! I can't bear to hide my light under a bushel, so don't worry!

Mind you, Rennie, it's damned funny talking through a woman, you know. Damn funny. Don't forget I have all those shining fellows around me saying, "Don't hurt those vocal chords, or out you go!"

No. I'm not finished with the world yet. I like to hear myself talk and I like to hold the attention of my listeners. I've got plenty to tell you about, make your ears tingle and your hair stand up straight on your scalp!

Rennie: I haven't much hair left to stand up!

G Robey: I am talking to the audience, my dear fellow, you're only the actor. I nearly said playboy, but that wouldn't have been correct! Yes, I could make them roll in the aisles, I could. I still have that gift.

Well, they have told me I must stagger off now. So thank you very much for giving me this opportunity of making my entrance. What a lovely word that was in the old days, when I waited for my cue and made 'my entrance'.

Now I'll give you a clue .... with my cape flung behind my shoulders and my cane and my moustache curling and quivering, another little idiosyncrasy of mine, I had a habit, completely unconscious habit, of putting my little finger into my ear drum and vigorously turning it round as if I were trying to dislodge a goblet of wax! That was me, Rennie!

Ella: Robey?

G Robey: Ha, ha! I said my moustache. I meant to say my eyebrows and stopped at the last moment! I wanted to tickle his fancy a bit longer! Now what an honour I'm paying you, baggy pants and all!

Well, you know Vi is with me too.[2] We'll get her to sing, yes. Damned hard job to stop her on this side, let me tell you lads and lassies.

I'm off now on my way. A lot of the old gang are here to wash away the earth. Well, goodnight.

It's a long road that hasn't a turning, Rennie, and it's a long road in Blighty[3] that

---

2. *Vi was his wife 1869–1954. She was a music hall artist and actress.*
3. *Old name for England.*

hasn't got a pub too! Thank God for that. Well I'm off …

I can't get out! That's why I keep on saying "I'm off". I can't get out of this body properly!

What an experience … talk about marmalade jam, I'm in it right up to my neck!

There's Angela telling me what to do. Wait.

Now, I've got it, I've got it!

Angela: Well, you see who you are attracting Rennie! It's going to be a lively circle. He got us all laughing. He is very happy. A good man, yes a good man. Well, that was a pleasant interlude!

Actress
"The battle is going to start quite shortly between the dark forces and the light"

This was suspected to be Gertrude Lawrence although she never actually says who she is.

Gertrude was an English actress who lived from 1898–1952. She worked much in the theatre with Noel Coward and was famous for saying:
"My candle burns at both ends, it will not last the night
But my foes and my friends, it gives a lovely light."

Good evening everybody.

Ella: I know that voice darling!

Actress: No you don't know me, but thank you for calling me darling.

Ella: I thought it was Angela for a moment.

Actress: No, tonight is strangers' night. We asked for this and permission was given us because we see everything that goes on. Those of us who were fond of hearing ourselves talk on the earth plane, we feel we would like to come back and just have a tiny weenie little chat with you, if you would be kind enough to listen!

I can't hope to reach the heights of many of the charming people who have spoken to you. But if you can take a lesser light like me, or even a hooded little lantern, to say thank you for letting me come and hear my own voice again. It is great fun for me.

I don't mind telling you at all, I was an actress. A well-known actress indeed! In fact at the drop of a hat, I could quote Shakespeare for you. But I think I've got stage fright. I feel not quite sure of my delivery speaking through a strange voice and a strange throat. It's really all very exciting.

I'm not too high up, I think I'm on the third plane. We call it Summerland. All very beautiful here and we stage our own plays you know.

Ella: So I believe, wonderful.

Actress: I came to tell you there's a great hubbub going on in the spiritual planes over the battles being fought, that the earth people know nothing about yet. We have warned you about them.

When I say 'we', that's a great impertinence on my part, but then I am always an eager listener so can say 'we'.

I can echo what they have said to you. The battle is going to start quite shortly between the dark forces and the light.

Well, the battle has been joined in good earnest and the prophecies will all be fulfilled. Then God knows, the world will be a beautiful place. It may not come in your lifetime but don't let that worry you, the promise is there.

I can tell you this too, that if the world is happy and clean and nicely washed, those in spirit are equally happy, they have nothing to worry about. They are always worrying about the plane they have left. They come back, life after life and you can't help getting fond of the old pub! Yes, so you come back for another little drink. Sometimes it's bitter beer you choose, or it's light ale, or champagne, like I did in my last incarnation, which I am glad to say *is* my last incarnation.

I am being nudged on my elbow, I have to go, it's just because it's Christmas and they allowed us to come through and speak.

I do bring great light with me because I am so happy … and so … Oh, Bless you!

Charles: Pardon me for sneezing.

Actress: Yes, that is why I said, "Bless you!" We don't sneeze up here, but I can say bless you for everything. Well I do! I bless you all, each and everyone.

The blessings of the Lord Jesus Christ from those marvellous, heavenly blue eyes of his.

There comes a light. Oh he is here! Yes, he is here. The light there never was on land or sea comes from those eyes of his. I have brought red poppies with me. There is an allegorical meaning of red poppies. They grew on Mount Carmel's slopes when the Lord Jesus walked there.[4]

With that lovely thought I must bow and say goodnight. Don't give me a curtain call for they won't allow me back once I have left the body.

Thank you so much, lovely to meet you in person. Goodbye my nice new friends, you've been such a very nice audience.

Nanette: Well, we're very glad.

Actress: We used to know the moment we walked onto the stage whether they were 'with us' or not and if they were, we were able to give of our best.

Au revoir … au revoir!

Angela on good and evil forces as Lana appears

When someone opens themselves up to evil forces, there is a definite tentacle hooking in the possessing spirit to the aura. You cannot easily open the door and show them out again. I swear from what I have seen, sometimes even the Master Jesus can't get them to leave. It is a hook, like a bat has at the end of its wing. Yes indeed it is so, and the possessing entity, when on earth, would have been of intense magnetic power for evil or for good. But it is often put to evil.

[Angela breaks off for a moment … and then]

4. *Mount Carmel in Haifa, Palestine.*

Oh, bless you, excuse me for a moment, the Master Jesus is here. His love and his blessing to every single being. He went round touching you upon your third eye (instead of the top of your head) where he placed his forefinger and his little finger. I have never seen that done before. He brought the two fingers together and touched you.

So you get your pourboire[5] from the Master and much love.

I don't mind telling you, I like to tell you, that I go quite shivery at the knees when I see him! He always has that effect on me. I get goose pimples you know! Yes, I feel so loving, so adoring and yet ... oh, I don't know ... so tiny ... teeny weenie next to this great being.

Yet he makes you feel that you are a queen when he speaks to you. He is one of those marvellous beings that when he is talking to you, you feel that you are the only being in creation. He makes you feel that you're all important to him, that is his great magnetism too.

He has just given me a playful tap on the back of my head!

5. *A little gift.*

A Shakespearean actor comes to bid farewell
"I gathered laurel wreaths to myself with much satisfaction"

I greet you.

I am trying hard to reclaim myself as I did upon the earth stage when I was a Shakespearean actor. You will forgive my failure, in this particular appearance upon an unknown stage to me, to reach your standard that you might expect from an actor. So you will make allowance for any discrepancy?

It gives me great joy to be able to speak in this august gathering. I refer to the holy one that I see. This is not meant to be offensive to you, dear ladies, but it is the truth. There are few people upon this tortured earth plane to whom I could give that accolade. When I speak of august people on earth, I pick without hesitation the one whose body I use at this moment. I place my finger on her and say unto you all, verily sitteth one who weareth a laurel wreath upon her brow, not won in battle and bloodshed, but in sheer goldness.

I have not come here to extol her virtue. I have merely come here because they told me this is one way of clearing myself from the earth station where I have lingered over long.

When one has won for himself (it sounds so pitifully futile when I say this) laurels for acting, heaped upon me when on the earthly stage and when one passes to this side of life without much knowledge of what awaits one at the end of life's journey, a little of that world glamour still clings. One bids farewell to the earthly self with much regret.

I do not hide this from you, that I valued my reputation as a great actor. I did! I gathered laurel wreaths to myself with much satisfaction and I realise now how egotistical I was. In my own opinion, I venture to tell you that when I strutted the boards that is Shakespeare, there was not another who could compare with me!

I was probably alone in that opinion, but I was on Olympian heights as an actor. Now I have come to bid it all a long farewell!

I have hung around the theatres where I heard applause ringing to the rafters and struck my heroic pose as I acknowledged the shouting and applause of the stupid crowds. Oh, yes, there was always a contempt in me when I gazed down upon them with their huzzaring and clapping for more.

I have been seen at one of my haunts quite often, but now it's time to say good-bye and a long farewell to it all and I must confess that at the ultimate twelfth hour, as it is for me now, I go with gladness.

So wise are those guides who have brought me here tonight, that I leave this earth plane without regrets.

I had little else in my life beyond my theatre. Very little. You would not know the weariness of soul that attached me towards the end and the mockery of it all. You know the old saying, 'The king is dead, long live the king.' Well, it is the same in that profession which was my life, my bread and my wine.

I knew if I ever toppled once, I was toppled forever, for the slide down is long, the climb to the top is painful and arduous. But oh, my god, the fall from Olympian heights comes overnight and I realised I was beginning to have one toe hanging over those perilous places, for I was tired.

It is difficult to let go of that which has been the wine of life for you and that is why I am what you call earth bound.

I knew nothing of the life hereafter, I was much too occupied with my own importance and my success. I am much wiser now. Oh, so much wiser. For unbeknown to all of you, I have been part of an unseen audience here and that is how I have won my release from my earth conditions.

My appearance here tonight is to tender you my heartfelt thanks. Were it not for this room, I would still be groping in the mists of illusion. But I am free now and shall depart shaking the dust of old earth from my fleeing heels!

Wish me well on my way, on my winged flight into beauty and reality. It is about to take place from this very room! I have been taken and I have gone tentatively, I must confess, to partake in a glimpse now and then of what awaited me. For I had not sinned in any way except in my self-love, which consumed me.

Now, I can call you my dear friends, because I have grown to love you. One cannot feel any other emotion, for this room is surrounded and steeped in love and I go my way a happy immortal!

It was mercy that has been shown to me in this room and it fell on me as the gentle rain from heaven. Thank you.

And I say *au revoir* for we shall meet, I know, when you come one by one to join the great majority. I, by that time, with great diligence and great study, hope to have progressed on this eternal path to heights of glory that I cannot even conjecture.

Do you know, I practised what I was going to say here tonight for many hours before I ventured into this body. It is many years of training that has given me this aptitude to speak, but I do not mind confessing to you all, that what I have said was totally different from what I had arranged to say!

Farewell.

Horace Walpole (1717–1797), writer
"The quality of mercy is not strained"

He was the forth Earl of Oxford, one of the most gifted, loveable and outspoken personalities of the 18th Century. A very merciful man, hating cruelty in all its forms, animal or human. In 1750, he made known his horror of the slave trade, became an MP for Cattington, Cornwall and voted against it in Parliament.

Amongst his wide range of interests, he wrote essays, verse and satires such as *Letter from Xo Ho to his friend Lien Chi at Pekin*. His literary reputation rests chiefly upon letters that deal in a most vivacious way with party politics, foreign affairs, art, literature and gossip. His first-hand accounts of such events as the Jacobite Trial are invaluable.

Walpole, known for his unusual sense of fun, once went to dinner at Lord Beaufort's with a garland of sweet peas on his head! On another occasion he received his guests wearing a wooden cravat by Grinling Gibbons and a large pair of spectacles that had once belonged to James II. He took much pleasure in what he called his 'youthfullity'.

"The quality of mercy is not strained, it droppeth as the gentle rain from heaven upon the place beneath and it is twice blessed".[6]

I greet you all. Let me leap ahead and tell you my name is Horace.

All: Our greetings to you.

H Walpole: I shall not tell you what is erroneously called my surname, I shall titillate your appetite. I'm not Horace any more. In fact, I have to think quite hard to remember that part of me.

Joan: Were you a writer?

H Walpole: Yes.

Joan: Walpole?

H Walpole: Yes, you are very clever. Well, now the cat is out of the bag! I came to add my few words to you all here, where I feel extremely happy. The whole theme

6. *The Merchant of Venice, Shakespeare.*

tonight is mercy, for this quality is extremely lacking on the earth today and we, in spirit, see a light that accompanies mercy.

There is always great rejoicing, for mercy is one of the attributes of the most high. Now that might be misleading, for if I say to you, 'God's mercy' then I mislead you, inasmuch as this, that I plant in your minds the idea that God is aware of giving mercy. This would also postulate that God was aware of cruelty on the earth plane. The absolute reverse is the case. God is all perfection, God is all love. When He creates perfection, it is so perfect because there is only perfection that comes from the perfect. It sounds complicated, but you understand what I am saying. He has no knowledge but this love. True love compounded of so many facets, amongst which, perhaps, the most wonderful of all, mercy.

It is a beautiful word, but it can also be a very cruel word. One word can mean two things, had you thought of that?

'I have you at my mercy now as the point of my sword is at your throat' or, 'Down dog, on your knees and beg for mercy'. Do you see?

I come too, to raise my voice and say you must and will go forth as apostles. That is your role, what you have chosen.

Now this word mercy, think of it always and when you come across people whose actions repel you, have mercy in your heart and mind and know they would not act in this manner if they knew how wrong they were. Therefore, do as we do in spirit, regard it as ignorance.

I have progressed greatly. I can say this to you without any boasting. After all, how can you live amongst these great ones and not progress? It is quite impossible, it is as contagious as fever.

Therefore be merciful in your thoughts, much more so even than in your acts. For when the great majority of people upon your earth perform an act of mercy, I have no hesitation in telling you, there is a small degree of smug self-satisfaction in being merciful. There is a slight aura of glory attached to the man or woman when you hear people say, "He is a most merciful man".

Oh, yes, don't deny me your thoughts. The ego is there. But to be merciful in thought, that is a different proposition for it springs from the soul and is unseen by mankind.

That which is inside the man, the heart that *thinks* mercy, that is true mercy.

So in future, should you find you are prone to condemn in thought, instantly, for your own sake and for the one who stands condemned in your mind, substitute that thought for one of mercy. For if he were fully aware he would not so act.

This quality of mercy, which has been quoted here tonight, is not strained. No indeed, it carries its own vibration, which is so powerful that the very man on whom you might be casting a condemnatory glance will benefit instantly without even being aware that it is emanating from you.

Remember, it is not strained. It goes straight out.

Remember too, that when Shakespeare was writing, it was not his mind all the time, it was sheer inspiration that brought forth some of the most beautiful thoughts and language in the world. Perhaps for those very words, 'The quality of mercy' he gained immortality upon the earth for himself.

Am I too dogmatic? I am only trying to tell you a very vital truth about the power of God. You hear the old oath that men swear 'by God's mercy'. There is no need to say God's mercy, they could simply have said, 'by mercy', for that is the power of that word.

I have been warned not to speak at full volume so I content myself with the thought that I am audible. Am I?

Group: Yes, very clear indeed.

Horace: I am not like the Shakespearean actor friend, I've not come to seek release from the earth, I found this myself when I was here. I had a very sound sense of logic and viewing the whole set up I was able to deduce the truth, like Sherlock Holmes. I know his creator extremely well in spirit!

My deduction was correct that God is mercy, do you see? Not God's mercy.

God is mercy because mercy is God-like.

Thank you.

Angela talks of Shakespeare
"We have a poets' corner"

Only a few people know that Shakespeare was inspired. He knew it. Oh, yes! He knew it. Well, where do you think he got it all from, Ella?

Ella: There has certainly been much controversy.

Angela: Yes, but as we have said before, the world reveres Shakespeare as the author of all the plays and sonnets. I revered him. What does it matter whether Bacon or Shakespeare and all the other claimants to the title, wrote them? It doesn't concern you. We know the truth. Forget it! For if it had not been for Shakespeare it wouldn't have been written! So we'll leave it at that.

But it was an inspired group. Oh, yes. Occult practices. They got the fright of their lives too! You cannot play around with forces like that if you have men whose character cannot bear the strong light of the other world. If you go looking for fame and fortune and things like that and not for God, then you will reap the harvest. You sow the wind and reap the whirlwind, you know. But it is all forgotten. It's all in the dust of his grave, but will all come to light because truth will out.

Just like the truth about the bible and what a topsy turvy world there will be in the ecclesiastic circle, what a rolling of heads and bishops' crowns there's going to be. My goodness me and about time too!

Well, there are rules that have to be obeyed over here as well.

We have a poets' corner to which we all belong and congregate, which Rennie is going to adorn one day, too.

[Rennie laughs]

You know, it's the same with musicians, they have their groups. As you know, like seeks like.

Do you know, there has always been a little devil hidden somewhere inside of me and every now and then little horns push over the tables! You know, when a famous poet came to our side who was awfully full of himself.[7] Well, when he arrived with beard and waggling eyebrow I went up to him and introduced myself and I said to him, "I too used to write poetry". He said, "Hm, yes, quite pretty stuff".

I was so infuriated I nearly hit him! I really did! He became my *bête noir*,[8] which, you know, we're not allowed to have, being a guide. So I've had to struggle to overcome this *bête noirishness* of mine. But I got over it. Now we're quite friendly because as I once said, he has been cut down to size.

7. *George Bernard Shaw*
8. *French meaning 'black beast'.*

Frédéric François Chopin (1810–1849), musician and composer
"I came in on a wave of thought"

Born in Zelazowa Wola near Warsaw, he first played in public at the age of eight and published his first works at the age of fifteen. He died at the age of thirty-nine from tuberculosis.

Bonjour Madame et Monsieur, c'est lui Chopin lui-méme. I did come because of the music played here. I did come because of the love this woman had for my music. I think I came in on the wave of thought, sent in from her mind with my name.
   Merci beaucoup Madame et Monsieur.

Angela

Hello. This composer was Tara's favourite when she was young and had to practise long hours. When she heard his music she was thinking of this and him. He wears silk stockings and knee breeches, the clothes of his time. He has spoken at one time or another at other séances.

Olive Schreiner (1855–1920), writer and feminist
"I am well on my way now and I have my child at last"

She was born in the Wittebergen Mission Station at the Cape of Good Hope. Daughter of a German Methodist father and English mother, she grew up largely self educated. At fifteen she became a governess to a boer family near the Karoo desert and later lived in England where she wrote the novel *Story of an African Farm* under the pseudonym Ralph Iron. She also wrote: *Dreams, Dream-life and Real Life, Trooper Peter Halket, Women and Labour* and *From Man to Man*. In 1894 she married S.P. Cronwright who took her name, wrote her biography and edited her letters.

⌐ Olive came through for us three times. This is a compilation of all her appearances.

I also held a pen in my hand. It's Olive.

Good evening my friend. We've not yet met, have we? No, but I give you a glad handshake and welcome you to this company.

⌐ Betty was here today for the first time as a newcomer.

Olive: Nobody ask me any questions because I refuse to answer! Just in case someone had a question. I felt it pinpointed in the air!

I'm only here to say that I'm so grateful that I have gone on so far ... I wish I could tell you how wonderful it all is, but you know I might get all mawkish and sentimental as I was in my books. So we'll forget that.

Now, as you know, I knew all about this subject before I came, so it was no unknown territory for me, but I must say I got so many wonderful shocks! It is far beyond my preconceived ideas of the glory and the splendour of it all that I feel sorry for the people on the earth. The only thing that comforts me in my pity for you is the lovely awakening you will have, you will see?

So my pity is really a blending of love and an anticipatory participation in watching your faces and the dawning of the realisation of the glory, which you have won for yourselves. Pedantic, am I not? No, I must not use that word 'won', it is quite ridiculous. I am going back to that theology 'your reward in heaven' which my father hurled at me morning, noon, night! A subject of dispute between us, as you no doubt know.

Well, I'm on my way now and I have my child! You will have read of my macabre habit of taking her little coffin wherever I went. Now, I am with her. Yes, we are together at last and it has been worthwhile waiting for this re-union. Oh yes! As I told you, I am waiting in anticipation for the glad awakening when you all come, which doesn't mean there is going to be a sudden holocaust and you are all going to be swept away together! One by one they journey onwards.

I won't be melodramatic and say, farewell, I am just going to say *totsiens*.[9] It's been lovely knowing you.

To you Nanette, I omitted to say welcome back! Don't worry about anything. That is so easy to say on the earth, don't worry, when that's all we poor mortals do from the time we draw breath until the day we die! When are we free from worry? Even so mild a thing as the weather! I wonder if it's going to rain, I shan't be able to go out, worry, worry, I am getting married tomorrow, my veil will get wet and my flowers will wilt and I'll look a mess!

Oh, dear!

Au revoir, totsiens.

"We miss that fame!"

I see myself as I really am, not as I saw myself on the earth. I see the truth now and I've come to tell you all, I am sure you'll be happy to hear I am a much more contented woman now. A much happier woman. I was not discontented, please don't think that, but I went on with my foolish dream about myself on this side of life. Now I see myself, face to face, clearly and not through a glass, darkly.

I now realise the happiness. I know the other was a phantom happiness. Mine is reality now and I am released from the earth too, because obviously had I not been released I would not have come down, even though it was to square things up with Tara. I could have gone on and thought, 'well, it doesn't really matter, I can tell her about it when she comes over', but I was still attached. That is the invidious thing called fame! Whether it's in a small degree or in a great degree, it holds us to this earth because when we pass on to this side we miss that fame. We do miss it!

Look, let me make it very brief. Say that I am thirty years of age on earth, then put me forty years ahead and I'm seventy. You can take it from me, one doesn't learn very much in the interim! Do we really improve ourselves? Hardly at all. We are content, just as I was, to sit on our toadstools of fame. But in thirty or forty years in spirit, you don't sit on a toadstool, because people don't hang around like a swarm of bees trying to tell you what to do, what to think. No, they are too busy with their own concerns.

This is not selfishness but it is the plan that everybody has to develop from within. It must come from within you. Or you can sit quite happily there on your laurel wreath with which you have just been presented. Bit of a prickly seat!

There is so much to see. It's a lotus-eating life at the beginning so, my dear, a hundred years can pass and you don't change … and then it begins. For we are not meant to live quite like that forever.

9. *Afrikaans for 'goodbye'.*

You know the railway crossing, when the train is coming, a warning bell gives a tinkle and you feel faintly discontented. You know what is going on, you feel restless, you've got to do something, go somewhere. That is the beginning.

I'm talking personally, but I have compared my own experiences with a lot of them here because I get around a lot. I'm gregarious. I like people, particularly men, Guy!

So it follows this pattern. A great, great spiritual being wouldn't pass through to where the average one goes. They would pass through without even knowing it. That is how it is for the very few on earth, the great and shining ones that are hidden in human body. They will know nothing of that at all for they will go straight to their places waiting for them on the fifth plane. But for the average, it is all very pleasant. Believe me, a most delightful spot. There is nothing you lack, absolutely nothing. You can start to work right away, instantly, if you wish it. But then again, after a lifetime on the earth, you may not want to, so you stroll around finding your bearings. So begins the long, long saga of your upward climb. A most delightful proceeding!

I'll be there hanging around when you come!

We never knew why she had to square things up with Tara. Sometimes two souls need to meet. They might have known each other previously, or an opening might have been made for them to work together in the future after they both had passed from their earth bodies. Tara never spoke about it.

"I am penitent"

I did not come to lecture, but you had good tidings, so I am not going to add to it, it's done me good and I am penitent.

Self has to go.

When I first came, did I not tell you of the penalties of fame? Let me tell you the hateful truth that when one has any kind of fame one tries to cash in at the slightest provocation and I cashed in then. Not that it brought me glory!

You have enough experience of me to know I am very impulsive, very headstrong and when someone has been injured, away I go!

So I told you that I am not likely to be appointed to be a guide, nor am I likely to be just a helper. The first time in my life not seeking publicity!

Yes, confessions are good for the soul. Don't bother to put me on the sewing machine.[10] I don't speak words of philosophy or anything, I talk about myself mostly!

Quite unimportant.

I do my work and am happy. So don't give me any further publicity on your tapes!

---

10. *She called the tape a sewing machine as it stitched all the words together.*

Rudyard Kipling (1865–1936), English Nobel Prize winner
"There should be no such thing as patriotism"

Born Joseph Rudyard Kipling in Bombay, India, he was educated at the United Services College in Devon, England. His first novel was *The Light that Failed*. He wrote the brilliantly successful collections of verse, *Barrack Room Ballads* and *The Seven Seas*. He was a Nobel Prize winner for literature and his short stories include: *The Jungle Book*, the classic animal stories, *Stalky and Co* and *Kim* and the children's classic, *Just So Stories*. Other famous stories include: *Soldiers Three, Kirby* and *Captain Courageous*. He was a doctor of Philosophy in Athens, rector of the University at St Andrews in Scotland and served in Irish Guards regiment between 1914–1918. He died at the age of seventy-one.

Good day. Although I am a constant visitor here, I find it troublesome to use this voice.

You know I had an impediment, a stammer, which I overcame like Socrates with Demosthenes pebbles in the mouth. This is the second time I have spoken through this body. I know you are consumed with curiosity as to who speaks!

I had not a little fame. Fame may be the spur to victory, mankind has a habit of clawing the person who seeks it!

"Oh, east is east and west is west, and ne'er the twain shall meet
till earth and sky stand presently at God's great judgment seat.
But there is neither east or west, border nor breed nor birth
when two strong men stand face to face, though they come from
the ends of the earth."[11]

I wrote a lot of poppycock! There should be no such things as patriotism!

Heroes going to war to fling young men into battle. Patriotism! I was rolling out this nonsense thing of how noble and glorious war is.

Entry into spirit is a great leveller of human beings, something of the tragi-comedy watching them with the garland of fame. I refer to Winston Churchill as an example. He revealed himself as an egoist. Pathetic to watch him when he found himself shrouded in the Union Jack. "You surely know me?" But passers by all busy with their own business murmured, "sorry" and hurried on. He scarcely realised that what he had done counted for very little in spirit. After years of patient observances of fame there is hardly one of us who does not get puffed up.

11. The Ballad of East and West – Rudyard Kipling

There has been a run on the poets in South Africa, birthplace of Tara. I heard that name in India when I studied eastern mysticism, but my wife didn't like it, so I dropped it. Tara, name of goddess in Hindu, meaning light.

One of my unbroken rules on earth was no favouritism, so they will wonder why I am such a constant visitor at these meetings.

Very pleasurable.

Memsamhib![12]

---

12. *He had spent a lot of time in India, memsamhib is 'madam' in Hindustan.*

John Masefield (1878–1967), English poet and novelist
"A tall ship and a star to steer her by"

John Edward Masefield was born in Herefordshire and educated at the Kings School in Warwickshire. He joined the Royal Navy, but ill-health brought him to shore where he became a journalist and then writer. His sea poetry includes, *Salt Water Ballads*. His best known narrative poem is *Reynard the Fox*. Other works include: *The Widow in the Bye Street*, and *Noel – the Hawbucks*. His plays include, *The trial of Jesus* and *The Coming of Christ*. He became Poet Laureate in 1930.

I hope I can manage this, but I know you will be tolerant with me and not tell me to go. I can't get this right, it's not so long since I left your … my, earth!

I was very weak and feeble, not in my mind, thank God, but certainly in my tired body. So when I come back and use an earth body, I feel the dreadful lassitude and lethargy of my dying days. So please, will you understand?

I will make my stay as brief as possible. This is part of the clearing system for me and it is only because I had a good working knowledge of life after death that I am here tonight. I hope you can hear me quite clearly?

Ella: Yes indeed, very clearly.

J Masefield: Forgive my laboured way of speaking but it's the best I can manage now, so thank you for your indulgence towards a very old man.

I quote you a few lines:
"I would go down to the sea again, to the lonely sea and the sky and all I ask is a tall ship and a star to steer her by."[13]

Translate for me and substitute the tall ship for the tall man who was my star who steered me home. That is the man known as Jesus Christ. This, my tall ship, who brought me safely into harbour.

I have asked to come tonight to tell you to pin all you have on to him. As I did. You will know now who I am and if you have ever read any of my work, you will readily be able to discern that I was a firm believer.

That is a moot point 'believer' that word …

---

13. Title of this poem is *Sea Fever* by John Masefield

I had a deeply rooted knowledge of reincarnation, also. I was mystical in my outlook. I practised meditation when the desire took me, not regularly as is the case of the mystic, my life was too full for that, but I was always drawn to the spiritual side of life. In my long life at sea I learned under the great canopy of the star-studded night. Once in a glorious while, I saw stretching out into infinity … dare I say it … I glimpsed the face of God.

Therefore, my slow departure from my harbour of peace was not tedious to me because I knew the words of Tennyson:

"I would meet my pilot face to face when I had crossed the bar".

So my friends, so I did.

I've come back to tell you, hold fast to Him and know too, this irrefutable fact, something I believed in my watches at night, love is the ruling factor of the cosmos.

Like blossoms that grow on the fruit tree, each one alike and yet different. Each one of the same tree, the same life, the same love that brings the blossom into fruit. So it is in spirit. Unceasing love, the tide that flows on and never ebbs. Never! Love … selfless love … never asking, only giving, following in the pathway of Jesus. You must be patient with me that I harp over much on that name but I have seen him and now my glory is complete. Therefore do I call him, 'the tall ship' that brought me home back to my eternal resting place.

Thank you and if ever you should read my poem about the sea, try and recall what I came to tell you. The truth, the shining truth.

I am tired now and I do not wish to bring about a condition of fatigue in this human body. The moment I leave it, I will regain my joy in living and being my true radiant self.

Nanette: Many thanks for coming.

J Masefield: May you always sail on calm seas. Thank you.

Elizabeth
"There is no such thing as hellfire"

She introduces herself only as Elizabeth. This may be Elizabeth Barrett Browning (1806–1861), a highly successful English poet who married poet, Robert Browning, settled in Italy and threw herself into the Liberation Front from Austria.

Good evening, I am Elizabeth. I may sound a little quaint in my delivery. It is quite an undertaking to follow in the wake of this very forceful person who has just left.

I haven't come to say anything very much, except to say, go on as you are for you are on this pathway he spoke about.

It is quite beyond the imagination of anyone on earth to know what God has in store for his children, no matter what they be, or where they come from. For ultimately, each one must find his or her niche and place in the empire of God which is limitless.

I have travelled far, for you must remember I knew about the life immortal before I left the earth plane and was well prepared for it. But even I … my imagination falters at what must be beyond that still awaits me, small wayfarer that I am.

No one is forgotten, no one is left uncared for. There is always somebody waiting to tend those who come. As you have been told before, the call for help must come from the soul itself, it cannot come second hand.

Just as Angela has said, 'go within'[14] and that 'within-ness' will send out a call for help, you can be sure there are legions of loving, merciful souls to help, no matter how low people may have sunk in the mind of mortal man and woman. They are not left without someone to help them on their upward path.

Do not be confused by theology. Do not be misled by what passes for religion upon earth. It is due for a great shake up, because the great and wonderful truths that should have come through the Christian religion have been glossed over by the church. We are not allowed to say anything about anybody but we cannot wear blinkers and hide from ourselves the fact that there are many who wear the black coat of the clergy who are totally unfitted to speak the word of God. We must remember too, that they are victims of a system that has been in existence for hundreds of years that has become like a clamp on humanity. Certainly in my time, we were not allowed to question. Too afraid even to think! That fear is still in existence in the world today. A great many illiterate people have the fear of hellfire, of burning eternally in the flames of hell by which so many churches have bound these people by terror.

So it is with the greatest joy I am able to tell you — *there is no such thing as hellfire!*

Of course, you know that yourselves. But it will be mooted abroad quite soon and this overwhelming fact will be removed from suffering souls.

I see it when these souls come over, if they have committed one small sin or broken a commandment, you do not know what hell their lives can be. Waiting for

14. See the Indian Sage, Meditation chapter, page 248.

eternal damnation. Or it can take another form of saying to God, 'I have done my worst, do as you damn well like to me now'. These are the words they use when they become defiant. They think they are damned anyway. This downward path becomes the immediate result of the teaching of the church. But it will change.

As John Masefield has said that God is at the helm and all's right with the world.

Good night to you all.

Thank you for putting up with me!

Writer
"I will give you the esoteric meaning of the Lord's prayer"

The group surmised that this was Evelyn Waugh (1903–1966), probably through Tara or Angela. As I have said before, often these names would be given to us later.

Born into a family of literature, Evelyn's father worked for the publishers Chapman and Hall. He had a fondness for the Victorian novel and a loathing of Dickens. With his tone both cynical and clever, he was ostracised for his homosexuality. He loathed Britain's political culture at the time, eventually to become almost entirely at variance with the outside world. His first novel was *Decline and Fall*, and amongst other works he wrote, *Officers and Gentlemen*. His masterpiece was *A handful of Dust* and his most famous book, *Brideshead Revisited*.

It has been given to me the most pleasant and sweet duty of expanding the true meaning of what is known as the Lord's prayer. I will give you the esoteric meaning, although I do not like this word, it has been vulgarised and much plagiarised.

Contrary to all dearly held convictions, this prayer was in daily use many centuries before Jesus Christ set foot upon the earth. It is one of the oldest cries from the human heart for understanding. It has been incorrectly translated and handed down from generation to generation, losing the true meaning of its glory in the passage of time.

Well, if you will be patient with me I will to the best of my ability give you the true meaning.

Will you repeat the beginning of the Lord's prayer please.

All: Our Father who art in heaven…

Writer: Stop. You have made a mistake.

All: Which?

Writer: I will explain to you.

There is no 'one Father', there is no euphemistically termed 'heaven'. All is one. There is no fabled heaven to which we are denied admittance if we break one of the commandments. No, it is all His realm.

One Father, which art in heaven. It is four great beings who came from the vast outside to give the truth to the dwellers on the planets of the solar system. So they are grouped together under one word, Father. This has a different meaning in the original term that was an invocation to the four great Lords, for their minds were as one, one for all and all for one.

That is why we, in the totally wrong version say, 'Father who art in heaven'. Where is heaven and where is hell? In men's minds and no other place.

The phrase should be, 'Lords of all, who dwell in glory and majesty supreme'.

[To Michéle he says]

I have just been told that you attended a church school. We have them in my native land too. We hope you benefited by your stay there!
Will you give me the next line of that prayer.

Michéle: Hallowed be thy name.

Writer: Thank you. Hallowed be thy name ... So holy it cannot be revealed. Too holy for the tongue of man in his ignorance to utter that collective name for the great Lords. Now child of the church school ... continue!

Michéle: Thy Kingdom come, thy will be done.

Writer: Thank you, that is enough. The dream that emerged from the great cosmic mind. Not the four whose names are hidden. Could there issue from that mind aught but beauty?
In bringing into being the planets, came the dream of beauty for the creatures he would put there. Note I am not alluding to our Father which art in heaven, to express his glory over which he alone is king.
'Let thy kingdom come.' Omitting that word ... let ... and the sentence loses its mystical meaning.
Thy will be done on earth as it is done once again in that mythical heaven.
What was His will? To live gloriously ... gloriously through love. That is the only emanation from the mind of God. Only that one emanation, love. Love in its purest, holiest essence. You only have to gaze upon a flower, a tree, an animal, a human being and you see the manifestation of love in all its different stages.
I might say in the course of one day, if I were back in my earthly body, I love my wife, I love my children, my dogs, the word of my own brain, I love that sunset, I love listening to a great work of music, I love to gaze at a beautiful painting, but how often did I say, 'I love gazing on the face of my neighbour?' Is not love evident in the most savage animal towards its young? Is it not evident in the lowly ant? Why is it lacking in the created world? Thy will ... universal, all embracing, all giving love, and don't think it is too difficult to attain. Continue.

Michéle: Give us this day our daily bread.

Writer: Is it not given to us in every shape and form to keep our physical body on the earth? Yes. It is there. But it also means give us our daily bread of the spirit and that really means being thankful for that which gives us sustenance.

Michéle: Forgive us our trespasses.

Writer: Is there any necessity to ask of that Great One forgiveness when I told you

He knows only love? Love so perfect that it can see no imperfection in its own creation. There is no need to plead for forgiveness. It is there pouring out, the giving … the forgiving, the giving of love. Now do you see? Continue!

Michéle: Lead us not into temptation but deliver us from evil.

Writer: Wait one moment … this is where I almost wish to laugh!

I am portraying for you this God who sees us as perfect, which is what we all will attain some day. Can you imagine the stupendous impertinence of man lifting up his voice and saying to the Father of creation, 'Lead us not into temptation!'

Do you all laugh with me with a tinge of sadness that turned me away from the church. That one sentence, 'Lead us not into temptation' … we will forget that hateful part. We will continue. I wait.

Michéle: What about 'Deliver us from evil'?

Writer: Ah! Evil is ignorance. A human being is evil only through willful ignorance. If we were to define the word evil we would spring a trap for ourselves. For what is evil? What I think is evil today, the young people would laugh at me for being a stupid old fuddy duddy. Am I right?

Michéle: It depends what you think is evil.

Writer: Aha! That is my point! Who can define evil? Who? Not we poor children on the earth. But as you have all sought and found the truth, so it is there for every child of God. 'Seek and ye shall find', 'Knock and it shall be opened unto you.'

Therefore that really means, deliver us from the consequences of our foolish ignorance. Lead kindly light. Apt? Continue.

Michéle: Thine is the Kingdom, the power and the glory.

Writer: I will not elaborate that theme. It is correct what I have said or told you about the kingdom, the power and the glory.

'Amen' means so let it be … for the time is ripe and at hand when men will turn from the husks of swinedom and find the jewels of the kingdom.

Thank you for being patient with me.

Angela continues after Evelyn Waugh departs

Another little grain of knowledge to your shores from the vast shoreless ocean of knowledge. May the blessing of God rest sweetly on your brow.

Ludwig von Beethoven (1770–1827), German musician and composer
"I come to thank her"

Beethoven was born in Bonn and died in Vienna. His first music lessons were from his father, but he is thought to have received lessons from Mozart and Hayden. He first appeared as a child keyboard prodigy at eight years old, but suffered deeply from depression caused by increasing deafness. By 1817 at the age of forty-seven he was all but stone deaf. The cause was never established. It could have been nephritis or syphilis, as there was no cure for these illnesses at that time. He died before his work was complete, hence 'The Unfinished Symphony'.

Tara, through her deep meditation or sleep state, would communicate with 'out of body' spirits or souls. Beethoven made her feel particularly depressed and heavy as he had a dark vibration about him.

Now the time has come when this is all kaput and I so anxious to speak. I come this day to the *gnade frau*[15] in whose body I sit.

I thank her with *mein* heart for what she has given me. The other day when I came in her sleeping room, I was *kommen* here, so they take me to her and they put her in · sleep and she released me.

Nanette: Yes, we thought this is what happened.

Beethoven: I come to thank her, for I make her feel …

Nanette: Yes, but she understood.

Beethoven: Thank you, *danke*.

Angela interrupts to relieve Beethoven

I must just interrupt because our last speaker wants to depart. He has been in the mists since he left the earth. Not really in the deep mists, you know, but not able to

15. *Means 'holy woman' in German.*

advance because he was feeling his life's work wasn't done and feeling the world hadn't treated him properly. All the feelings people often have when they come over.

So you can tell Tara the darkness that came over her was his deafness and the horror of it, do you see? That is what had bound him fast.

Well, you have seen how we have released a number of them and unfortunately, you will not believe me when I tell you that much of Beethoven's gloom, much of his bitterness and resentment has influenced the music of today! Yes!

Chopin has spoken through Tara and in direct voice I heard her say that he has spoken through several other mediums. He released himself but then he was a different temperament. When he comes down, which he does now and again, you have a wave of quite different music coming ... you can thank Chopin! Yes you can.

When the other comes ... discordant, jangled ... well, then you know who you can thank!

There is another one, which we released from the same country as this one, Wagner.

Yes, yes, all the distortions that come are from disappointed, talented people who have not achieved enough for their personal vanity. So they brood on and on, sending down the thoughts and vibrations. They all go down and you get all the discordants.

Yes, it is so, and we have to release them.

Percy Bysshe Shelley (1792–1822), English lyric poet and writer
"I am an old soul ... the rose is my emblem"

Shelley, best known as a leading figure in the Romantic movement, was a friend of Byron. He attended Divine College in Oxford and was expelled for his contribution to a pamphlet called, *The Necessity of Atheism*. He eloped with sixteen-year-old Harriet Westbrook, and moved to Dublin where he set up a commune. Later he wrote *Queen Mab* when he fell in love with Mary Godwin, with whom he also eloped and married. Harriet drowned herself. Shelley was devastated by the death of his son, William, and after the publishing of *The Revolt of Islam* he left for Italy where he spent the rest of his life. *Prometheus Unbound* is considered his masterpiece. His works are too lengthy to list here, but *Hellas*, a war drama, was inspired by the Greek war of Independence and was his last work.

Shelley and his companions were drowned in a sudden squall after returning home from visiting Byron and Leigh Hunt in Livorno.

"Hail to thee blithe spirit.
Bird that never wert ... "[16]

Yes it's Shelley. I greet you all. So happy a blithe spirit when I wrote that poem. I became part of that little bird and soared like a bird.

I have to speak in a whisper for I have been told to be so careful and not to trespass on the hospitality of all those here. I do not have a very masculine voice, so it doesn't worry me to speak *sotto voce*. As you might say I had a streak of feminine in me, what you call 'left over' from a previous incarnation in which I know I was a woman.

I felt the feminine strain so strongly quite often during my sojourn on the earth as a poet. It doesn't shame me or make me blush that I tell you now that I had very feminine hands. Very delicately fashioned, more for playing the spinet than pulling the plough! But I used to look down on my feminine fingernails and feel a queer streak of pride in me, thinking they resembled little pink shells.

You think I lack humour? Why not read my poems.

Shelley seemed a very earnest young fellow. Shelley *was* a very earnest young fellow carrying the cares of the world, oh, so strongly on his shoulders, thinking he

16. *An extract from one of Shelley's greatest poems, To a Skylark.*

could start out on a crusade to make the world a different place to live in. How sadly he failed in that attempt. But let him take courage in reflecting that today his poems are still read and enjoyed.

That is my reward, perhaps, because I now know that I was sent, I did not come.

Why should I leave my embowered place in spirit to come back to this dreary earth? I was sent an unwilling messenger, but I came and unlike Caesar, I cannot say I conquered. But I came and left soon.

Oh, yes the death wish was there. On the day on which I knew it was the end I made no struggle to keep life in this body. I was too thankful to soar like Ariel into Olympian heights and to find my niche back in the lovely sequestered home which was mine in spirit.

I am … and this is not blowing my own trumpet, not at all, there is no need for me to do that … I am an old soul.

I was with Pythagoras in Greece. I was with many others whose names live on in the sands of time and no amount of tears or water will erase those names. Shall we add Shelley? With the pink seashells for nails?

Ah, Shelley, Shelley. You know I am a blithe spirit? … I am … I am. I am a blithe spirit!

It was my blitheness, my gladness, my joy at knowing I was God that made my stay upon earth so unhappy in my last life. My unhappiness at school, my father couldn't understand this captive from other worlds whom he tried to cage and tame to his way of thought. He thought I was a rebel. I was just a lost blithe spirit.

I recaptured the thrill, the joy, and the magnificence of it all when I listened to the birds singing. I could hear, could you believe me, the veil between myself and spirit was so thin, that I could hear the flowers singing. Oh, yes! I could hear the songs of the flowers.

I did write about a plant, I called it a 'sensitive plant' but it did not convey what I received from my beautiful little bonny friends, my flowers.

The rose. That is why I am here. The rose was my emblem. It is still my emblem and it will ever be.

One day, when I was holding a rose in my hand, I gazed deeply into that heart and in a moment I was transported. It was difficult to say that I passed into a trance or was caught up in spirit, as they say in the bible, but I had a vision. The vision I beheld was the rose, which seemed to swell and grow and grow in size. Deep in the heart of the rose was the face of Christ.

Now it has been said by some that I was an atheist. Never, never. I was so aware of God. It was the God of the people of the earth that I couldn't believe in. Ever at school having God thundered into my ears, this vengeful, cruel God who was ready to snap up little boys like a dragon and crunch them in his teeth. Could I love this God? When I heard the flowers singing his praise, could I adore that vengeful God? When I listened to the song of the waterfall and the song of the brook, could I?

No, I could not.

But the God I knew, the God I had not forgotten, the God whose image I had brought with me into my mother's womb, that was the true God.

No. I was a God-worshipper.

But that God I kept secret in my heart because had I tried to explain to my contemporaries! 'Imagine', they would have said, 'Well, we have thought Shelley mad and now we know it!'

So I kept my great secret locked in my timid heart and it was only that day when I beheld the face of Christ in the heart of the rose that I knew I was being rewarded for my undying devotion, my adoration of God.

You did not expect that Shelley would speak here. I am quite certain that this beloved instrument will be overcome with surprise when she hears I have spoken. She was very fond of my work when she was a child. An older woman inspired by me taught her to love my work. But later on, not so many years later, she transferred her affection to Rupert Brooke and Shelley faded into the background.

She has given little thought, scant attention in the years that have passed but I have not lost contact with her. I came to her through that poetry for I have known her from the days of Light.[17] I came with that band as a camp follower, not a leading light, so I have never lost sight of her.

[Turning to Guy, Shelley continued]

I would be glad, my dear friend, if in the days to come you could perhaps buy – no, I would not like to put you to expense – borrow a volume containing my poems and peruse them. Having met face to face, perhaps you would understand then, why I am here today and what my life meant.

It is a great trial for the children of the Light when they are encased in a human body into which they do not fit. To maintain an orderly way of life when every nerve is straining for release and yet deep down in the reluctant heart, the rebellious heart, you know you cannot go.

After my vision of Christ, or Jesus as your preachers call him, I knew him. I knew my time was short. I knew that my entreaties had been given ear to and that my case had been considered before the 'council'.[18] I knew the mercy of the Christ had said, 'Let us call this tired soul home'.

One day I hope to welcome all of you, as you have welcomed me today.

I am no longer the puny weakling that I was upon the earth plane struggling with ill health. For when the soul and heart are not at peace, the earthly body will suffer and my earthly body did. I was thrashed so, on my puny little bottom, with a cane. There was little substance between that cane and my bones. That was to drive out of me the evil spirit that was bedevilling this soul.

Yes, that is life.

I am a blithe spirit! Why do I recall anything as depressing as the clergy? Away with them! That will come to pass and what a happy day it will be for this planet spinning so sweetly in space!

I deliberated on my way down, I halted my flight and gazed down upon this dark cloud surrounding it, completely enveloping it. You would not behold that for it is visible only to the eye of spirit, the cloud of evil. But beyond it was luminous, for there are gathered on the earth plane and around it, great ones. Great ones of spirit

17. See Chloris page 140.
18. A group of higher minds that monitor the earth.

with their loving hands outstretched in blessing.

I am confident of victory. Confident.

In all my descent into matter, or to put it in plain words, in every birth I had on the earth plane, I have always been fully aware of the battle between the children of Light and the forces of darkness. I have cried out against evil in my poems. Read them and you will see.

Remember the *Flower Song*? *The Bird Song*? I twitted Keats on his, *Ode to a Nightingale*. Was it rivalry to my lark?

I just came for a moment, swift as a swallow in my flight. I have been here before and I noted acutely and watched this process of using the body and I impart to you my own blithe spirit.

Angela continues on Shelley

Shelley could see what was going on very clearly. If he could not see clearly, he only had to wish and it became magnified for him. You see?

You know, he still is so exquisite. He speaks about the song of the flowers, that's what he is like. A lovely melody himself and so beautiful. He is one of the rare ones. Now and again, in a moment of extreme ecstasy, we, even in spirit, see a light there.

I can't put it into esoteric language because the meaning is so profound. That light, shall we say, denotes the four corners of the universe, indicating a spirit that has had experience not only in our solar system, but from far beyond in space.

How can one name the age of these great ones? No! One can't. But if you are privileged to see the shining symbol there, then you know you are gazing upon one who is out of our solar system entirely.

Angela refers to Rupert Brooke and others
"Shining youth, rather think of them in their glory"

Rupert Brooke (1887–1915) was an English poet, born in Warwickshire and educated at King's College in Cambridge. He travelled extensively and fell in love with a native Tahiti woman called *Taata Mata*. His first book of verse was, *Poems*, but he was known for his patriotic war sonnets after joining the British navy in WWI. His war sonnets sold in such great quantities that the war supply of paper was exhausted and the journal in which he was publishing, *New Numbers*, was forced to close down. He died of food poisoning at sea.

We know what is coming because the future is the present and becomes the past. It is one happening. If it wasn't in the future, it couldn't become the present, which couldn't become the past! It's one picture. It's inevitable. But we, being a little farther ahead, can see what is coming. Well, it was a loss but Shelley had to come.

It was like Rupert Brooke. He had to leave the world at the age of twenty-six years. A great loss to the world from the point of view of beauty and of words and so on. But he had to come.

They come, these beings who have a special something. They just come for their youth. I suppose it's better to remember them as a shining youth, as I have heard Tara say and forget that they would become portly and bald! Rather think of them in their glory.

Think of bonny Prince Charles and the great beauties of the past too. You see them when they get old and raddled, better that they had died when they were young and beautiful. Some women who come over here who were famous beauties and toasts of the empire, you don't know what they are like!

When they begin to slip from that throne, it is agony for them because it is all they have fed their ego on. Their vanity. Then they realise it's gone! Then their spiritual bodies shrink, they really do! Yes, not many survive that debacle, I can tell you. The loss of beauty and fame.

If only they knew how futile it all is. If they could understand that it meant nothing and must pass, they would take it and enjoy it but not agonise over it when the first wrinkle appears!

You know how they go on, Nanette. It is quite ridiculous! Some have very beautiful souls and it shines through the wrinkles. They still say, "She was beautiful when she was young". But she is more beautiful now.

3

Convents, Monasteries and the Church

Chapter 4: Convents

Kathleen's story, an Irish nun
"One gives oneself up to a merciless system that should have been abolished many years ago"

Kathleen tells us that she is Irish in her story. Although spirits do not speak in accents, the pitch and tone of Tara's voice would vary from person to person.

Necromancy, we were told, was the work of the devil and all his imps. I asked to give utterance to my thoughts today. I'm not sure whether I will be successful, but I have seen such kindness extended to other strangers who have spoken, that I am not as nervous as I thought I would be.

I have been allowed to be present at so many of these meetings and I see it is the work of God and his angels.

My name is Kathleen, I had no other name. When I entered the convent, I surrendered my name, my lands, my money and now I realise ... my true personality.

After the long years of training and the way they filled our minds with an entirely erroneous picture of life as it is lived in heaven ...

But I will tell you my story.

I was a big, bouncy, healthy girl when those gates closed behind me. Little did I dream, in my enthusiasm and my love for the holy mother and her son, that the gates were closing on my soul as well. Bars were placed across my soul. I could not escape.

Later, I didn't even wish to, you know. It is all so artificial, so completely false. It is all such a tragedy.

I have come because I have been informed that where I was in my convent, the country is in a state of turmoil over the question of religion.

If you look back upon the history of the world, you will see that most great wars have been fought over an ideology or a religion. Holy wars, or any name they give them, you will find the excuse is made that they are for the advancement of man. But the root base is always an ideology.

I do not come today to declaim against mother church, I merely come to speak about the system that for many centuries has turned thinking people (I refer to the unfortunates who are known as nuns) into automatons, without thoughts of their own and later on ... without feeling.

I don't think it is known beyond the convent gates, the lengths to which they will go to indoctrinate the thought that there is but one church and only one. That is, the Catholic church.

Please, I am not here to bring this church into ill-repute, I am merely telling you how hopeless it is to escape from their theology or their group once those gates close behind you.

It all seemed so romantic. It all seemed so beautiful to me, egged on by my family, to give myself up to God.

But, one doesn't give oneself up to God, one gives oneself up to a merciless system that should have been abolished many years ago. It should never have begun.

Truth is distorted in the most invidious and insidious manner. It is glossed over with pretty words, fictitious teachings and they call it, 'the truth of the holy church'.

I am a normally intelligent woman, thinking at last for myself, at long last!

You see, in a family like mine, who was devoted to the church, when a member decides on a life of solitude (you will notice I harp on the words 'behind the closed gates') that member is feted, fawned upon and made to feel that he or she is one of God's elect. Even if one has qualms about the finality, one has not the temerity to disappoint the family because the family glows in the thought that it has brought into this world one of the elect.

If they only knew ... if they only knew.

I plunged in with my enthusiasm, I have remarked about it before. I was known for my zest for any particular subject that caught my wandering thought, so that when this one wandering thought was caught and held captive by me (that I would like to give myself to God) I entered my prison house. Prison house of my body and prison house of my soul.

I noticed after a year that my enthusiasm for that which I had imagined to be a holy call was wearing thin, very thin. My first doubts began to march in on me like an army invading a territory!

I was made to perform the most menial tasks. I came from a wealthy family and believe me, the things that I had to do ... I don't think we would have asked the scullery maid to do. But I did not rebel. My once beautiful hands, my only vanity, became rough and red, calloused and bleeding. My knees, after endless hours of useless scrubbing of floors in the bitter winter of Ireland, were cracked and painful, even to the touch of my rough garment.

Having been cosseted and coddled by my family, I approached a senior nun and quite naturally asked for help with this condition. I was roughly spoken to. Yes, this is hard to believe that nuns can be so cruel. I was told it was all in the service of the blessed Lord Jesus!

I retired to my little cell, full of pain. Believe me, if you have not experienced the pain of fingers that are burst open and bleeding, chapped with chilblains and nothing is done for you!

Well, I rebelled in my soul for the first time that night and angrily said to the blessed Jesus, "I don't think it is fair of you to demand this of me. How am I serving you by scrubbing my hands on flagstones? My getting soaked through and wet and never a word of sympathy for me in my pain and distress?"

You think that I am mewling like a cat, now, in self-pity? No, it was a healthy young body rebelling against unnecessary pain. Having been coddled always by my doting mother if I fell and cut my knee, this stern, cold, unfeeling attitude chilled me to my already chilled bones.

I was now inflicted with a homesickness that nearly destroyed me.

However, I was spoken to by one of the very few kindly ones when, in a moment of extreme misery I knelt before her and said, "I cannot endure this coldness towards my distress and my pain".

Then she said, "You know, this has been the burden that every true child of God has to bear. Segregated from the rest of the world, it was known as acidy in the medieval times. If you are a true daughter of God and of the blessed mother, you will endure it without complaint."

I looked up into those mild, blue eyes and asked, "Did you endure this too?"

She looked back at me and said, "But of course, my child. How else would I understand you?"

I thought I had found a refuge in her. I thought I could go to her and unburden my soul.

Thereafter, a priest who visited us once every six months arrived and I, thinking I was talking to God, told him of all my afflictions, my unhappiness and my rebellion against the system. I also confessed I had been to my friend and received from her sympathy and understanding.

The sequel to my confession nearly sent me into a complete, I realise now, nervous breakdown. The Mother Superior sent for me. The priest had betrayed my confession and my punishment for that was that I was never permitted to speak to my friend again. I was told that she had been banished to her cell for fourteen days and nights!

I am not relating a story of what happened in the convent in the medieval times, but in this century! I only left eight years ago and passed into spirit.

I will not dwell upon my unhappy years. In a way I left long before my period of departure really arrived. My soul could no longer endure this. I approached my family before my novitiate was over and they gazed at me in horror. They almost looked upon me with loathing, for it would be an unheard of thing, for this girl who so gladly and loudly announced that she had felt that God was calling her … how could they now give her even a glimpse of hope that she could escape every human feeling!

I was assigned to the most unpleasant tasks even when I had become a bride of the church. I dislike using the words 'bride of the holy Jesus'. It is a mockery. I would look down at the ring upon my finger with hatred. But, I dared not take it off and throw it away, my punishment would have been confinement to my cell on bread and water and probably a thrashing … You don't know what goes on!

Perhaps it is only in Ireland, which is ancient and behind the times. I cannot speak for other convents, I speak of my experiences in my own pitiless prison house. You know, we were told that if we had a rebellious thought or if we broke away from the system, even in thought, all hell loomed for us!

In Ireland, at the moment, there is bitter dissension they tell me and I am delighted! I am raising up my soul in a plea and prayer to God that at long last, light is being let into these iniquitous places. You see, they sally forth in their sweeping robes and you think what tranquil faces they have. I was one of them and can tell you that the tranquillity is simply that the soul is dead.

They are, as I saw it there, the walking dead!

They have thought hell waited for them. We were told of a young nun named Katherine[1] who in her misery flung herself off the ramparts of her convent and from time to time we were shown frightening pictures of the hell and hellfire which she would now be experiencing. An abject lesson for us to remember!

Every day and night I prayed, "Holy Mother of God take me. Please God let me die ... let me die."

So heartrending were my prayers that one bitter night, in winter, I caught pneumonia and God called me for the first and last time and I answered the call.

Did I find hell? No. I found only joy. God was everywhere present every moment of the day and night. We have no day or night but I merely tell it like this because you are still of the earth as He had been every moment of my stay.

It was all so beautiful. I came over from the convent so firmly with the thought planted in my mind that perhaps this was just an in-between stage and I would have to go to hell to be punished for my sinful thoughts. So I asked a very kindly being and he said, "Hell is only of the mind my child ... there is no such place."

I came to tell you that this system is being attacked and it must go. It belongs to the dark ages of man when only fear existed. If there is a hell, I never saw a glimpse of it or met anyone who had been there.

I am so happy now and thank you for listening to me.

Angela comments on Kathleen's story

No man can be as cruel as a woman can be at certain times and in certain circumstances. It seems that when women are all confined together like that, the very worst in them comes to the surface. Well, they are trapped, and like a trapped animal will always snarl and show its worst side through fear in a restricted and unnatural environment. All very sad.

We have places that resemble convents in spirit and many nuns who pass into spirit wake up there and feel no shock or strangeness. You must remember that from their lives in a cloistered atmosphere, they have forgotten any other way of life. We have people there to restore them to health and strength, mentally and spiritually.

Do you know, sometimes the new arrivals think these lovely places are the work of the devil and all the loving helpers are simply in the guise of the devil. Oh, dear me!

This is where, believe it or not, our difficult rescue works takes place. You cannot

---

1. See author's story on Kathrine, the soul as the eternal recorder on page 88.

shake them out of the thought that hell is waiting for them, for they are taught that devils appear in beautiful guises, even as angelic beings waiting to destroy them. For they had always expected the Virgin Mary to be there with her arms out in welcome.

We have such a time with them. It is pathetic in the extreme. But the cleansing and the enlightenment comes and those cleansing tears ... how your heart would break if you could witness that moment.

It is no easy task for a woman who has been a nun to use a body like this beloved instrument. For as I told you, anything to do with this subject was called necromancy by the church and she was bold enough to come down and tell you her story which is one of countless legions as I have remarked before.

Kathleen, with her knowledge and pretty blue eyes, is now head of one of these convents in spirit.

Nanette
The soul as the eternal recorder

One day Angela brought Katherine who did not speak through Tara but Angela spoke for her instead. Apparently we had been nuns in the same convent long ago. Katherine, it seems, had been responsible for my death by incarceration, within one of the convent walls. Now was the time for her to seek and receive my forgiveness that she might be cleared of the pain and guilt connected with that day and move on, peaceful at last.

Fortunately, I have never in this lifetime suffered from claustrophobia, although I have always believed such a death particularly horrific.

I understand that many phobias are the result of past incarnations when a terrifying death was experienced. It can happen that a situation in this life could trigger the soul memory and bring about the ancient fear once more. The soul being the eternal recorder of everything in every life.

This picture shows ✝ her in her garb though she was later de-frocked.

Sister Frances Mary Banks M.A. (Died 1965)
"I was a great friend of Smuts"

Formerly Sister Frances Mary of the Community of the Resurrection, Grahamstown. For fifteen years she was principal of the Teachers College near her convent. Frances became author of several textbooks on child psychology, and also wrote the book, *Teach them how to live* from her experiences as a tutor at the Maidstone Prison in Kent, England. Three weeks after her death in 1965, Frances was able to make contact with her close friend Helen Greaves. Through her she communicated her newfound knowledge. It was all written down and published in Helen Greaves' interesting book, *The testimony of Light*.

I am one of those sometimes called here 'a passerby'. But from the moment when I first came to look and listen, I have never passed by. How can anybody pass by this scene of so much beauty, light, wisdom. Shall I go on *ad infinitum*? The so-muchness of it all!

It isn't very long since I died. What a stupid word, we must change it in our minds to 'since I was reborn' and do away with that ugly word ... die. That is a negative word, which should have no place in man's minds.

It may surprise you to know that I was a psychologist. Don't try to find out ... No, why should I hide when so many years ago I met Tara and I saw her latent potentiality and the light, which even then shone so brightly in her.

I will not attempt to hide my identity. My name is Frances Mary Banks. Preface it with th. '''', which I wore like a yoke on my back in my earth life. I was a Sister. A nun in the Anglican church here in this lovely country where I know you are seated at the moment.

It is not long since I left and working as hard as I did for the spiritual welfare of the human family, I can't give up that urge.

You know, Charles, I suffered a glorious fate on the earth. I was defrocked for my belief and faith and knowledge, which I preached about in my nun's garb. I speak easily, don't I? The habit is there ... not the nun's habit!

Now, I will tell you a little secret. I was a great friend of Smuts. He used to say to me, "You are the only woman I know who has the brain of a man". A doubtful compliment! But I know what he meant because, you see, I had taken many degrees and we could talk on many subjects.

I read a great deal. I probed, never satisfied. I searched, on and on and you know,

I haven't got the answer, yet, to many of my own questions. I have to wait. To each one his time.

It is quite delightful to be able to speak. Will you give my dear love to this girl and tell her how little we knew, when we stood under the tree and spoke about the doves, that one day I would speak through her! Isn't life strange. Despite all her clairvoyance, I know that never entered her head. Mind you, despite my knowledge and reasoning power, it never entered mine. Well, here we are.

I would deem it a very great favour if I could engage your attention for a little while again on a future occasion, Ella. For I was a churchwoman, then I was a free woman. I could tell you about the pain and agony of that changeover. Not for me a chameleon change. The worst thing for me was that I had to grow my hair and wait. Never having been blessed with an abundance of hair it seemed to me that mine would never ever grow again!

You will well understand and readily believe me when I tell you, as my transition from a nun into being one of the people again was troublesome. I had always had the greatest respect and love for the one we call Jesus Christ, but it was difficult for me, indeed it is for everyone on the earth, to visualise the real Jesus. Apart from the medieval conception of him, in which the artists all copied one another so inevitably, you look and say, 'that is Jesus'? It gives me great joy to tell you, the reality is quite different from the picture, quite, quite different! Perhaps the one he brought himself, through Tara's hand, is the nearest approach for there is no pain, there is laughter and there is manliness.[2]

Ye Gods! It used to worry me that they made such a mix about him in those pictures. If they had only used their minds and worked it out for themselves. The hard work! No man who did what he did in three years could have looked as they pictured him. No. What a wonderful revelation you have before you when you come to spirit and behold him in his ... well, what other word is there but glory and majesty. Above all, and this may stagger you (although why should it) his humanity is so wonderful. He is a humanist and I love him with all my strength and power.

All the others are very great and beautiful but in the Christian mind, one is so imbued with the thought of Jesus that the others take rather a lesser place in one's conception of glory. Oh! Don't believe for a moment they haven't got their full quota of glory and majesty! They are all God anyway!

Now I must go. There is just a little time allotted today.

Thanking you for all your good work. Unbeknown to yourselves, coming together like this, in this atmosphere of piety, sincerity and love, the influence spreading out into the ether is colossal.

Good night.

---

2. *Tara did a spirit drawing of Jesus – See page 119.*

Chapter 5: Monasteries

Angela introduces Fracalo, an Italian monk who was burnt at the stake

There had been a slight hiatus in the circle when an unknown entity tried to take control of Tara whilst Angela was speaking through her. Angela withdrew to lead the intruder away. In the meantime, another spirit was called in to take her place in order to maintain the power in Tara's body until she returned.

Beatrice fills in for Angela
"When it's all over, the meetings, great discussions take place"

My name is Beatrice. I was known as Bea, although that's not going to interest you now. I often sit here you know. I have been allowed to come through, I don't know why, but, it's to do with the man who just walked out of the room here. I saw him go, but that will be straightened out in a moment or two.

So, if you can put up with me for a short while, I'm no great shakes but at least I can keep the power by just talking.

It happened at a most unexpected moment with us all sitting here agog, also being trained and taught in matters ethereal and matters heavenly, and suddenly they pounced on me and said, "now go in!" We have watched it being done, so we know exactly what to do.

Joan: So is this the first time you have ever come through?

Beatrice: Yes, it's the first time and I'm not doing so badly, am I? Mind you, my best

91

friend is holding thumbs for me, but I'm not frightened. I have not been over for so very long.

There's this man back again, he is most insistent. I'll see what Angela is going to do. She is leading him away again, he looks so tearful. He has still got his long brown robe on. I can't place him at all, you know. Many of us come to this side and we know sweet blow all and then we are slowly indoctrinated. That's not an apt word but it is fascinating to me, because it is new territory completely! It's all very fascinating.

I want to tell you something I bet no one else has told you. When it's all over, the meetings, great discussions take place. Oh, yes, the school isn't over when you toddle off to your beds. Great discussions go on, for even here it is very difficult to convince some people that they are dead. Those are the ones they are so careful with, because truly, you can upset them very badly indeed. Those who go around with ear plugs in, looking for that mythical heaven, you know, which the psalmists and the padrés ... there's one about two arms' lengths away from me ... have to be very careful what you say about padrés ... but between you and me they do gabble a lot of tripe, don't they? Not even any onions to dish it up with! When you come over here, you'll see for yourself what it's all about and realise the tripe!

Never mind, I'm enjoying myself. Angela has taken him now. He has quite a 'thing' around him, what do you call it? An aura. Yes, well, he has quite an aura of his own. I don't know why they won't let him speak. I expect there's a valid reason for it. He caused quite an upset in the apple cart.

You think I'm slangy and racy? I was like that on earth and I haven't changed yet! Just a minute, I got so interested I forgot to give power. I must go now. I haven't the faintest idea what I've talked about.

Nan: Perhaps you'll come again?

Beatrice: No, I won't come again, I've got nothing to relate about my life. Nothing absorbing or interesting.

Nan: Well, good luck on your journey.

Beatrice: Yes, thank you. I'm not going to lag behind. Goodnight. I will listen to myself later, on that machine you are playing. We do, you know.

Nan: How marvellous, do you really?

Beatrice: Course we do! We don't flap home when it's all over. Of course, you do realise that for us there are no walls, no physical obstacles. We don't see that vibration at all, so it causes us no discomfort. Some of us just squat on the floor, others stand, some just lean around.

On some nights when the great ones come, the word goes around and we are banished, we lesser fry. We wouldn't understand one word anyway.

Goodbye.

Angela speaks of Fracalo, a heretic burned at the stake

Hello, hello.

Now I expect you are all wondering why this all happened just now ...

The monkish man, he was burned at the stake and now he wants to come and get clearance of the earth. We can't let him tonight because Tara is not so well. She is tired you know and he would drain her too much.

He was an Italian monk who took a long time to burn. You know, what they called the 'slow roastings'.[3] We can't let him come, but we will help him, he can come another time.

He was in darkness for a long time. Three hundred years ago he was on earth and you see he stood up for the truth. But he found that what he thought was truth, wasn't truth at all. So, you see, when he came over he felt very confused and people like that wander off into the mists. It becomes very wearisome following them up and if you say, 'hey you' they turn and look at you and scuttle away.

Ella: How very sad for them.

Angela: Yes well, if I had my way and I was on the earth plane, God forbid, I would open up great universities of learning for the teaching of spiritual facts. What really happens to man after death. They would know what to expect and how to live. All this useless garbage that is implanted in their minds at school. The only true knowledge is how to live, how to die and how you live after you die. What else is there? Earth-life and rebirth into your natural world.

Well, when you come over we will have a conducted tour and I will show you the misunderstandings, the lies, (that's not a word we like to use here), but these ghastly lies have changed the lives of otherwise potentially very good people. You see, they tell them this and they tell them that and because they wear a gown or if it is a bishop who wears a mitre, then it's all gospel truth! Then we have to undo the work!

Not that we complain, but it would appall you to see how mulish they are, because it is put there from birth, generation after generation, cycle after cycle. The same weary round they tread like squirrels in a cage, round and round and never find the way out. Well, they are the same way, the whole thing is too great and too vast for them, then, in the transition period. Not all of them, some are deeply into it.

Forgive me if I'm not full of bounce tonight, the brother has left me rather deflated. I hated to say no to him because he has watched others coming through and being released and he cannot understand why he isn't allowed.

You see, if we allow him to use this body and he has not used it before, he will immediately recall all his agony and probably smell his fat burning. So we can't, but we will find some other way, don't worry.

I had to be awfully persuasive, because he stood blocking the airway around Tara and he is a big man. He must have taken an awful long time to burn.

Nan: How ghastly ... dreadful!

3. *Slow roastings in Spain occured during the 1400's.*

Angela: He told me they hung him over a slow fire. Yes well, that's why we have these karmic laws.

Annabel: I wonder why this happened to him, what were the circumstances?

Angela: Heretic. He was called a heretic. They did dreadful things in the church, every church, not one is guiltless. Oh, no! Just one moment please …

It was that monk back again. He came round the other side. Well, I have handed him over to Ronnie, he will take care of him.

Please don't think we are being heartless, but it will do no good at the moment. You see, it's his mind. For three hundred years he just heard the crackling of wood and he can't believe he is going to be released from it. We don't have to bring him through Tara to be released, we do it in other ways, but he certainly has watched other people being released and he wants to do the same thing.

Ella: There's nothing we can do in meditation for him in some way?

Angela: No, not at all. There is a group around him now of great spirits helping him. Amongst them, let me tell you, is the very one who ordered the burning! Yes, well, that is how it is on our side.

Fracalo, that is his name, he has this craving to unburden himself, just as people on earth say, 'I must unburden myself to you'. Well, he wants to unburden himself of all that he suffered.

His memory is so vibrantly alive there, so we can't let Tara undergo it, but he cannot see this. We cannot say nay to anyone who wishes to come to the circle and listen and be educated, like Beatrice and many others, but he doesn't understand, you see? He hasn't used his mind for three hundred years, nor his tongue, which would be so rusty, he wouldn't be able to get the words from her mind.

So it makes it very difficult for us.

Do please believe me, it has upset us very much indeed. He has lurked in the shadows for quite a long time. But don't worry, he will come right, we'll look after him.

Chapter 6

The Church

Methodist minister and religious reformer
"I once butchered for the bastard"

It was revealed to us later that this was John Wesley (1703–1791) who formed a group of four to plan a new religion. The first half of the 18th Century in England was a time of moral disorder and corruption in high places where crime was rampant. By the end of the 18th Century, a religious revival emerged in the form of the Methodist Church, brilliantly organised by John Wesley. According to the historian W. Lecky, it purified politics and created a wave of humanitarianism that led to the abolition of slavery and to penal reform.

To forgive is to be on the side of the angels, in a double sense. If you can accomplish this most difficult of all the human emotions, even when you feel you have been wronged or insulted, rightly or not, and you learn to forgive all those things, you truly will be on the side of the angels when you pass into spirit. Do you see what I mean?

I am quoting a very cogent point here and a very great truth that the act of forgiving (so beautifully demonstrated by the apostle) is your entrée into the higher lands of spirit.

To hold in your heart and mind a grudge, as Olive so clearly put it, is like a millstone around your neck when you come into spirit because it is revealed to you. You can notice that you shall be the one very often to say to the person who harmed you, 'forgive me for bringing you into that frame of mind that made you do this to me'. See?

Don't always think that when someone does anything to you that you are truly the injured one. Very often it may be an angry thought, maybe your own, that brings into play the desire to hurt in the other person. So you must forgive.

Look deep into the unconscious. When you are aware, go back and think what started it all and you will find, most times, that you are the aggressor bringing about the desire to hurt you in that man or woman. Ask forgiveness from that person for rousing an unhealthy symptom of the lower side of man's nature.

You understand that with arrogance and egotism in the average human being, the resentment, like black treacle, viscous stuff, comes pouring out into the etheric and starts a sorry tale. For that action, and I'm talking of when the resentment is deep, when you say, 'I can never forgive them, never', this black fluid pours out and wraps itself round you like a winding sheet. It clings fast until you can say whole-heartedly and divinely, 'I forgive you'.

That is only one half of the action.

The rest should follow immediately and you should say, 'I ask your forgiveness'.

It is a double action. The wrong doer and the wronged. Two people.

Don't ever forget the weapon that is your tongue. It is more deadly than the asp that killed the Egyptian queen, for that finished its work quickly and finally, but you don't! Think it over.

Yes, I should be a tremendous taskmaster and I am. I was a great reformer. A religious reformer and it was not until I reformed my own religion in a following life that I realised how blind I had been!

Man, know thyself. Man, reflected in everybody else, yourself in everybody, God in all of you.

So for your own comfort, think of these words constantly, when you feel downhearted, when you feel trodden upon, reviled and disliked, 'there is only God'.

Far better to come prepared in mind, intellect and in spirit, to cross the bridge in perfect safety than to find it buckle in the middle between your world and the world in which I live. Is it not infinitely worthwhile to get yourself a passport that admits you straight away into the realm of God than to hang around a beggar at the gate?

Believe me, I speak of this for I, too, was a narrow minded, bigoted and tyrannical man in my thought of God. I persecuted.

I was not a cruel man physically, but I freely admit, I played with my tongue and I saw only the dark side of God. I cried out, "Woe and betide you, all of you, if you stray from the path!"

I was and still am, quite a glib word maker! I painted lurid pictures of hellfire and satan with his fork in hand. I did, I did!

I think you have gathered by now that I was a minister of religion.

I'm sure I can vividly remember on one occasion, when I was giving forth my imagery of hell, two women in my congregation fainted in the pew (probably too tightly corseted) and I was gleeful! Branded as lambs, I saved them from burning, which I told them they would be condemned to if they did not change their ways!

Oh, I kept that on through my whole long history. Each Sunday, out I thundered, 'Beware, beware, repent before it is too late'. I was louder than John the Baptist in saying, 'Repent, repent, for vengeance is at hand'. I would point a finger at them sitting before me and say, 'Mark well these words, see that you put enough in the plate today, for I know just those who are able to put in a substantial amount and those who can't and I can see from here what you're doing!'

Oh, I was feared. And I was delighted!

It was only after I had passed into spirit that I could count those lost or straying sheep and the burning brands that I had rescued on less than three fingers on my one hand, which means two!

The others rejected me completely. I was fanatical. Yes, had I been a priest two or three hundred years before that incarnation, I know I would have had no hesitation in applying the boot. You know what that means? I would have put them on the rack. I would have done anything to make them say, 'I believe, I believe'.

Oh, how blind we are.

I did not do this out of wickedness or through wicked intent. No, I only wanted to call them to God. Can you believe it?

Now I know that not one of them forgave me for the fear I had put into them of hell. None of them were particularly evil, nor were they particularly good, but I had implanted into them that dastardly fear, so that when they came to spirit, they remembered my words.

As the ages and the years passed, they began to see how wrong I had been. Do you think they ever forgave me? No. They condemned me and they had to go on a long time before they could forgive. They haven't all done so yet.

So, partly to assuage that I had been so wrong and partly to flee their wrath, I took on the body as a preacher. This time with a clearer vision and preaching ever 'Forgive'. For I had not yet been forgiven and I knew the agony!

So there you have the action. They couldn't forgive me for the fear I had implanted and by hating me, they held themselves in the dark hell that I had brought them into.

So I came down then and was known for my tolerance, my love and harping, 'love thine enemies, forgive, open wide the gates of your hearts lest the gates of heaven be closed against you'.

Quite aptly put. I told you I had a good command of words.

I am rather a peculiar being, because differing from the greater majority of reincarnated people who go into different nationalities when it is necessary in order to further their progression according to their desire, I have remained rigidly English. I have almost persistently reincarnated into England because if I were to tell you who I was in the time of William the Conqueror, I would abash you by what I did under that banner!

I have tried to undo but made a mess of it each time. You must not forget I butchered when I first set foot on British soil, as you call it now. I butchered for the bastard, as he was known. You know that William the Conqueror was called, 'the Bastard'! Perhaps somewhere in me, amongst all that blood, the divine awoke for the first time. I had not incarnated much before then. So, down the centuries I reincarnated in Britain, sometimes in Wales.

You might search, please, when you go to England, watch well and you will see a statue of me like this, for this was my sign. I would place my finger across my lips and say to my congregation, 'Keep your lips sealed against words of anger'. A little idiosyncrasy of mine. But it seemed to drive it home, you know, to put the finger across the mouth like so and keep the mouth sealed against words that sting like scorpion's tails.

Keep your mouth sealed against words like swords that pierce the heart and mind. Thank you.

[With that he placed Tara's finger across her lips as if sealed. Then he left.]

Reverend John Weatherby – Country Parson
"To be bored is a far greater sin than to drink. It rotted my gut not my soul"

You've had actors, crackpot professors, scientists, doctors, but I swear you've never had a country parson before!

Here I am, the Reverend John Weatherby!

I was listening to what you call the records of the meetings here and none of you is over sympathetic to priests. Well, I was a vicar.

You could wonder why I am gracing your little group with my presence today. You know, this room where we are today is in the form of a confessional. A very different reason from the one for which it usually functions so brilliantly well!

You are all agog to hear what I am going to confess!

Mine was not really even a venial sin. No, mine was a dreary round routine of a work that bored me to death. God, bored I was! I would stand in my rickety pulpit and look down on those moon faces looking at me and think, 'God! How you bore me'.

Due to circumstances, the usual thing, my bloody family, no room for the third son, 'Oh, chuck him in the ministry and be damned with his soul. Anyhow, we've finished with him, let the bloody church fend for him!'

Well, what use was I when I began? So boring. Not to the glory of God. The bloody burden of my soul! Yes. It's good for me to swear. I couldn't do that until I left the pulpit and got out of that cloak and cassock of mine. God! If you had to listen to the wail of that organ! Oh, that wheezy organ and the wheezy woman who played it! Oh, the boredom of my country parson and my boring wife. Equally boring, boring life and boring wife!

I don't have to be loyal to her, she pursued me like the hounds pursue the fox and she caught the fox, the goose!

We had no children in our rectory, but by God we had an outdoor privy! The worst punishment inflicted on me splashing through the mud. Oh God! The door didn't fit properly, nothing fitted properly and I fitted properly least of all, into a work chosen for me by my 'loving family'!

I am another who suffered for the honour of the family but (now comes my confession) I am still living in that hell of boredom! I got no advancement. Other fellows were passed over my head and given the plums whilst I stayed stuck fast with my feet in that pathway to the privy!

Then you mouth platitudes. I knew what a farce it all was but what could I do? I could do nothing. I couldn't escape. Trapped in that church, as surely as those nuns they buried alive for answering the call of their bodies and looking for a man. That was how I was trapped.

Well, I did the only sensible thing to do, I became a gal ... orious secret tippler! Aha!

At last I found my way out of boredom. At the beginning it was glassful by glassful and the bloody bottle by bloody bottle at the end. What a lovely life! Aha! What a wonderful ending it was.

I had to hide it from my parish, little did they know that many a time in my pulpit at my feet was my comforter! Not the comforter I preached about, but a lovely bottle!

What is your name my good fellow?

Charles Orfang: It's Charles.

J. Weatherby: When I say that, I am not speaking in a lordly manner. I merely mean you must be a good man to sit here and listen to all this.

Charles Orfang: I am enjoying it.

J. Weatherby: Yes and I'm enjoying the telling and repentance, although, I don't quite know why I am, but I'm here to confess. Let me tell you, my good lady, to be bored is a far greater sin than to drink. A little drop and you'll love all those moon faces looking at you. That is what I had found after the first half of the bottle had gone down my gullet.

So I come to the end of my sermon and it is this; never allow yourself to be bored.

I drank. It might have rotted my guts but it didn't rot my soul.

Well, you would like to hear what happened at the end of the Reverend John Weatherby, wouldn't you?

[All agreed]

J. Weatherby: I went out on a fiendish December night to the bedside of a person dying, who should have died ten years before and her family and I would have been happier had it so happened. Well, I had taken the trusty bottle with me, locked up of course in my bag.

I can remember what a lovely memory the last one was. The downing of a good half bottle! I stood on the edge of a field with a small river about a hundred yards beyond. I had parked my tin pot of a car somewhere in the dark and instead of finding my car I sank away without a bubble! Found myself here, dead!

I have to go now. Would you have liked me to come to you holding my oily palms together? Would you have liked me to come to you with an obsequious servile grin on my face? No, I come as I was.

Angela followed immediately

He is such an utter darling. I cannot tell you what a delightful being he is. He is the soul of kindness and a deeply, deeply religious man, who couldn't stomach the hypocrisy of his church and the narrowness of it all. He was actually a brilliantly clever man and it was again one of the tragedies of family, where he was not allowed to do what he wanted to do. He would undoubtedly have made a name for himself in science. Yes. That is why he is so happy now because he is, at the moment, working with the scientist who came the other day.[4] They are working together and now he has found his niche, but coming down into the body he would naturally resort to mannerisms of his last days on the earth planet.

---

4. *Presumed to be Professor Oliver Lodge. See page 220.*

Archbishop Cosmo Gordon Lang of Canterbury (1864–1945)
"How the light came to dwell amongst you"

A Scottish Anglican prelate and Archbishop of Canterbury. He was born in Fyfe, Aberdeenshire. Principal of the Aberdeen University, he entered the Church of England in 1890, became the bishop of Stepney and canon of St. Pauls, was appointed Archbishop of York in 1908 and Archbishop of Canterbury in 1928. As a man of wide interests, he was accepted by all parties in the Church of England and was both counsellor and friend to the royal family.

This information is a compilation of two occasions that Cosmo Lang came through to us. In the late twenties, a church commission was set up to investigate spiritualism and whether or not to give their blessing on it. However, the findings were never published. Cosmo Lang contributed to the findings being quashed. Tara resented the fact that the findings were never published.

This meeting tonight has been convened on high to serve a dual purpose, that you three loyal adherents to the faith may be thanked.

I have not used a physical body, a medium, so have received the most horrendous warnings from my colleagues in spirit that I must handle this human instrument with far greater trepidation and care than I assigned to the mechanical instrument in which my voice heretofore has been recorded.

My name is Lang.

Group: Oh!

Archbishop Lang: Yes, I expected that 'Oh'. As I told you, your instrument also recorded that 'Oh' on the ether when she saw me and was not at all inclined to allow me to use her. But Angela stepped into the breach and she brought under control the meeting between herself and myself.

Last night was extremely fortuitous because it had all been pre-arranged. You know, of course, that we have no idea of time in spirit, but I use those words with definite consideration and aforethought. I planned the meeting last night because for a long time she held in her mind resentment against me for my attitude. I might say almost in self-abnegation, for the attitude I struck against spiritualism *per se*.

As I shall be working with her in the future it is essential that she and I can work in perfect accord with each other and that all resentment against myself is dislodged.

I make a pun on Lodge's name! I overheard a conversation that we had no sense of humour. I bubble with it my friends, even to the inexorably bad taste of making a pun on my friend Professor Lodge's name![5]

So, it must be dislodged from her mind. Knowing her extremely well, she will probably clamour to hear what I have to say about her, which will surprise her.

---

5. See Professor Lodge on page 220.

I am a frequenter of this hallowed place. Yes, I have studied her in trance and out of trance. I have been an intruder in her bedroom when she was in meditation. All unknown to her, for I have kept my identity well concealed knowing that I would have as frigid reception as I had from her this morning.

Let me hasten in my own self-defence to say that I was greatly misjudged.

It was only after great heart-searching and burning that I withdrew from the peoples of the world, the findings of the church on spiritualism.

Spiritualism was cluttered up then, as it is today, with all kinds of nonsensical farragoes of which I highly disapproved. I claim no clairvoyance or prophecy but I knew deep within me that the day was not yet at hand when the churches could give out that this was the essential part of Jesus' teaching. But I knew that the day would come.

I am still enthralled with the man called Jesus. Since being on this side, meeting him and knowing that one of his most endearing traits is his sense of humour, I am quite sure that when he kicked the fig tree and stubbed his toe that he used an appropriate swear word in Aramaic that turned the air blue that day!

He was the instigator of my entering into my holy orders.

How that word 'holy' is abused. This instrument knows the true meaning, the true worth of the word holy, for she knows the true experience of wholeness of spirit.

Through my student days and throughout all the days of my ministry, I followed the pathway of this great pathfinder, Jesus. It was a great shock to me working under the aegis of my church with so much concealed, to learn of its narrowness. If we should pass through the lychgate⁶ as we enter the church, there should be a greater opening of the spiritual eye and the spiritual ear. But alas, there is a shutting down.

It was also a great shock to me, when I passed into spirit, to find that my beloved saviour was crucified not for his faith, not for his belief in eternity and in the Father, but that he was considered a political danger! That is the truth.

As is happening on your earth plane today, when every man (and I include my churchman) lives for himself and what he can get out of life, it was the same then. The Jews feared the Romans. The Romans feared the Jews and make no mistake they did, for all the might of a nation can crumble under the fires of fanatical people. Ravenous, greedy, unscrupulous beastly men. Yes, I had to revise all my thoughts on that dreadful happening.

Oh, if one could only open up the eyes of man, open up his heart and let him see what a gift this life is. To use Jesus' words, 'the life abundant'.

If you would only turn to us, there would be no more wars, no more hate. If they realised that when they come over into spirit, even the crowns and the mighty will tumble down into the pit and they can take with them nothing but what they built up within themselves.

Unless man hears the last sound of the war drum, lest he beholds the last snare of the hunter and turns away back to his God, his world will be destroyed.

That sounds a tall order to you does it not? But it is man who will destroy his world.

---

6. A lychgate was a roofed gateway to a church used for sheltering coffins before the priest arrived.

If this happens, do I see any hopes of him building it up again? No. I am afraid that the end of the tether has been worn out and is frayed.

Can you imagine that man can be so blind? If you could see from this side of life, I think you would literally drop dead in your tracks!

The group of great scientists with whom I work come down to try and help. After all, that was our task upon the earth. I do not claim any divine power for myself, I do my work for the good shepherd to bring the straying lambs into the fold, to try to open up happier horizons for mankind by investing things, such as machinery, to lighten the burden and make life a little brighter.

So in both ways, in religion and in science, we were motivated by the desire to help mankind.

Alas for me to have to say this, but truth will out. I failed as a shepherd.

Those great inventions of the scientists, how many of them are not now being used to exterminate man? The all over picture of humanity in the world at the moment is dismal, or worse still, a terrifying sight.

However, I would have you know that no soul is rejected by God. God cannot reject that which is his creation. So no matter what eons may pass, there is not a soul that will not be reclaimed and brought back to God.

There are worlds without end, planes of existence, fields of knowledge, avenues of learning and great vistas of unimaginable beauty waiting for every created being. The search for perfection is endless, for who can say, I am perfect? No soul has been given that insight into himself. No, his inner sight will always be directed towards God who is perfect.

I go into deep and weighty matters here, perhaps I should let the veil fall at this juncture of our acquaintance.

I come as I am now, a very ordinary man, stripped of the trappings of my high office and therefore, at last, will be able to meet my fellow beings on an equal footing.

Do you think I did not detest the servility, the subservience paid to my high office? I knew it was an empty thing, which I would have willingly tossed out through the window. Oh, do you think I did not have long thoughts on the subject? Believe me, the climb to the top is fraught with pitfalls. What does our poet Khayyam say? "Pitfall and Jinn"[7], that means a trap. I thought it meant an alcoholic drink! The climb is fraught, perilous.

We brought one of our most humble parsons[8] a little while ago and even he said, 'I was passed over and left'. Well, that was a dreary parish, I know. Yes, we brought him to let you gain an insight into the workings of the Anglican church. I, least of all, blame him for the consolation he found in the bottle. As he said, "It did not rot my soul". We brought him to let you see that a man can still remain great in spirit no matter what the vicissitudes of his life (a favourite word in spirit). Indeed, you will be glad to know that he has risen greatly in spirit and is closely associated with myself in our mission now. A great spirit there.

We will hearken now to the instrument.

---

7. *This gives us an indication that Omar Khayyam will be coming through.*
8. *See Reverend Weatherby, page 99.*

I shall be watching her reaction. I know what to expect fully, but I want to state to you right here and now, here is a soul without flaw. Here is womanhood of crystal purity. Here is a soul who can go no higher.

This opinion is more than fully endorsed by the greatest of them all under whose surveillance you have been since she, I might say, graced your home.

Think these words over when you are seated alone and know that it is your inestimable privilege that the master Jesus guided her towards you.

Spiritually the picture is flawless. Physically she has suffered and paid the price. The toll that all greatly endowed spiritual beings suffer and pay when they sacrifice.

I stress, sacrifice. If I had a blue pencil here I would underscore that word a hundred times. The sacrifice they make in taking upon themselves the physical form again to help their fellow beings!

In every life, the light was there and it has never diminished, though she in her present state is unaware of this. We cannot place upon her shoulders too much responsibility and too much recollection of what she has accomplished in the past. Better to let it lie fallow in eternity, so that when she returns now to grace us, she will know.

Only then, will she be stripped of the burden that went with the bringing of the light. The rays on which this soul works only are the concomitant features of truth, comfort, love, light, thought for others and help, given at all times, never refused, in small measure, in large measure and flowing over.

Now you know why she was chosen for this great mission; there is no other upon earth planet, nor with us, worthy enough to do this.

Ideally, she should have been withdrawn from mankind. Ideally she should never have borne children. Deep in her heart she has felt this, but dismissed it loyally in the deep love that she bore the children of that wedlock. She should have been withdrawn from mankind and the tarnish of mankind.

Blameless and without blemish, the life she has led!

But how can you persuade an independent soul like this one that this would have been the way made easy for her? No. Due to some mistaken loyalty to the past, she came and insisted in being associated with those whom she knew in all the past, to bring light to them. There was no need for this, but ever on the earth plane, we fall short of the ideal, do we not? So she, having free will to follow the pathway, she chose, bringing upon herself contamination of her own purity, the attendant ills of the human body.

Well, enough on that subject. I merely wanted to tell you how the light came to dwell amongst you.

Had I been in the pulpit now there would have been a clock on the wall to remind me to bring my sermon to an end. But there is no clock on the wall. Just a very lovely 'human' alarm clock called Angela who has pulled the bell and tolled my departure from this body.

I thank you.

4

Philosophies of Life

Chapter 7: Christians of the Faith

Unknown teacher
"I will rest in the Law not the Lord"

Angela: Glad to have you with us Michael.

Unknown teacher: The words of the Psalmist say:
   "I will wait upon the Law and renew my strength
   I shall mount with wings like eagles
   I shall walk and not grow weary
   I shall run and not grow faint."[1]

   I am here for a very short time. I hope I can manage this. I was told there is always a welcome for the newcomer.

   I came to interpret for you the true meaning of those words. For the time has come in the cycle of the earth's periods. It always does. Otherwise, as it has been told you many times, stagnation occurs and there is no progression. It must be so in an ever-changing world.

   The scriptures say, 'I will rest in the Lord'. It is not so, no. It is the Law of the creator that is the great supply house of energy such as health, happiness, prosperity. Life giving, wealth giving, giving all. Why should you be denied prosperity? Is it against the law? No, it is in full accordance with the Law. Therefore the supply is there in the Law. There is a great and never failing reservoir of this power of the Law. The Law is accessible. It always was, but man did not reach out for that which God gave so fully.

   Now listen to me or my visit is a failure. Take my words to heart and ponder them, one by one like pearls upon a ribbon. Go inside of yourselves and reach out with

1. Isaiah 40 verse 31.

both hands, with your heart, mind and thinking powers. Say unto God, I know that you have placed there for each and every one of us this storehouse of all we need. Give unto me that which is my due. For each man, child and woman there is their due. This is the Law of God.

God is the creative mind. He is a geomatricician and a mathematician. Everything is worked out by numerology. Oh, not your conception of numerology, the creator's conception.

You think He put you here to die of starvation, mental, physical and spiritual starvation? You think you look after your people like that? To let them die of three starvations? No. Then why do you think the great Master of it all would treat his created so?

Jesus got one small glimmer of light when He said, 'You are all important to God, not a sparrow falls but He knows not it, not a hair of your head that is not numbered but He sees'[2]. He had the wisdom, but the meaning has been lost. You understand this, little man?

Michael: Yes.

Unknown teacher: Then keep it in your head, it will stay there longer than the head of the adult. Let it go down into your subconscious and it will be remembered for the rest of your life.

What? Oh, I must not name myself!

Now, after you have glutted yourself on the feast of good things that the Law has in store for you, then can you say with knowledge, 'I shall mount with wings like eagles'. You will become king of the etheric realm when you know your own power. When you are linked with the storehouse of power through your knowledge of God so you have watched the eagle rise into the air. Be ye eagles and know it is there for you.

Do not be depressed, my brother Charles. Oh, what you do to yourselves when depressed, if I could show you a mental picture of what you do to your power of spirit you would drop down dead with shock! Could I show you what you hand to your inner power of the spirit and the mind. If you would only see yourselves as an eagle receiving the air with wings of God.

Now we have finished with the air, we come to the earth, 'I shall live, walk and not grow weary'. Ah, with the knowledge that you have, when you are tired, you must sit down and reach out for strength in the physical body. The eagle is the spirit. The weariness of the walking is the physical. From the physical effort that you put into your daily work, you will see how it is given to you.

Those who believe prosper because they believe. Is this not so?

Guy: It is so.

Unknown teacher: Yes. Now we say, 'I shall run and not grow faint'. This is metaphysical that in the running you stretch out. So with this knowledge, if you can

2. *Paraphrase of Matthew 10 verse 30 and Luke 12 verse 7.*

reach up, you will not grow faint when the revelations are made to you.

I only give unto you the way of life. You have sampled it and found it good, yes?

Guy, continue with that full confidence that what you ask for will be given to you, for you have seen the apple that would poison you if you ate it. So discard it because you believe in the Law.

Forget your flesh and let your spirit and your soul soar up to God like the eagle. You too, Michael, then you will come into calm waters, my little man, and you will restore your strength.

Now, do I make myself clear or have I come in vain? All I want to tell is, think of this Law, not the Lord. Oh, no, no, no. It is the Law. Spell it out for me.

Charles and Guy: L–A–W.

Unknown teacher: Thank you, thank you. You think I don't know how to spell it?

[Laughter]

I want you to spell it so it is before you in letters of flame, fire. Remember the Law is there, given by God. Everything is perfection, you know.

Ha. I have no patience. Now I must go.

The Prelate
"I came to speak of God, God, God"

The prelate apparently heard one of the group ask, "What is God?"

I came to speak of God … God … God.

Were you to say that ten times tonight in a speacial manner, the power of this room would be magnified to such a degree that the atoms would shatter, so I just speak of God.

What prompted that question? Was it ignorance, longing or curiosity? The truth now, nothing but the truth now?

[The group explained that the question was prompted by the desire to understand the creation of the rose.]

The prelate: The rose has always been the flower most intimately linked with the Godhead for the fragrance and the beauty. Is there another bloom, another flower on the earth that finds its way, so soon and so straight and so quickly to man's heart as the rose?

Oh, I defy you all to tell me of one with such universal appeal. You cannot, for there is not one so regal as the rose, so tender, not one so suffused with light and colour as the flower of love. The rose.

Now I take you back. I am permitted to do this. I take you back to the dawn of your world and give you one guess what flower bloomed first, the rose, the sign, the creation. His glory had taken the planet into the palm of His hand once more, guiding His force, His power. So now you know the significance of the rose … God's flower.

I cannot put God into a brown paper parcel for you and tie Him up with string and seal each knot so that the mystery cannot be solved. No, no, there is no mystery. Man himself put that there. Can we shape Him? No, no, we cannot encompass Him. When the hour comes, when the moment comes, the realisation of God comes up. The soul knows that from God and God alone come each and every one of us.

The past and the future are all in the stream of life and God introduced his highest form of creation, man. Thoughtless man, cruel man.

Through the murk and the mire of each man's past (do not put a feather in your cap, don't think each life was a fairy tale ablaze with light) the soul has to be purified. The beauty is there and the ugliness, fear and love is there. Then the soul gropes his way back, slowly, to God. When the soul gives heed, it cries within and wants to know, 'Who am I? Where do I go? What is God?'

He is your lodestar and as the magnet turns to the north, therefore you will turn to the lodestar. Then you get the first inkling of what God is.

It does not do to ask of one another what is God, for you have yourself and only yourself who can find the answer.

You may find it in a flash, in a moment of tragedy when you cry for the first time in your life, 'God help me'.

Let me bring that question down to the level that is the trial of your creative power. God is simple. A perfection.

Why should He hide himself from His created beings? No. No. There is magic in His glory, divine beauty in His love. If you can approach Him and tune yourself to these words, 'God is'. Then add a great corollary … 'Love'.

Then you have God. Ever great, ever present, pervading all. All comes from Him. Therefore find Him.

The great master Jesus said that we should go within. God is 'within' each one of us. He also said unto you, "He who sees me beholds the Father".[3]

"Blasphemy" they called, "Blasphemy! He likened himself to God".

Now, he knowing that he himself within his body, not the envelope, not the skin, but the great being within, was part of Him, came from Him.

After all, are you not all children of God? Are you not?

Although I must admit sometimes you behave like children of beelzebub, the dark one! Yes, you have all eternity to learn about yourselves and your relationship to God.

God is patience. Oh, the great patience of the most high.

How often did they not come to me as a prelate in dire distress, in times of misfortune and say to me, 'Why has God punished me like this? What have I done to Him? I pray to Him, I give to the poor, I do all I can to find favour in His eyes and look what He does to me. Surely He could reward me and not punish me like this?'

I would reach the point when my hands would leap up in my bosom and in that moment would have torn my robes from me because I was unable, totally unable, despite my high office, to answer that question. Therefore, I made the supreme effort of my life to come to this gathering tonight because one child asked, "What is God?"

God, my young friend, is the ability to forgive unto seventy times seven.

God is the ability to play the good samaritan and to love those who hate you, who despise you, because the power of love will turn away the power of hatred and make those men and women better people.

That is God.

He is giving and with never a thought of reward or gratitude nor of receiving in return. Never go back to the good you have done. Do it and forget it, it will do its own work. Do not recall the goodness for that goodness should well up from the heart without thought. The giving without thought.

Likewise, never go back to the bad you have done, because it only makes the bad stronger, it feeds on itself. Don't dwell on it, don't give it life. Do you see?

Do not call back sadness of the past, because you feed on it and it feeds on you.

Now let the good stream out and go its way. 'The rolling stone gathers no moss'. Let it roll on clear, gathering no moss. Am I paraphrasing that old saying? I just want to show you that a good deed goes on and can gather nought to itself, for its goodness shines on.

Do not go from here my loved ones and say, 'I must give'. Oh, no, that will not help you. No hothouse flower is being forced. No, never in such a manner. The heart

3. John 14 verse 19.

that will give without thought – that is God.

God, my young friend, is happiness for he knows no sorrow.

God is laughter, not malicious laughter, but joyful laughter that wells up to and from the soul core, for that is where God is in you.

God is beautiful music.

God is the wind in the trees.

God is in the rain falling on your crops.

That is God.

Nanette
The Essenes

It is believed that Jesus was brought up in a brotherhood of a group called the Essenes. The fundemental principles of the Essenes were taught in ancient Persia, Egypt, India, Tibet, China, Palestine, Greece and other countries. The teachings have been transmitted in the most pure form by the mysterious brotherhood of the Essenes that lived, during the 2nd and 3rd centuries B.C. and the 1st century of the Christian era, near the Dead Sea in Palestine and Lake Mareotis in Egypt. In Palestine and Syria, the members of the brotherhood were known as Essenes and in Egypt as Therapentae, or healers.

Essene communities lived a simple, ordered, communal way of life, always near lakes and rivers. They lived according to the Law and were neither rich nor poor with all personal monies distributed as needed. They were vegetarian, grew their own crops, fruit and vines, but did not drink wine. They prayed before meals and ate in silence. They took ritual baths at sunrise each day, after which they always clothed themselves in white garments. They valued music and and considered education extremely important. Their studies of ancient knowledge included the healing arts from Egypt and astronomy from ancient Persia and Chaldea.

They would receive visitors from time to time and records of their way of life have come to us through some of their contemporaries: Pliny, Philo the philosopher, and the Roman historian, Josephus Solanius. Some Essene teachings are preserved in Aramaic in the Vatican and certain texts are found in the collections of the Habsburgs in Austria. Nestorian priests from the 13th century brought writings out of Asia when they fled the hordes of Genghis Khan. Fragments have been discovered in Sumerian hieroglyphs of eight to ten thousand years ago and there are symbols that hint of knowledge dating back to an even earlier time.

The Essenes' principles are reflected in the Zendavesta of Zoroaster, the Vedas, the Upanishads and the Fundamental concepts of Brahmanism. Indian Yoga systems sprang from the same source. Pythagoras in ancient Greece also followed the same principles, as did the Alexandrian School of Philosophy in Egypt.

I myself knew little about the Essenes until Angela spoke of them but can highly recommend the books written by Edmond Bordeaux Szekely, who achieved the massive undertaking of translating the Hebrew and Aramaic texts on the Lost Scrolls of the Essenes.

Among other great teachers who came from this brotherhood are Elijah, John the Baptist and John the Beloved.

I have always believed that the Essenes and the Albergensis were of the same group, although the Albergensis became known much later on in history.

Angela speaks of the Albergensis
"The truest followers of Jesus"

The Albergensis, also known as the Cathars, were from Albi, north east of Toulouse. They were a powerful religious sect who flourished in the 12th and 13th centuries in the south of France and Northern Italy. They were known as 'the pure ones' because they renounced the Catholic church and baptism. They lived and preached in their ritual a life of chastity, poverty, vegetarianism and simple piety. Their theology was based on a belief in the universe, which was thought to be heretical. Their belief system taught that people's spirits were imprisoned in material bodies and transmigrated from one body to another until they merited heaven. They were well organised and gained many converts, emptying the Roman Catholic churches, which posed a serious threat to the Church of Rome. They rejected their authority and sacraments and condemned their hierarchy. Believed to be in league with the devil, they were accused of encouraging debauchery and unnatural vice.

The church did not carry out the sentence of death, instead the condemned heretic was handed over to the secular arm and was usually burned at the stake. In Spain, the final ceremony was known as the *auto de fe* meaning, act of faith.

In 1208, Pope Innocent III (1160–1216) declared a crusade against the Albergensis which led to a merciless war and lasted twenty years. The Spanish Inquisition continued until the final execution in 1820.

Have you heard of the Albergensis? The truest followers of Jesus. These great and noble people lived in France and saw man's heart as a rose.

Have you heard of them? If not, please, my friends, find a book about them.

They withdrew from what you call your orthodox Christianity because they shrank back in horror at the bloodshed and the murder and the appalling cruelty of it. They founded their own wondrous group, mystical, meditative and finding truth in the heart of the rose as the heart of God.

They were wiped out by orthodox Christianity in the period of a few centuries, 25 000 of them were wiped out in a year. It is a sorry tale, this shedding of blood for the Saviour.

I would have you know, thoughts sent up with sufficient intensity imprint their image on the ether and surround your earth. That energy is used by the dark forces. It can be used for floods, fire, earthquakes, pestilence and viruses.

It really seems a little unfair that we should be engaged in this battle when we should be enjoying our paradise. The crippling effects of fear and anguish, never absent because of what man does. Done by man and man only, working hand in hand with lucifer, or arriman, or satan. He has many names.

Do you know what his object is? To gain control of this planet from which he was banished. For as the mason created your planet he, a shining angel, one of the brightest of them all, boasted when he had almost completed it, that he and he alone had done it, forgetting the Great Architect of all. Then the battle began and brought about the malevolence through that banishment.

You have your creepy crawling things that bite, poison and are filled with venom.

This killer instinct in some of your animals and this fight instinct in man, is not God-given. No, it is man-given.

But the light and the power of God is just that bit stronger than lucifer, so in the end, we conquer.

But I repeat, why should we have to do it? These great masses of angelic beings and highly developed human beings who have become radiant, why should they leave their heaven and sally forth again to rescue man in his foolishness? Without the power given out by the thoughts of man, satan would have no power. He feeds on the emanation of the spirit blood. He fed on the emanations of the blood spilt by Jesus, crucified in a bestial manner.

Have you any idea what ensues? The actual nailing on the cross.

When you think of that noblest being, the angel of Light that came to the earth (you know, he was with God before your planet was created, he was with God in full glory as he is today) and he came to give you a way to live, that was all. He did not come to give anything new. He merely came to give you your due, your age, that you could find your true abundance, your full glory.

And you, your gratitude! You nailed him. It is one of the lowest forms of execution you have upon the earth for after a while, man's natural functions can no longer be controlled as he hangs upon the cross.

So that noble body was be-smeared by his own urine and faeces. Flies sitting in their myriads on him when he knew the sorry mess his body was in. That is how you would send the prince of peace out of this planet?

You have never thought of that, have you? Man's bestiality at its lowest. Cowering from the Light that came to make it clean.

Spirit drawing by Tara

Disciple John the beloved comes to donate an Easter message
"Easter, an empty ceremony"

Lana, the name given to Jesus in spirit, had given John this Easter message to pass on to the world.

'Why weepest thou? Must thou shed tears because I live? If there be tears, let them be tears of joy.'

It is difficult for me, not having given voice on earth for two thousand years. Try to understand, unknown tongue to me, I am a man. I come at the request of Joshua (Jesus) to donate an Easter message.

It grieves my Master that your world mourns his death on the cross. He, not wishing this to be done, not wishing to be crucified again says, it is all wrong, all foolish, all empty, as empty as the tomb, the sounds of mourning and grief.

Joshua is triumphant, *in gloria*, not on the cross!

"Why weepest thou?" he said this to the woman in God.[4] Why seek the living among the dead? Now Joshua says to the world, "I live".

No, not for him, the tears of grief.

How can it uplift man to gaze at God when eyes are on the tomb? Did he not say, 'Though you destroy my body, the temple of the soul, yet in these days will I lift up my body of spirit and live?'[5]

Oh yes, yes my children of God, the Christ liveth in splendor and exaltation. Lift up your voices in love and not in grief. Thou art grieving for something that never was ... a dead body on a cross?

Why weepest thou? Do you think it pleaseth him, this empty ceremony? Do you think he loves to see the image of his crucified body in your minds? No. Then why do you do it?

You cannot tell me why, but John can tell you ...

It will pass away. For the pictured image of Christ on the cross has kept your world in despair. Why not have that day of joy and see him in beauty and not on the cross? Do not keep him enrapt like an infant in ceremonial cloth. You deny the adult Jesu[6] in robes of glory and light. You make him a dead child in swaddling cloth.

4. *Mary Magdalene after the crucifixion.*
5. *Paraphrase of John 2 verse 21 and Corinthians 6 verse 19.*
6. *Another name for Jesus*

No. You must let that go.

Every year you go to a weeping place because you think that is your duty. Do not do this!

Rather think of that morning in the garden when the woman[7] saw him released from the tomb.

I give you this Easter message from him, "Rejoice my children, Hosanna to the all high".

7. Mary Magdalene.

Spirit drawing by Tara

The Apostle Peter speaks of his testing time
"To forgive is divine"

I came to tell you that to err is human, to forgive is divine.

Did he not forgive me when I betrayed him three times?

He did not forgive me because he thought he had to. No. He was divine.

His forgiveness was not planned nor was it out of duty to reveal to us what he should do. It came from the centre of his being. The forgiveness flowed out as it flowed out hours later at the 'tree of shame'.

To forgive wholly is the divine in man overcoming the animal that is why I come to you to say, remember, do not hold back, always forgive whole-heartedly. Let that river of love flow, then you are God. Do you see what I mean? I want you to hold very fast to that thought in the days to come. Be not smug in forgiving, forget self and let it go. It is a cleansing river.

When my death came, in my pain, I too could forgive them because I had seen a divine quality in man working in Jesus. So when my time came that quality overcame the rest of me and I knew even in those hours of pain that man is divine.

I was free of earth for I could forgive divinely and in doing that, I let go my human self that had erred so often. Be not misled by history about me. I tried to defend myself when I was guilty of betrayal to him and of the betrayal of the divine in me, but it was only in the death agony that the revelation came and I realised it and how the crucifixion could have been a different story.

That is why I wish to say to you, "Forgive before it's too late".

I don't know whether I make my meaning clear. I was not gifted with speech on earth, I spoke haltingly as I am doing now. Wisdom did not flow so I could not cast pearls before swine! But I try now to give a little wisdom I learnt in the last moments on the cross.

The years with him and the years afterwards brought very little wisdom to me. I have no shame in saying that because even man today cannot see his true glory. Yet he knew and forgave us.

In the moment when he tested me, he asked me who I thought he was? I had the only flash of insight I ever had in all those years and the years that followed when I said to him, "Thou art the Son of God".[8] Even I didn't know what I was saying.

It is regretful that I must leave you and cannot come to speak again, but I have not changed much. There is a great need all over your world. The time is at hand, when the divinity in each man will be called upon to reveal itself and the first act will be to follow these words, "love thine enemies",[9] which means forgive them.

Thank you.

8. *John 18 verse 17, 25, 27.*
9. *Matthew 16 verse 16. Speaks of Simon Peter.*

Spirit drawing by Tara

The Disciple Andrew
"Tara refers to me as the silent one"

Tara refers to me as the 'Silent One' in those days on earth. The twelve were continually arguing and debating amongst themselves. I stood aside and kept my own counsel and when on the rare moments the Master and I had time alone together, we spoke and laughed much.

Angela on the Disciple Andrew

He was the most intelligent amongst them. Lana took strength from those strong men. Also, they did not at once return to the Master when they passed into spirit. They had much to learn before they could do that.

Spirit drawing by Tara

Lana brings healing and gazes back to Palestine days
"This group is God controlled"

During our years of sittings together Lana came a few times to greet the group. The three that were gathered here on this day were myself and my two children, Michéle and Michael.

Forgive me if I speak softly and take care with my natural power so that Tara can accommodate me without being destroyed physically, or else I could not have come. Bear with me, be patient, the cord holding her, attached to her form, is stretched to breaking point. But I am here and I declare unto these three who are gathered together in my name, 'You behold the man'.

[There was a surprised and joyous welcome]

I thank you for that tribute. I am not lauding, beloved, in saying that this Tara came to manifest God. She does not look for reward, she comes only to help mankind.

Now I do not propose to repeat the adage of the pearls!

Thank you child for your laughter. Faith is laughter, love is laughter. Do not think the man Jesus never smiled nor laughed? Does it seem strange, too good that I declaim myself? Why should it be so? You so happily accept those who come before me by a certainty, great souls like Budrain[10] and the orator who burst forth into speech. Is it impossible to believe it is I? You either discredit yourselves or me.

But I come in simple manner. Not as a divine being, so falsely perpetuated or as the figure of suffering so ruthlessly placed on a perfectly executed cross, meticulously carved by a non-existent carpenter. It was a tree, a stump, driven in the soil and rock. I merely carried the branch. No cross was carried. Only those who betrayed me carried a cross and do so to this day.

I was eavesdropping on Angela and was able to hear Tara give voice to her opinions, which is why I came to enlarge on this issue, so she may hear this when she returns to what she sententiously calls 'earthly tenement'.

Budrain says the word comes from Rome, meaning four different levels of building which housed many people. My oratory was a more simplified form, not endeavouring to give human intellectuals, but hearts, the greatest influence. God.

I came to let you know beyond a shadow of a doubt that this group is God-

---

10. Budrain is the name given to Julius Caesar in spirit. Angela informed us that he was a guide of Tara.

controlled. Whence came the power to produce the water?[11] A symbol too of mine, of my life upon the earth. A deeper symbolism than perhaps you realise.

Now you may give me your hand for a moment. It is time for me to depart but it is also a long time since anybody could say to me, 'Go'.

[Turning to Michael]

You are well beloved in spirit child. Go in peace.

[We thanked him for coming]

It is my privilege to acknowledge your blessings, which I take with me.

I note it is a habit with you to be kind and to speak to we who are visitant unto you and to end by saying, 'Bless you'. But do not be deluded for a moment that we do not in turn enjoy being blessed.

[A dove started to sing in the tree outside. Lana turned to young Michael ill with asthma]

Michael of the Holy Covenant, do you hear the bird of peace at my words? I pour on those gathered together in my name, all those seen and unseen, the blessing of the holy spirit, the balm of Gilliard.[12] You will bend your small head to me my child, ever as I said, "Suffer the little children to come unto me".[13] Even as I once beheld you, so I bless you now.

[Turning to Michéle]

Your name in feminine form is that of Michael, the Archangel. Do not stain this name. The vibration of a name becomes peculiar to him or to herself. The glory and effulgence of that name, let it be a beacon for you and your brother for the service of man.

This world is at low ebb. When I gaze back to Palestine days, I thought the world would end. How warped was my own outlook. The territory was so small and yet seemed to encompass the known world, doomed to extinction due to man's way of living. I am at this time close to the earth and realise it was like a gnat's sting compared to now and what has befallen man. It is more like that of a serpent!

It is strange to be speaking through a female body, I have to be so careful. I am not exempt from this either!

I go now. My blessings and love. There is no need to stress these words when it is yours always, even should you not ask for it nor wish for it.

---

11. *Refer to page 14 Chapter 1, 'How it all began'.*
12. *A special healing ointment.*
13. *Luke 18 verse 16*

Guardian planetary spirit
"The materialisation of the water in the footprints"

None of you know me but I know you. From the moment of inception of your being, when you are going to be brought down to function in human bodies on this earth, I am one of the guardian planetary spirits of earth. You find this difficult to accept?

Those present: No, not at all.

Guardian planetary spirit: That is good. I have been present in thought at your meetings and I will deem it a great favour if you will relate to Tara that it was I who brought about what you call the materialisation of the water in the footprints in your room here. For I, being in charge of the elements of earth, could produce that element of water. When Tara pleads for water for the earth, it is I who answers the call. Yes, it is I!

It is with the greatest difficulty that I am in speech at this time, for there is another being using the body and the tongue and the lips of Tara. I am not in the body but I am projecting my thoughts into he who so kindly acts as my proxy. It would be impossible for a planetary spirit to use an earth body for we would shatter it into the void! But it is I who truly speak though my voice must come through another who can know how to use Tara.

This might explain certain tribal beliefs that rain dances are so powerful that they have the ability to bring rain. These prayers have been known to be answered.

Speaker from the age miscalled 'Victoria the good'
"Why can man not take that bright star of Bethlehem forever in his heart"

Can you hear me? I can't pitch my voice any louder.

I have come at your festive time, but as you know it is a fallacy as it has been remarked already. But it does definitely bring with it a feeling of goodwill. That is the anomaly of the whole thing. Why, if man has it in his nature, his capability, his propensity to feel goodwill and something akin to affection, can he not feel this goodwill throughout the rest of the 364 days of the year?

I speak of the year from the so-called Natal Day.

Now why can man not take that bright star of Bethlehem forever in his heart and show there is God in every man, woman, child and animal? God in all creation.

I suppose one can go on hoping that the future will bring a change in his outlook or at least in his way of thought and attitude that he adopts for everyday life. To try to live what the great one called, 'the abundant life'.[14]

Man has the abundance of living as God intended his children to live, not as birds with clipped wings, but free as the gull as it soars above the sea in its ecstasy of light. It was never denied.

When Jesus Christ came to the earth he said, "I come with a sword". Oh, how misinterpreted that man has been in his sayings! He did not come with a sword to fight, to be martial, he came with a sword to clear away the rubbish, the debris of past religions. Religions which had soared and died and gone into the forgotten, but had left faint echoes of darkness and superstition and all the horrible part of a dead religion that clings onto a man, leaving a concept, not of God, but of a devil and hellfire! That was the sword of peace he brought to clear it all away. To give man the abundant life.

If the preachers and clerics would only go through with their minds alert and not stuffed with the nonsense from their seminaries and their religious schools about the teachings of Jesus Christ, they have only to remember those words.

Now you have the thought of the militant Jesus Christ, which is wrong, so you have confusion in men's mind. You have the churches, the fellowship of churches, but oh, they have such a ravelled sleeve with all the stitches dropped and the pattern is all wrong and out of place! Due entirely to ambitious clergy.

A little while ago, when I asked if I could come here, I went into what is called the Akashic Records[15] and looked back on the lives of the popes and I am sure you good people would rise up on your feet with your hands thrown up in horror were I to tell you what some of them did! No lives could have been filled with greater evil; lies, adultery, theft, torture. You name it and I'll name you eight popes that were guilty of the most heinous crimes that man could think of, all under the canopy of mother church!

Well, I've not come here to lay a calumny against the church. I merely came to try and tell you as a group to hold that star of Bethlehem fast in the centre of your

14. *Praphrase of the Psalms and Matthew 10 verse 34.*
15. *Akashic Records, see page 228.*

forehead and go forward, knowing that God is at the helm of the good ship planet and nothing can foul the rudder.

Always try in as gentle a manner as possible. Never force your convictions on other people unless they lend you a willing ear, no matter how much of a crusader you are. If the impulse is there to bring the light of reason, correct living to everybody, do not do it to people who are unwilling to listen, for they will tear your beautiful words and rend your soft hearts. Don't do it!

There will be signs and portents in the future that will convince the most hardened atheists. Well, I warrant you as I sit in my seat, any of those miscalled atheists at the first sign of danger to their lives, or those they love, their first words will be, 'God help me'. Automatically it will just come, for it is in man's soul from the time he came as a spark from God, the knowledge of God, and you cannot deny God.

So when the earth mind is confused with grief, with pain and sorrow, the soul mind takes over and calls out to his creator. Who else can help him? Who else? Only God.

We are not omnipotent. We have not omnipresence, nor are we omniscient, but God alone is perfection. How do we know what perfection is? We cannot even hazard a guess.

On children

It is a strange thing, the love bond between parents and their children. Despite the look of civilisation, as we call it in our pride today, this bond between the head of the family and the children was far stronger, deeper and sustaining than it is today. For there was no breaking away from the home, there was no turning the back on parental love or influence. It is sad that those beautiful concepts of father, mother and children seem to have gone over the horizon, never to come back and therefore you have unhappy children.

It is not always the children's fault, it is the fault of the parents as well. Everything seems to have become too much of a bother! There is a lassitude and lethargy all over your world due to pollution of your air, your water, the very food you eat. Now I do not quote from your newspapers but from the findings of scientists on this side. You do not realise yet just how polluted your food is and this can bring death.

Well, I must not dwell on that. It is all very sad and now the great reaper must come and cleanse all of it away, the refuse and the dirt, mentally and spiritually, so that there is a renaissance again of man's soul, man's outlook! Oh, yes, this has been a dark age!

I lived in the age of she who was miscalled 'Victoria the good' [16] Yes, I lived at that time and I know by virtue of the position that I held, I know the injustice of life for the poor. How the children suffered. It doesn't bear repetition, so I am not going to tell you. I must take my leave, thank you for listening to me.

Joan: Will you come again?

---

16. *The sixty Glorious years of the reign of Queen Victoria I 1819–1901. A time of extreme Imperialism when many of her subjects were suffering in poverty.*

Speaker: I should like to come again, but time is running short before the sittings end. But you have been greatly privileged and I think you realise this and are appreciative of the great spirits who have come down to your earth to speak. So willingly they come down. Nobody asks them, nobody in spirit orders you to do this or not to do that. They might suggest to you but as you have a free will on the earth, so you have free will in the spirit planes too. Your opportunities are so much more wonderful and so much more numerous than they are on your little earth.

So believe me, if you could see them when they come in their glory and their majesty!

These words have been used time and time again in this room to try and let you hold fast in your mind, the manner of people who come to you.

Bear this radiance with you when you go out and look at each man and try to see the God in each man and woman you pass in the street, no matter if it is a beggar, a prince or a king, anybody.

Remember you all are of God.

Remember also these very potent words, "Whatever ye do unto the least of these, ye do unto me".[17]

Thank God I no longer dwell in body form, nor will I ever seek reincarnation, not even in the brave new world that is coming when all will be so beautiful. Not for me, ever again.

And now I bid you all good night.

17. *Matthew 25 verse 40*

Lana
"Where is the concept of parents honouring their children's outlook on life"

I would love it if you could hear my voice as I spoke on the mountain. I dare not speak with any volume of sound, as I am truly not within this body. I am, as it were, projecting my voice into her voice parts.

There has been, I hear, some discussion on the commandment, "Honour thy father and thy mother".[18] I would ask, where is the concept of parents honouring their children's outlook on life?

It behoves parents to entirely disregard the link of the blood beyond the call of bringing the body into the world and guiding the way. The parents have no right to keep a hold on the soul, embodied in the spirit, which belongs to God.

You on earth and we in spirit must co-operate.

'Honour thy father and mother' have never been given to mankind because they place people in thraldom. Those words were supposed to have emanated from the mouth of God. This was never so. How much submission could have been erased from mankind had that commandment never been.

We were brought together in this last incarnation to serve God and mankind, "judge not, lest you be judged, condemn not, lest you be condemned".[19] Let no chink come into the armour of love and light which you have girded round yourselves. When those who are the servants of God are tried to great extent and arise victorious, then it is a triumph for the children of Light.

When you read the Ten Commandments, you realise they have all to do with the material side of man, therefore not of God. Nothing spiritual about them. They were brought about merely to bring an orderly way of life, necessary for those times. But you will notice these commandments instilled fear and if not adhered to, punishment would follow.

But you are responsible only to God. Be comforted as God is with you always.

I have been told by the ever-watchful ones, I must make my departure. The cord is wearing thin and neither my love nor power could replace it. My penalty for being called 'the Saviour'.[20] Did I ever name myself 'Saviour'?

[Turning to Charles Orfang]

Lana: Thank you for that manly 'No.'

When you were on earth at that time it was you who said, "Our master never claimed that".[21] Memory will ring one of these nights.

[Then to Michéle and Michael]

18. *Exodus 21 verse 12.*
19. *Matthew 7 verse 2.*
20. *Originally, the Hebrew form of Joshua meant 'helper of Yahveh'. The latter form means 'to deliver' or 'to save'. Therefore 'Jesus' came to be known as meaning, 'Saviour'. ('Mystical Life of Jesus' by H Spencer Lewis PHD. FRC.)*
21. *This must have been Charles Orfang in a previous incarnation.*

Think of me beloved, not as a man unattainable, but as a brother. A real friend, a member of the great white brotherhood, an elder brother. I will not leave you comfortless. Turn to me in the high places of your mind and make contact with me. I will reward you well.

May the Law shine on you and beyond the portals of your hearts.

I go now.

Think of me when I spoke these words, "I am the way, the truth and the light".[22]

I spoke not of myself, I spoke of my Father, which is in Heaven.

Angela

Could I but portray to you that divine being. Those dear eyes that beam love and protection. A man who went through the experience of the love of a good woman, children at his knees. How could he understand so deeply if he had not? He well knew the phases of human existence, he also had his temptations …

---

22. *John 14 vs 6.*

Nanette reflects on the life of the Nazarene from spirit communication
"Jesus died at the age of 76 in Srinager where his burial tomb known as Rauza Bal is maintained to this day"

I have threaded together a few facts of his life, which were given to us at various times over the years by different communicators including the Master himself. Sometimes spirit communication would happen off record. Tara recounted many tales of her private meditation sessions where she was privy to certain information later detailed to me. She also wrote down many of her experiences, which were passed on to me after her death.

Eons ago, Jesus was one of the pathfinders who brought the light of knowledge to our earth from an older and more advanced sister star.[23] This planetary spirit and great brother of mankind has descended again and again into matter, to light the way for us, to show the joy of living in the light of love for one another. His last incarnation was as a Galilean, born in the natural manner to Mary, a Jewish maiden and her Roman soldier. Mary was given protection by the wealthy Joseph who later took the boy Jesus with him on a visit to Cornwall in England where Joseph was a trader in the silver mines.

French chronicles, from the 1st century, speak of Joseph's visit to England from the near east. The dearly held belief that Joseph was engaged in the metal trade led to the old saying when pouring molten metal in Somerset, 'just as Joseph did'. Another Somerset saying was, 'as sure as Christ came to Priddy'.

Jesus grew up to be six foot two inches tall, with honey-coloured hair, blue eyes and a penetrating gaze that could see into the very hearts and minds of men. He was known for his sense of humour and whimsical smile. A man of passion and great humanity.

Jesus was introduced to eastern teachings during sojourns in India and Egypt before his return to Palestine.

He became an initiate of the Essenes, married Mary Magdalene who was also a member of the Essenes. Two children were born to them.

Jesus did eat a little meat and drank wine, both of which he found necessary for his strength during the arduous years of his mission. He once said to us, 'One must be sensitive to the needs of the body and sensible in your outlook on spirit'.

Jesus had to work hard to heal the many mentally and physically sick. Very few were instantaneous healings, they depleted him too much. Very often he was so tired he would have to go into meditation and withdraw into the high place or the 'holy mount' within his mind to regain his power and energy.

It was a demanding life in many ways. Only to John the Beloved and the quiet and steady Andrew could he open his mind.

One day when he came to us he said, 'In my wake, I admit to my sorrow that men twisted what I came to say and carnage, fire and destruction followed!' "I came with a sword."[24] How they misunderstood, I did not come to destroy, I came to cleanse and

---

23. See references to Chloris and Atlantis pages 140 and 188–190 respectively.
24. Mathew 10 verse 34

cut away the old dogmas, superstitions and ignorance and to exemplify the Law.'

When we spoke to him of reincarnation he told us the quotation[25] was really "Expiatation is mine" and not "Vengeance is mine". Expiation meaning to atone or make amends.

Why do souls incarnate in untenable bodies in the first place?

"The sins of the fathers shall be visited unto the third and fourth generation?"[26] No. It is the "third and fourth reincarnation".

Reincarnation was abhorrent to the church and so references were deleted from the bible.

He believed that if you develop yourself enough you can overcome karma.

On the aspect that puzzles so many, the Holy Trinity, Lana answered, 'Do not be misled by false dogmas which will scatter like chaff before the winds of truth. There is no Holy Trinity as taught by your priests. The Sons of God and the Daughters of God, my beloved ones, is your Holy Trinity, nothing else.'

Regarding the Holy Communion, the Last Supper was only to be a private meal between friends. In the last days of the Master's mission in Palestine, he really did believe he could endure the crucifixion. He thought he could survive and become the leader, but he saw the situation and withdrew. After all, two thousand years is only a drop in the waters of eternity. During those last days he learnt of the futility of the plot and the uprising of the Jews. There would not have been one left alive through the revenge that would have come from Rome, there would not have been a stone left standing in Jerusalem. The Jews wanted Jesus to fight with a sword but his sword was one only of peace.

He was to die, not for his spiritual teachings but because he was a political threat.

He had to work cloak and dagger to get messages to Joseph who was well informed in advance as to what the plan was. He, who was to sustain Jesus and the disciples with the wherewithal to carry on.

Joseph purchased the valuable healing ointments that were to be used by the two Essenes who were to attend Jesus during his three days in the tomb.

The sky was cloudless that day over Golgotha and the sun was shining when Jesus, with a wreath made from the white, five-petalled wild rose roughly placed over his brow, made his way towards the 'tree of shame', carrying the branch on which he was to be nailed. This was not as depicted in paintings with nails pierced through his hands, but through the wrists, so that the flesh would not tear, and a nail through his feet. His nose had been broken and he suffered great difficulty breathing. At some stage he also had a rib broken. The words he uttered on the cross were, "I forgive them" not "Father forgive them".[27] And it was, "My strength, my power, why hast thou forsaken me?" as opposed to, "My God, my God why hast thou forsaken me?".[25] For even with all his yoga training he could not overcome that physical pain.

His friends put myrrh into his mouth to deaden the pain. Being a soporific it made him pass out. Thus after three hours, Longinus thrust his dagger into the side of Jesus and pleura was in full operation as blood and water flowed from him.

25. *Deutoronomy 32 verse 35, Romans 12 verse 19 and Hebrews 10 verse 30.*
26. *Exodus 20 verse 5.*
27. *Luke 23 verse 34.*

Believing him to be dead, the soldiers did not perform the customary act of breaking the prisoner's legs. It was now the eve of the Sabbath and they allowed Joseph and his friends to take Jesus away to the white-robed Essenes who were waiting to care for him for the next few days while he rested in the cave.

It has been explained that when Jesus emerged from the tomb he went into the garden where he met Mary Magdalene who ran to embrace him. He hastily said, "Touch me not", because the wounds were still painful. "I have not yet gone to my Father".[28] In other words, 'I have survived, I am not dead but very sore'.

If you look at the verses of Luke 24, 36, 39, 41 and 43 it would seem to prove that Jesus was very much alive when he asked for food and was given a piece of broiled fish and a honeycomb.

To avoid discovery and re-arrest it was necessary to meet his friends in the utmost secrecy. In fact, Joseph hid him for eighty days prior to Jesus' return to India. There are literally hundreds of books depicting Jesus' time in India, some of which are mentioned under the Further Reading section on page 274.

Thomas (disciple Doubting Thomas) and Mother Mary went with him to India but it was an arduous journey and Mary died before reaching their destination at a little place later named *Murree* in her honour.

I have been told that the sepulchre called *Mai Mari Da Asthan* – the resting place of Mother Mary – is still there.

Thomas continued on with Jesus to Srinager in Kashmir, where he stayed for some time before making his way to southern India to preach for the rest of his life.

On his arrival in Srinager, Jesus went immediately to the King of Kashmir and sought permission to stay and preach to the tribes of Israel who lived in that region, not many miles from the tomb of Moses. (The *Ka Ka Pal* or stone of Moses is pictured in the book *Jesus in India*. *Ka* meaning eleven. It refers to the twelve tribes of Israel, excluding the Levites. The stone, believed to have magical properties, can only be lifted by eleven people placing one finger under it while chanting *Ka Ka Ka Ka*.)

After explaining the nature of his teachings, Jesus was made welcome.

In a modern edition of *Jesus in India*, interesting photographs of the original manuscripts dated 15 AD report his encounter with the great Raja Shalewain before 78 AD near Srinager. It explains that the raja was impressed by the wisdom and saintliness of the fair complexioned person dressed in white. Verses 17–32 also speak of the past sufferings of Jesus when he appeared in the land of the Amalekites as the Messiah.

Jesus became a revered and much-loved figure until his death at the age of 76. A shrine was built over the burial stone, known as the *Rauza Bal*, meaning Prophet's Tomb at Srinager, where it is still maintained to this day

There are clear photographs in the book *Jesus in India* of the outside and interior of the *Rauza Bal*, the tomb of Jesus (*Yuz Asaf*) showing the decree made by the grand *Mufti* in Kashmir to officially confirm the site as a sacred shrine.

I have myself visited and photographed the ancient and finely carved screen around the tomb within the *Rauza Bal*. I have also walked in the valley known as *Yusmarg*, the Meadow of Jesus.

28. *Mark 15 verse 34.*

In another book, *Jesus died in Kashmir*, included are pictures of those who call themselves *Beni Israel*, children of Israel, who still hold the Yusmarg Meadow of Jesus sacred, as they believe that he accomplished his mission to find the ten lost tribes. In this lush and beautiful land with its snow-capped mountains and shimmering lakes, the generous earth gives in abundance almost every known vegetable, fruit, woodland and field of flowers.

This place is not far from Israel. I have often wondered if this was not, perhaps, his Promised Land.

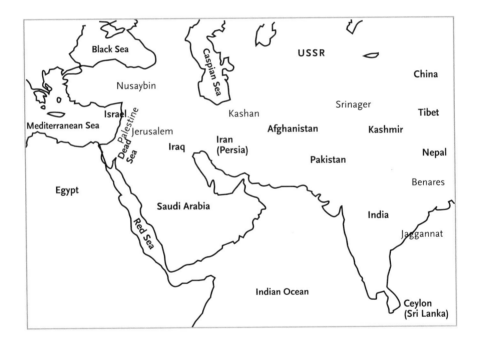

Chapter 8: Hindu Spirits

Sarojini Naidu (1879–1949), Indian feminist and poet
"When will the light ever beam in my land again"

Known as the Nightingale of India, she was born in Hyderaba and educated at Madras, London and Cambridge. She published three volumes of lyric verse: *The Golden Threshold, The Bird of Time* and *The Broken Wing*. She organised flood relief in Hyderabad and lectured and campaigned on feminism and the abolition of *purdah*[29]. Associated with Mahatma Gandhi, she was the first Indian woman to be president of the Indian National Congress in 1925. Imprisoned several times for civil disobedience incidents, she took part in negotiations leading to Independence and in 1947 was appointed Governor of the United Provinces.

Sarojini came in very depressed about what was happening in India at the time. This discussion took place around 1968.

I greet you my friends. This is Sarojini Naidu. You do not know me, Mr Rennie, but I have spoken much with your dear wife and daughter. There has been much talk of me in London where she is at this moment, which is why I was attracted to go and have a peep at her!

I have not been in contact with the earth plane since I last spoke at Narrow Waters because I have withdrawn to try to alleviate the position in my own country of India.

---

29. *A screen or veil that secludes women from public viewing conceiling them from head to toe including their faces. A practice used by Muslims and various Hindus, especially in India.*

Ella: She met someone at a diplomatic reception who knew you.

Sarojini: Yes, that is correct. Someone who knew me very well indeed. It was all arranged!

I greet you all at this time of goodwill upon earth. There is definitely a tidal wave that goes round where there is a softening of the heart and there is giving and there is receiving and it is good that it is so.

We too have our great festivities in my nation as you know, when we light the lights and have the night of worship for the light, so we are sympathetic.[30] There is much that is similar in all religions of the world, great similarity.

I am still seeking my flute-like voice, which I can't contrive to bring about speaking through Tara but there has been talk about my voice with Nanette. During my days in India they used to say, I had a 'lute-like' voice!

Ella: Yes, these friends spoke particularly about your lovely speaking voice, also that you spoke eight languages!

Sarojini: That is so and no *chi chi* accent! But I did not attempt all the dialects of India. Ah, India! When will the light ever beam in my land again?

Mahatma Gandhi is here and quite desperate too. It is sad that the knowledge has been clouded over by the struggle for life. Graft, misuse of money, corruption from one end to another. You would weep tears of blood!

Indians will have to revise their way of thought as they have been in a state of inertia too long. The present prime minister[31] is strangely bereft of compassion. Power can do dreadful things to the soul. I try to instill the understanding of what it is like to die of hunger, but she turns a blind eye. There is a great shock coming to her.

What to do? The light has set. Is there anyone in my land who is likely to succeed? I can't see it, the lotus lily no longer blooms. It has sunk its head out of sight.

But I must not charge the atmosphere with sadness. I cannot stay long. One is allowed only a little time tonight and I am delighted to come and make contact once more.

But it is a fact that the longer one is over in spirit, the less the inclination to come down and experience the heavy vibrations of the earth.

I was tired in the last days of my life there. I showed myself to Tara once. Drawing from a well, she could see that I was drawing from the well of wisdom and that I had become young again. Even in my new found youth, which is never lost of course, it is only the earth body that grows old, not the spirit body, but even coming down to earth vibrations like this, the radiance fades for a short while. Even the great ones that come to speak, they too have to go back every few moments to refresh. They would never tell you that but I have no hesitation in telling you. You can appreciate the sacrifice they make to come down to help. They do not regard it as a sacrifice but it is! To come from the verdant freshness of it all and then to be embroiled in the

---

30. *She is referring to the Hindu festival of Diwali, which occurs around 4th November every year.*
31. *Indira Gandhi.*

dark night of the world. I do not mean the physical night, I mean the soul night of the world in darkness.

The Master Jesus, as you know full well came to my beloved land of India, so even the Master, once embodied in the flesh, testified his way on foot through the flesh to the heights and to the imperium. Even the Masters have to go through the experience, for when the time comes for them to build their own new solar systems, they have to experience the whole gamut of human emotion.

I must go now. Although I very seldom indulged in a little wine upon the earth, if you do on your Christmas days, drink then a toast to Sarojini!

My fond love to you all.

Angela

Allegro after *largo!*[32] She is so beautiful. Pure Atlantean.[33] A wonderful light. She tries so hard to succour the land of her birth. She never had to labour over a poem, the words flowed like silver!

---

32. *Allegro meaning 'light', Largo meaning 'gentle' or 'calm'.*
33. *See Chloris, page 140.*

Mahatma Gandhi (1869–1948), political and spiritual leader
"I must acknowledge, I failed"

Born Mahondas Karamchand Gandhi, later he was given the title *Mahatma* meaning, great soul. Educated in India and London, he became a successful lawyer and leader in the South African Indian Community. His personal philosophy significantly changed when he abandoned western ways, material possessions and dressed in loincloths. Known for organising campaigns of non-violent resistance against discrimination, he finally secured an agreement with the South African Government to alleviate Indian repression. In India, he campaigned for a free and united India, including his famous two hundred mile (320 km) march to extract salt from the sea in his protest against salt taxes. Although this finally led to India's independence, he was imprisoned twice and ultimately shot while holding a prayer and pacification meeting in New Delhi in 1948.

I wonder what you would do if I told you who I was! I may before I leave.

I know this Tara. I have materialised my late body to her and have entered into her meditation and presented myself. I don't think I cut an attractive figure!

This is the first time I speak through a human body other than my own and I am finding it not a very agreeable sensation, so I do not intend to labour on in speech. I was known for my long periods of speechlessness. I hoped to achieve conquest by silence.

My label ... a failure, put onto myself by myself, for I must acknowledge that I failed.

What a reversal of opinion, what a revision of my own faith, my own credence in what I believed! What I had to undergo when I found myself in spirit. Dear me!

You expect halcyon days when you leave your body behind. You have prepared for this by starvation, by silence, withdrawal. You think, I am in communication with God.

It requires much more than that to place yourself in communion with God. Had I known as much as some of the great beings who have spoken to you, I could have written quite another tale!

I visit my own land now and see that which I thought so suitable was totally unsuitable! Havoc has followed my credo. So I must ask myself the vital question ... and I shall flee from your presence before you give me your reply, in case it is more than I can bear.

I had to return to the earth for I cannot progress. I am like Tantalus and Sisyphus,[34] ever the elusive.

Well, this troublesome thorn in my flesh, the vital question is, 'what did I believe?' When I said, "I believe", and I quote what I believed, in Gandhi and no one else!

You know who I am.

Yes, I am disguised in the way I talk because I have been warned not to be my foolish self in this body. I do not quite know how to manipulate the organs of speech. But I had to return and I think after listening to that sage,[33] I will be released by myself and no other when I return to my place of meditation in spirit.

I have not yet left the vibration of the earth. I believed myself indispensable to the welfare of India and it seems I was quite mistaken … quite mistaken.

So I withdraw now and I thank you for your exquisite courtesy in giving me, like the famous Mark Anthony, you 'lent me your ears'!

I feel already lightened in my soul. Oh, we poor mortals, so rich in our immortality and so blind to the reality of it all.

Thank you.

34. *Tantalus was condemned by Zeus to live forever in the Abyss or Hades. Whenever he tried to drink water it ebbed away from him. Sisyphus was also sent to Hades and had to roll a huge boulder up a hill. But it always rolled back again.*
35. *The Indian Sage page 248.*

Lord Krishna (No birth/death dates)
"What you call God matters not"

He is one of the most popular deities in Hinduism, believed to be the eighth avatar or incarnation of Vishnu. Krishna is described as the prince of the Yadava tribe, friend, councellor, child and youth. He is proclaimed in the Bhagavid Gita amongst other devotional texts. As a young boy he is depicted as the foster child of cowherds, as a youth he becomes the lover of *gopis* (milkmaids) who plays with his flute and dances with them by moonlight. The love of Krishna and his favourite *gopi*, Radha, is celebrated in great Sanskrit and Bengali love poetry.

Peace on you, whom I cannot see in your earthly form. Only your spiritual grace is visible unto me. I hold forth in a tongue foreign to me, but like many others who come, I have been well tutored by Budrain.

I come into your presence on mother earth where it has been many moons since I gambolled. Perhaps to western people I am remembered more for my proficiency with the flute and playful amorous episodes with milkmaids!

Do you know who I am, lady, that you laugh? Yes, I am Krishna.

Yes, you might well say 'Oh'. Did you know of the immeasurable stages I have had to traverse to make speech here? Although it is not entirely for your benefit, it is for the light of God I come. Not for human persons, although I need to perform in the physical body. No, I come for the good of man collectively and for the clearing of evil.

Should she be offended with me if I called her milk maid? You know full well she is being used as a channel.

Forgive me, the effort of making the tongue work is great. I have just received word from one greater than I that the pathway was prepared for me to speak today by those others who preceded me here in this sanctuary. Then accept me for who I am and know that I, like the others, come to do the work of God and not the work of man.

There has been a mighty conference in the highest plane of spirit these last years. There has been a great coming and going out of spirit messengers to the little earth plane. Now when I, from my elevated position in spirit say and not in scornful tones, 'your little earth planet' it is because I see the whole and remember in the east we mention, 'the drop returns to the ocean and becomes one with it'. So it is with your earth planet. It is oh, most essential to the perfect running of the whole.

[There was a coughing spasm, after which Krishna continued.]

Forgive. The power I bring is great and the body is frail. It is so essential that the littlest one is in perfect condition otherwise the planet becomes like this body, frail.

I use this body in which I now uncomfortably sit as an illustration of what I mean. If I remove from the earthly body one small vital organ, the body will be cast into disorder. So it is with your small planet. If it disobeys the Law of God and brings about disruption and chaos within itself, it, as a member of the great body, will bring about equal disruptions in the main of it. Do you follow me?

It is difficult to speak with an eastern mind the western thought ... but it is one and the same.

I, like Sorojani of the lotus feet,[36] was also well known in one of our lives for the sweetness of my voice! You would be touched in your heart if you could see with what concern they are watching me to see I do not tax the voice of this beloved woman. They need have no fear, Krishna always loved the women. Why not? In India where last my feet were upon the earth, the woman is the divine mother, so I have brought into your presence today the divine mother.

You will not fully comprehend the immensity of this statement but it will become visible ... the bringing of the great divine mother in earthly form. You cannot behold her, beloved ones, but it will have an effect on the earthly plane, which will astound you.

You were well informed by Angela that a victory had been won for the forces of Light and did she not say you will notice in the weeks to come there will be no violence on the earth?

Well, you have seen that happen. There have been rumours of war between various countries and the world, the planet earth held its breath expecting destruction to begin any moment, but the crisis was dissolved like mists before the rising sun.

. Now Krishna, bringing into your presence the great divine mother, you will notice now what will happen and be thankful that I, Krishna, was privileged to come today and tell you this, for you have within your hearts the knowledge of what is to be. So you are elevated above the normal populace when you, in beholding the trend of life, can say with the knowledge of a smile, 'Krishna told us'.

My friends, which of the mighty on earth will believe you? You found it difficult when various great ones came to speak with you, to accept it could be those whom they said they were. But the truth that was in them and the glory that was theirs, left no room for doubt did it?

[A silent affirmation from the group, which was one of 'knowing' rather than vocal.]

I deeply regret I cannot greet you by your earthly names but I cannot descend in thought to that degree that I familiarise myself once more with the earth vibration. I merely enfold you in my loving arms and tell you, with joy, of the importance of the work emanating from this sanctuary.

36. Hindu people use lotus feet as a symbol of purity, enlightenment and perfection.

You have all been tested for any hint of spiritual pride creeping uninvited and unknown into your hearts. You have not failed this test because believe me, when one is admitted into our inner sanctuaries as you have been, the human brain and heart being what it is, it is totally facile for spiritual pride to creep in like the tempter your Jesus speaks of and to say, 'I have been picked out above people'. But for not one of you, nowhere is there even the faintest shadow cast upon your light.

Therefore I, Krishna and others like me come with joy to be amongst you, so you can take heart and think when two or three are gathered together in my name, there I am too.

The temptation of Jesus

Jesus, or Joshua, has asked me to cast illumination upon his own temptation. Exactly what I have been talking about now, when he, too, overcome momentarily by spiritual pride, was attached by what is called 'tempter'. He went up into the wilderness of his soul, no earthly wilderness, no barren place of planet earth, no, but the arid place within the soul when the tempter comes. He was, as you know, a Master. He had it in his power to reduce the mighty eagle of Rome, to trample it into the dust and to be forgotten. He had the power and the tempter came. Then in his soul, the wilderness began. Do you see?

Even a Master in earthly body is not immune and this is what Jesus wants you to know and understand. That he was subjected to this great temptation to let people say, 'He is above all'. Well, he did not succumb to the voice of the tempter and you know what he accomplished!

Let the great waters of wisdom deluge you

Well, my friends, you have not succumbed either. Hold within the fire of your hearts your hearth place, clean and holy and pure. No tempter can come nigh. In the fountain of your mind let the great waters of wisdom deluge you and wash away the taint of earth. Go forth and think you are upon a mighty mountaintop. That is what is meant in your scriptures when he says he went into a 'high place'. He went into the high place of his mind ... God.

Now go you forth too, into that high place in your mind and link yourself with God. For what you call God it matters not. There is God, available to his beloved children. It is you my beloved, who have separated yourselves from God. It is man who has done this.

Patience

Can we speak in the same breath and use the word patience, and say God waits patiently for his children to return to him? We can. For patience is a godly virtue. Man has separated himself from God, so he has cut himself off from the benign father-mother influence and love. He is like a child that has left his parents before he can walk properly. So he stumbles from one pit into the other. One morass after another, drowning himself in the mire, but the time is at hand when the soul will turn from darkness and like this little child, the footprint will resound as they march together on the way to God.

I have used this illustration, once again.[37] Wonderful footprints of great ones who have left their imprint upon earth's surface, never to be deleted, never to be erased but there for all eternity.

One brotherhood of man, one fatherhood of God, peace, love, glory.

I am not eloquent like the others that come. It is long since I descended to this little place. I would have you hallow earth in your thoughts and your heart. For remember, it has been the place where God manifested himself through the messengers of Light. Hallow this earth and hold it dear.

Yes, beloved children, remember the earth is a manifestation of God in his highest.

Do not say 'this wicked world'. The world is not wicked, it came from the source and it obeys the Law. It is man whose thoughts and deeds are wicked. When you speak, think deeply first, gaze about this world that the mind of deity has created and see its manifold beauty. Feel the ecstasy of life, watch the birds in flight and know you are seeing God manifesting.

You know, the cow is sacred in my land. There is great and ancient wisdom in holding this animal sacred, for it is the everlasting mother feeding her children with heavenly wisdom from her bosom. Therefore, my beloveds, do we not see the cow giving the milk of life? Not only to her own progeny but the children of man?

I cannot here delve into the ancient mysteries in which the cow figures so largely, but go you into the tombs of Cam, or Egypt as you call it now and there will be unveiled for you who have eyes that can see now, the true mystery of the cow.

I go now from my attentive audience. I will draw the light of love, the greatest force, not alone in your world but in the entire universe. The Law of love is honoured. When it is broken in any manner, individually or collectively, what chaos ensues!

I came to give you the blessing of God, deep-rooted in my own heart the knowledge of the perfection of the Godhead and the infinite beauty of the love for His creation. So I bring up my hands in the Hindu salute and say God bless you all.

[He brought the two hands together and touched the forehead in traditional Hindu greeting.]

Angela

He too brought the light with joy through playfulness and happiness. Hate and you will be destroyed by it.

Be joyous when you love.

37. *See footprint symbol under 'How it all began' and 'Guardian Planetary Spirit'.*

Chloris, the royal beekeeper
"So it became Atlantis ... *Is* ... being light. Is ... ra ... el – light"

And I say unto you that 'Gods became men and men became gods'.

There dwelt a race of beings endowed by the giver of all with the most wondrous heritage ... truth and light.

I am receiving your thoughts. No, I have not spoken here.

I was of this race of beings, we knew naught of evil, nor any of the ills that so beset your little planet. God-like we were, for we came fresh from the Godhead and had gained naught of guile. We came following our queen.

You were told of the goodly companions that came with her. I am one of those goodly companions, although I left your planet many aeons ago.

We lived in a community where peace and harmony and perfection reigned. What you would call heaven on earth. In time to come, when the light grew dimmer, we resorted to breaking of the Law. The Law of God.

Well, I will bow to your way of thought and speech and call him God too.

It is the Law that holds the whole universe planet in the palm of its hand and that Law is love. Yet, it pertains to my planet as well as your own. As well as planets you know naught about, including galactic space.

To go back to my own period of life on your planet ...

We fell by the wayside and many of us followed devious ways of the spirit and so punishment, inexorable and inevitable, followed our flight from light. Shall I call this colony, the goodly companions?

I cull my words in your language from a learned man who is standing quite close to me. You are surprised at my grasp of your language and the fluency with which I express my thoughts. I give you my name in that colony. My name was Chloris.

We brought with us on our flight from our planet, bees.

You did not know that did you? No. To this planet from our mature planet, came the bee, this most wise insect.

It has caused us amusement that your scientists cannot explain its orderly life, its mathematical brain that causes it to bring about its six-sided cell in such perfection. Also that the bee talks to its companions.

Well, let me tell you of my fall from grace.

I was the royal beekeeper. Allotted the task of caring for and acclimatising them to the poison of the earth. It was through this poison of the earth that their own venom developed – the sting – unknown in my planet.

While we were on my planet we did not die your physical death, we brought that requisite quality in our souls. Although we did not die here for a long time, during that time, we colonised that particular part of your planet where we built our city.

With the goodly companions, there were females and so marriage, as it is in my planet but not in the physical way of your planet. We resorted then to physical union on your planet and we bred children. Still, held we fast to our great and glorious heritage, tending the light of truth and the light of love. But as a miasma creeps up from the marshes of your planet and brings fever in the veins of the men on the earth, so did the toxin of evil from the earth dwellers invade our veins. And I, Chloris, was the first one to fall by the wayside!

It was I who discovered that from our God-given nourishment, the food of the royal bee, an intoxicating liquor could be distilled. I was responsible then, for the first time on your planet, to know what it meant to be intoxicated.

Now, I will go further and explain to you that on our planet we have our great seers. They, in their early days of training, are fed upon a particular plant (which does not grow and has not yet reached your planet), which brings about ecstatic trance conditions.

They were selected people, these seers.

We, who accompanied our queen were not seers, not one of us. But when I, in my intoxicated state, persuaded my companions to join me in revelry, we thought that we had at last found this great plant, or rather, essence, which gave men vision into the future.

What a disastrous error that was!

That was the beginning of our decadence. Our fall.

You have a vague echo of it in your bible history, 'banished from the Garden of Eden'. I give you the truth. We were banished forever from our planet, never permitted to return.

We spread, we separated, we quarrelled and we made war upon each other. Our queen with her council had long since left us. We went our diverse ways across the earth, spreading this iniquity of the essence of the bee, finding as time progressed, a stronger brew each time.

Fain would I not tell you this, but it is right that you know whence came the legend of your Garden of Eden or that part of your planet that we had turned into a veritable Garden of Eden.

We fled from it and left it a wilderness. It is now a desert place upon your earth, for we were visited by one of our airships, which destroyed it. Never again will there grow a mortal thing.

We had brought light to your planet and we had put out that light. Therefore the place of our sinning was wiped out.

Quite shortly, your scientists and your searchers will find out what brought about the desert,[38] which my friend standing here tells me is near China. Yes, truly were we punished in our Garden of Eden!

Children of Light – Children of Israel

Now I will pass over intervening years of time. We had not yet been granted permission to die physically on your earth, although we had died spiritually. We wandered, lost, separated, mourning and grieving in utter despair.

You have a parallel case in your recorded history of the man Jesus who went into the wilderness. He did not go into a physical wilderness, he went into the same wilderness that we went into, spiritual. He, being one of us, was tempted as we were tempted. He having come with the queen was stronger than we and he overcame his temptation. We did not.

I will pass over this aeon of time, in which the remnant of us, the children of light wandering in the wilderness, became the children of Israel. The children of light, still being punished, fleeing from the light, desecrating the most holy of holies.

I opened my harangue by saying to you, "and it came to pass that Gods became men and men became Gods" … I will now go to another portion of your earth planet, to us so infinitesimally small and infantile and I will come down to that continent known as Atlantis.

Atlantis

This has been much in the mind and speech of she whom you call Tara of late, due to our influence over her. She has no idea that we have spread above her this net of information, which we are now giving through her to you. I hope you are duly appreciative of learning the truth about the community of men on your earth planet, lost to your historians. Records wilfully, sinfully destroyed.

But the secret will be out soon.

The great tablets we brought with us were buried by order of our queen. She called to us. On my planet we call by mind to mind. She sent out the call and those of us who had not fallen as low as the beasts of the earth answered the call with joy in our hearts. The wandering in the desert places of our souls was over and so we joined her in Atlantis.

The name given, being the name of a particularly happy centre in our planet, Atlan.

So it became Atlantis … Is … being light. Israel … Is..ra..el – light.

Well, we established there again a small colony, which over the passing of the years became greater and greater and so the population spread and multiplied and our

38. Suspected to be the Gobi Dessert.

kingdom was of God. With the queen upon the throne, all the Godly virtues of light came back and once again we knew the joy of living 'in the light'.

So the aeons and the aeons passed over Atlantis. Great kings came from us, helped by the knowledge given them by the queen.

Now alas, by a misadventure I am not allowed to disclose at this moment, we learned of physical death and on that day was fear born like a monster upon your planet. From that day fear streamed out the awful sequel that has made this planet the war torn, unhappy, savage, cruel planet that it is. We, of Atlantis, are responsible.

Now, having eschewed the pleasure of the intoxication of the liquid distilled from the food given by the royal bee, we resorted to other ways of gaining power. With the coming of death and fear, came greed and cruelty. When an Atlantean man gazed upon his neighbour's wife, he slew his neighbour.

I speak of Atlantis as she was before God sent her beneath the waves at last. Then the last remnant where paradise was fouled was almost gone.

Gods became men and men became gods.

When I speak of gods becoming men, I speak of those great ones that came from my planet. Those men have become the gods of your tales of old; they were kings in my kingdom of Atlantis. Those who still retained the light, those who never besmirched and betrayed their heritage. So the rest of us became the men we had known before we became gods.

Then came the flight of my people from Atlantis.

We knew an evil in Atlantis of which you could not grasp even the first idea of its depth. You speak of earthly degradation, earthly decadence and earthly evil. Believe me, you are children at play compared with the fallen gods in Atlantis.

Well, an affronted God swept away the earth people who were trying to copy the superior being, which incorporates then the history of the little flood of one called Noah.

Ever the inferior imitating the superior, those who descended and founded the peoples of Israel.

As in Atlantis there were chosen those who would be saved from the pit of hell that swept it away. Even so, did those people imitate the gods made men and speak of a chosen few to save from the waters.

Am I making clear your so-called history?

[The group assured him so.]

And for you too, my friend?

Betty: I am trying very hard to understand.

Chloris: Never let it be said Chloris is still under the influence of the bee's liquid! I have tried with all my eloquence, which I have borrowed from another to explain to you that the earth, my friends, is but a babe in space. You are much busied at the moment trying to discover exactly what its function is in the cosmos in the universe.

143

You are in for many surprises! Perhaps man will walk humbled now as we walked humbled after the fall.

I have come to enlarge upon the words that if at long last the earth does not respond to the teachings of Light, even as our Garden of Eden was destroyed on your planet and our happy land Atlantis was swept away, so will your planet be destroyed.

But He has blessed it. He has stated that you will see the result of His blessing around the entire little globe. There was noticed a period of calm. No eruptions anywhere in the world for a time.

The mind of man must rise above the animal that he is fast reverting to in his spirit. He is growing into a mental giant and into a shrivelled dwarf in his soul. When that conditions occurs there is destruction.

I do not come to sow seeds of the fear, that destroyed me and mine, in your hearts. I come to tell you, as it has been told me, that prophesies made in this room or chamber or whatever you call it, have been accurate to the last degree. I come with a message of hope, indeed I do.

Let man once again find his light, his queen, for the soul of man is the queen of his body. Let him enthrone her and crown her with love. Stand fearlessly and say, 'Within me, I am of God, therefore I am light and I am divine'.

Do not be misled by me and think that we cherish you not, we do. Your welfare is of great concern to us, for upon your earth there are still remnants of us.

I speak from your spirit world, I have never been permitted to return to my planet. I left the earth for the last time in Greece, where I functioned as the oracle on the Sacred Grove.[39]

Once again did I dim my light! I possessed still the gift, which was an integral part of our being, our seeing. I told you of the seers, I told you that mind spoke to mind. So I committed the heinous crime of pretending I was light and concealed myself in that hole in the Sacred Grove and when poor, misguided men and women of the earth came seeking the wisdom of the oracle, it was I, Chloris, who spoke and was called 'Divine'!

Now that I have expiated my fall from light by my work in your astral planes, I am not insinuating that I am doing rescue work here. This is a visit of love. Most divine love.

I work with a few of my own group engaged in similar activities. I merely speak those words of portent to show you even the gods can become men through letting their light die out. The light of the soul, the light of God, the light of love which permeates the entire known and unknown of the void.

Break the Law ... and you suffer. Live by the Law and you bring about such happiness in all with whom you come into contact. I have learnt that in the hells I frequent.

I have no idea what impact I have made on you, none. I do not even know if you have received my words clearly. They merely are inserted into my mouth, as it were, a funnel coming down from Tara's mind and the words being sent down through the funnel to me containing my thought, which I have contrived to put out as clearly as possible.

39. *The Sacred Grove is in Delphi, Greece.*

I thank you for listening to me. You will remember the words of Chloris in the days to come when great surprises will be in store for you from outer space and when the soul once again reigns in glory upon the earth. Fear will no longer be the concomitant of your civilisation.

I go now and leave with you my love. A greater gift I cannot give.

Perhaps after one of my prophesies is fulfilled I will come again and you will give me greeting and say, 'Chloris, you are the light because you spoke truth!'

Then Chloris will be happy again. Yes?

Ella: Take our love with you.

Chloris: Thank you.

Whether Chloris ever came down to the earth plane again, I do not know. He did not come through our group.

Atlantis is dealt with in more detail under the Geology section where Angela explains that a new planet is coming into being and that landmasses will arise, one of these is suspected to be Atlantis.

Although, at first viewing Chloris may be difficult to grasp, it is interesting to note that the people of Israel are recognised as the people of Light.

Also interesting, is that it is reported that there was an oracle that spoke in Delphi; tablets are being discovered all the time; and scientists have never truly discovered why the bee operates as it does or how it communicates.

Chapter 10: Islamic Souls

A Persian mystic and prophet
"I always kept this sacred fire burning for Zoroaster, fire of the soul, fire of God – Light"

This speaker did not announce his name but was a follower of Zoroaster. He claims to have been a great orator and teacher who brought the Zoroastrian religion to the Persians. His grammar was not particulary good as he would have been translating from Persian.

Only earth stress brings me here. I was an orator and a teacher. I am sorry that I cannot express that which I wish to say in my own language. *Siga mala ah Allah*.

The world is in dire distress. It seems so to you my brothers and sisters of the world, as it did to me, so long ago.

I followed Zoroaster, the great master who brought light and worship of fire. I always kept this sacred fire burning for Zoroaster. Fire of the soul, fire of God, light. When you light the fire, the symbol of light, it will make you think of God-light.

The great forces of satan have ever been the battle against the Light. Sometimes darkness envelops the world. Sometimes, praise be to Allah, the God-Light conquers all.

I give you gold from Allah – truth – by revealing to you that the one whose body I now use was Zoroaster![40] Light. *Mazda*.

She talks much of the forces of light and darkness and devil, arriman. I come because Jesus asked me to come. The forces of light (*mazda*) are conquering now. The dark one and his black-hearted followers are falling away and sinking back into the blackness. Yes, the great battles in spirit! Satan now biting tail in mouth! In little

---

40. This was Tara in a past incarnation.

146

vessel of fire, like the vessel of your heart, you will safely warm. Burning you will say, 'my heart is burning with love'.

I worked much with flowers and roses there, where the little fire burnt with sweetness and purity. I was well known as Prophet.

Take courage in your hand like a Persian rose and know that *mazda* is conqueror.

The followers of satan have seen his fear and they, too, are biting tail.

Good God. God good! Sulaman, my horse is waiting for me … I go riding away …

Angela

Coming in a cloud of glory. You should have seen him!

The Aga Khan (No birth/death dates) – Title of a religious leader and Imam
"Naked I come, naked I go"

This title, the Aga Khan, was originally bestowed by the Persian Shah, Faith Ali, on Hasan Ali Shah (1800–1881), the 46th Ismali Imam in 1818. He lost his title following Faith Ali's death. Later, he moved to India and aided the British in the Anglo Boer war of 1839–1842. He was succeeded by his son who assumed the title of Aga Khan II and started the line of Aga Khans.

[After the greetings were over the Aga Khan turned to the Indian doctor visiting Cape Town.]

The Aga: The one who overshadows you is not of your race, does that surprise you?

Dr Chakreverty: No it does not.

The Aga: Good, well, it was he who applied for permission that you were brought here today, that your outlook could be enlarged and enlightenment could come to you, for believe it or not, you will be used in the days to come.

There has been a great assembly of spiritual forces brought down from the higher planes of spirit where, alas I cannot go.

I was an earthly man, much addicted to the material side and luxury in life but I endeavoured to follow through my responsibilities as the Imam. Did I fail? Yes and no. I failed with my son, lamentably, lamentably so. I neglected my duty as a father and a spiritual adviser to this boy.

Well, one cannot shed tears for that which is past. That may sound strange to you from the representative of this prophet, but it is true. We face each other when we pass out of this body, my young friend. No longer through a glass, darkly, but face to face. It was not a pleasant countenance I looked into!

You will forgive me when I recall earthly matters.

No word of censure was addressed to me on my arrival here, none. No reproachful look that I had neglected my duty was cast at me. No. It was I, who cast those looks at myself. I went into my innermost being and found there alas, a poor, weak man.

Gone my immense fortune, gone the jewels, and gone my dwelling places on the earth. I was of no significance! Stripped of my trappings as the Aga, I was as a cowering soul, naked as the day I was born. I have had to learn the full purport of those words, 'Naked I come, naked I go'.

That is why I am here today. I had to plead like a mendicant, I had to plead for this opportunity to speak here today. I … who … well, we will not dwell on past glory.

The dark forces

Armageddon, you have seen it in your newspapers, well, all prophesies that come through truth are true. At last has come what has been so foolishly alluded to as 'Armageddon'. The battle is on to the death of the dark forces. Praise be to Allah. The banners are unfurled and the armies of God, Allah to me, one God, the God of a thousand names. The march has begun.

It is from centres like this that the power has come. The power of spirit, you must understand my young friend, is impartial. It can be moulded into light or into dark. Oh, yes, not even Allah can withhold that power. His satanic majesty has had a long sway, but the shutters are being put up and the windows of his habitation closed.

Yet, do not think it will be an easy victory. No.

I will make a point clear to you, young doctor man, that is this; if a human being, manifesting the spirit of God upon the earth plane can gain a victory for light then there is a decisive victory against the dark forces. But it has to be brought through a human being or a group of human beings on earth. God manifesting through his highest creation, man.

My dear friend, I suffered under the same delusion, that the spirit of light is so powerful that it can control the entire earth and bring it into the light. Never was there a more foolish mistake made through the mouth of man! Had it been so, do you think we would have had wars, pestilence, murder, rapine and rape? Name it what you will. Had the shining ones been in full control ...

Then on the other hand, you must weigh, as they weighed me against my diamonds, the shining fact too, that had there been no battle between dark and light forces, there would be stagnation!

Do you follow this my friend? Or is it in direct opposition to your thought of spirit?

Dr C: No, it is not.

The Aga: You are a very advanced young man and a very advanced old soul, much blessed. I wish I had had a son like you! Can I give you greater praise?

No. I was a poor parent. Too much power and corruption sets in, inevitable. I digress once more on my puny self. Let me hasten to matters of importance.

One religion

I overheard your words to Tara that you were convinced there would be one religion for the world and that mankind would be drawn into this full realisation of the one 'God at one-ment', 'deity at-one-ment' with the divine mind, the cosmic being.

Well, it is coming.

The prophet manifested himself through a portrait through the hand of this lady, Tara. This was borne out. For in each man's heart lies the seed of eternal truth and in the eyes of the prophet – was truth.

Therefore truth spoke unto truth and my people said, 'It is well ... it is he ...'

Therefore the seed has been planted in that part of the world, has taken root and will grow into the rose bush in the land with which I am so closely associated, India.

Omar Khayyam (1050–1122), Persian poet, mathematician and astronomer
"Fear not, have faith for the dawn of light is here for the world"

Born in Nishapur, Khayyam – meaning 'tentmaker' as was his father's profession – was well educated and became an outstanding mathematician and astronomer to the Sultan Malikshah who undertook to reform the calendar. This led to the adoption of a new era, Jalalian or Seljuk, which began on March 15, 1079. His work as a scientist has been eclipsed in the west by the popularity of his book, *Rubaiyat*. This was first published in English in 1859 and translated by Edward Fitzgerald, who re-organised some of the verse quatrains, making it difficult to establish whether all the work attributed to Khayyam is really his own work.

"And lo! The bird is on the wing
    Come with Old Khayyam!" [41]

Well, you know, I did not deserve to win fame with that poem. No. I was the court mathematician and astronomer. That was a little 'byplay'!

Had it not been for your Englishman, well, who would have heard of old Khayyam?

I am now speaking through this very delicate mechanism of this precious child. I do not know how my voice is coming through, whether it is feminine, masculine, neuter! But when I say this child, the tale is passing sweet, great enjoyment, great luck and – dare I say it, for a philosopher to use this word – excitement.

When I spoke to her for the first time in her home I did not say who I was, for we do not always do so, but she instantly recognised me and into her mind there flashed the words, 'It is Khayyam, the writer, the poet'. And oh, my heart leapt with joy that the link held after all the passage of time.

Now we clear any misapprehension from your minds about my relationship with her.

It was deep love for this soul and intense regard for her piety and goodness. You might think, 'Well, here is another suitor out of the past!' No. It was entirely intellectual and spiritual that we were as twins, for I have been with her in the first band of Light.

41. An extract from a poem in the Rubaiyat

I gave a slight intimation of my intention to speak with you when the word 'Jinn' … 'Pitfall and Jinn'[42] was spoken here, I think a few meetings ago. Well, had any of you been astute enough, or known my poem well enough, you would have known it was old Khayyam announcing his intended visitation.

I jest, merely to try to tell you why I can use this body so easily, because I got attuned to earth's vibrations through the male instrument I used.

I merely came to say there is much good in man.

Have faith in the ultimate future of man, for in each man is the Godhead. No one is cast out, for God cannot cast himself out. Therefore, for what you term the lowest of the low and the most evil, always the beacon of hope holds out its welcoming glow.

I cast my eye around your earth planet, which was mine too, which I chose to descend or fall into. The fall of man.

Khayyam fell too, at his own desire to follow the queen.[43] I fell from grace.

In my following incarnation as Khayyam I sought what I knew to be the truth. But as you will read in that rigmarole of words, I never found the key to the door!

I sought the truth in the stars, in the sun and the moon. I sought the logical sequence of life. I sought truth in my intellect, the one part of me, my friends, which knowing how I had lost my light caused me the most intense and dreadful suffering that is possible for the human mind to undergo and survive.

From out of the abyss came the queen's light and her voice saying unto me, "Fear not, for the dawn is at hand for you".

My heart leapt like a living entity within my crouching body and for a fleeting moment once again beheld the light of the world and climbed out of the abyss. All because the queen stretched out the lifeline to me.

That is why I am here today. Privileged by Allah to use this body and to deliver this message which came to me:

"Fear not, have faith, for the dawn of light is here for the world."

Inshallah Inshallah

Salaam

Salaam.[44]

42. See archbishop Cosmo Lang, page 101
43. The Queen of Atlantis. See Chloris page 140.
44. In the name of Allah, peace, peace.

Spirit drawing by Tara

The lamp of wisdom, a follower of Mohammed
"All religions have a pivotal point like a wheel, a circle, no beginning, no end, which in Eastern symbology is eternity"

I came two centuries later than Khayyam did. This divine instrument has a drawing of me, which she did with her eyes blindfolded. I was known as the Lamp of Wisdom.

My name I would not give to you. It would convey nothing, but I would have you know that all those who follow in the wake of the queen, were you to translate the name, you would find it meaneth, Light.

Now I sit here very pleasurably, very comfortably, for the great Master himself prepared for me this place and here I am!

I was Islamic.

I studied deeply all the great religions of the world. I buried my beaked (oh yes – I had a nose like a beak) my beaked nose and my little beard. I buried my whole face (let me put it that way because most of my face was my nose!) into all the religions of the past. You could request of this instrument that she reveals to you my portrait.

I struggled to put upon my shoulders the mantle of Zoroaster. I finally ended, which was to be my destiny, by following the holy prophet of Islam, Mohammed.

After many years of concentrated study, I find, as I found then, all religions have a pivotal point like a wheel. You might say like the hub of a wheel and each religion a spoke going out in all directions to meet the circle of the wheel, which in Eastern symbology, is eternity. The wheel, the circle, no beginning and no end. You follow?

Do I try and emulate the great Master, Jesus, by speaking in parables? I do not mean to do this. I am not worthy to walk in his shadow but it is as I see it in all these religions, the one fundamental basis; there is but one God.

For you know the great pantheon of gods, which encompassed the world, until the great day dawned when those who came with the band of light, brought into the fallen man at last that there was but one God, the source.

There is truly a saying that a house divided amongst itself must surely fall. Well, through all these religions there runs that pure indestructible light, the one God.

So we will cast our minds back to the words spoken by Jesus of which he said, "In my Father's house there are many *mansions*".[45] It is the wrong word, but it has been accepted now in the Western world, literally. Let me paraphrase that in my words and say that there are many mansions of religion. You see? You follow me? Am I too Oriental in my way of speaking?

---

45. John 14 verse 2. The accurate quote is, "In my father's house there are many rooms"

[We assured him that he was not.]

Well, in my Father's house there are many mansions as there are spokes in the wheel. Now, if you take out of that wheel, one or two or three spokes, the wheel will collapse. So it is within eternity. You will have chaos if you have the great religions breaking and saying there is more than one God. No, they all merge and make straight for the hub.

Or let us rather put it this way. They all came from the wheel, the circle, the eternity and they made their way straight to the core. One hub to a wheel, one core to the universe, God.

Now, though they have the shining fact, the great reality of the one and only God, after the manner of men, they have divided their belief into little sections, like the segments of the spine. Now if you have the spine of man and you take away one segment, man can no longer stand upright. He will drop again to all fours, never to rise again.

So now must come the great age.

We, of the east, in our wisdom so much older than the west, (no boasting), we know that there are different ages for the world. This coming age, we are already in it, is the Aquarian Age. This is the age when man's intellect, instead of laboriously, oh so laboriously, finding its way up the ladder of thought, will scale that ladder, has scaled that ladder, from the bottom rung to the top in one leap.

Now that man has advanced so much with the intellect and the brain and reasoning power of God, if man combines that great knowledge he will accrue the greatness of God.

There are many things, that is a clumsy word, there are many facts to be found out in science in the next decade. Khayyam, as you know, was a scientist of the highest degree. He is honoured in his native land for his intellectual accomplishments. The time has come now when the spokes will no longer be separate. One by one, they will become welded into one solid wheel. One religion, one brotherhood of man, one road to the one God they know is there.

All that they have lost is a way to God, which should be universal. The cosmic truth, the all embracing, all illuminating light of God. The precious source, the jewelled heart.

Those   follow Buddha, they say, *Om Mani Padme Hum* – the jewel in the heart of the lotus. For when the lotus opens, there is its golden centre like the sun. That mantra has a double meaning; God, the jewel in the centre of the universe so no more will the lotus close its petals and hide the jewel, no; and the jewel will shine unclouded, perfect in the wide-open universe, which He, the great giver, has given to his children.

Therefore, let me, your humble servant, echo the words of my great Master and say, "Have faith. Let not that (lovely) silken cord that binds you to the nameless one become frayed and tattered and unsightly".[46]

You have the proof that the day is at hand. You have been told, I will not repeat this.

46. Ecclesiastes 12 verse 6.

Remember you few are in the vanguard of our heavenly armies, for you are taken out of your body, in the words of your poet, 'In the still watches of the night' and you are in council with us.

Owing to your earth bodies, it is difficult, we know, to retain within the earth brain the shining truth of the places you visit and the people you meet. That is why my Master and I have come to tell you not only to hold your head high, but the torch and the flame of hope within the heart, to you ... the torch is handed.

You have been tested and tried and we know you will never permit the torch to smoulder or go out. Nor will you allow it to smoke and befog the senses of man and the fatherhood of God.

Fan it with loving breath.

Fan it with the devotion to the one God who holds you all in the cup of his hands. I thank you.

Chapter 11: The Art of Zen Buddhism

Azu – A great master of China or Tibet speaks of Confucius
"The great dragon is awake"

Azu came through for us twice. Angela says later that this name is just a cloak. He says that he was from China, she says that he was from Tibet. Clearly he did not want his name revealed.

Confucius sat pondering under the willow tree in the little green bower while the branches hung like plumes over the little stream. Suddenly a light appeared in the bower and the angel of Light explained to him that he was a messenger of Light on earth, which he did not know as he was still attuned to the rites of the ancestors.

When one ponders and meditates in the surroundings of nature, it is comfortably arranged to have contact with the messenger of God.

So the reality of life came to Confucius and today he is still recognised as the great wise one.

You may come and see me in my lotus garden.

[Azu announced that a beautiful spirit canary was in the room singing rather noisily.]

I have to recognise that this voice has not spoken for over two thousand years and the hinges need oiling! My voice was never gruff like voices of the west.

Tonight I speak in a modulated tone as with the art of paint and brush. We had the art of speaking beautifully. We could make the sounds of falling water, a bird singing, a lotus flower with a special note in our voices. We learned about the love of God in old Cathay.[47]

47. Ancient word for China.

The beast walks there. No, there is hardly one land on the planet where the beast does not stalk, bringing agony and tears and loss of faith.

I was highly psychic like the rest of the race. We practised ancestral worship. Then one day, beneath the willow tree when I was in deep contemplation, enlightenment came to me and I knew the presence of the one God.

In my land of China today man's thoughts are muddled. There is not the clear stream over which the willow tree bends to look at her face in the water. The water is muddy.

Now we of the past are working very hard in that great and powerful country, that China with a legend of the past, which is glory and great artistry. Then it went to sleep.

But now the great dragon is awake! It is swishing its tail and blowing flames and smoke through its nostrils! We are trying to make it a paper dragon and not a real one!

Angela

He is one of the great masters of Tibet. That name is just a cloak. He is busy working there now, that is why there is this swinging away towards the west. It is going to gain momentum. You will see a change of tactics!

They are not enamoured of their head, the man who is there, their god. Well, they are finding he has feet of clay! They are a very ancient people with very good brainpower and insight. They may have been bedizened and bedevilled for a while but ... well ... we will leave them to their chop suey.

Azu
"One must temper one's wisdom and humour"

There was a great and wise one in China, much greater and wiser than Azu. He sat under the willow tree and it was there that he got his revelation in which he knew that the belief in the ancestors was correct but incorrectly used. The usage was wrong, yes?

The great one used to compose his writing under the willow tree in his beautiful garden. He wanted to impart his wisdom and start a class for the young males of the community.

When the lessons were over, the teacher used to strike a gong. There was one very clever young boy, but there was also a very big, rich boy who thought he could just do like this and then everybody must jump to attention.

[He claps]

The young boy was a great favourite of the wise one and he was naughty and mischievous.

This young boy did not like the fat boy who sat in front of him. The latter had a very fat buttock.

One day the young boy could not resist pushing his pen into the fat boy's buttock when they arose after lessons and the fat one rose in a great hurry!

The wise one was full of wisdom and laughter. You are not wise if you do not laugh at times. The teacher wanted to hide his amusement as he, too, was getting tired of the fat, rich one's demands. So he bent forward to hide his laughter and the fat boy thought he was bending over in grief and sorrow.

He dismissed the whole class and told the young one to stay behind.

The young one stood with his head bowed before him.

The wise one said, "My child, you have done what I wanted to do for many moons".

So one must temper one's wisdom with humour. You cannot be truly humble if you say constantly 'I'.

[The young boy was Ella in a past incarnation!]

5
Social Sciences

Chapter 12

Historical Figures

Oliver Cromwell (1599–1658), English soldier and statesman
"I left on the pages of history a foul chapter"

The son of gentry, he entered Parliament in 1628, became a mercenary, a corrupt and devious leader opposed to Charles I, which eventually led to the execution of the king. Cromwell's genius in military activities and ability to inspire armies ended in massacres extending to Ireland and Scotland. He supported minority religious viewpoints, particularly of Jews and non-Anglican Protestants, excepting Quakers. His foreign policy included dispossession of land. He dissolved the British Parliament to replace it by a nominated Parliament appointed by himself, and became Lord Protector of the Instrument of the Government in 1653. Having divided England, he was finally offered the crown and a new constitution. He declined the crown, but accepted the constitution with some modifications to increase his power, later becoming a great strain on Britain's finances.

"The Lord is my shepherd."[1]

How many of you have thought of the inner meaning of the words of that Psalm. I am no preacher nor am I a prophet. I am … no … I shall not give my name, for I was the perpetrator of vile and hideous deeds in life.

I come not to do penance before you. It is not needful for me to do this because long since I have been forgiven. There is no need to ask to be forgiven, the forgiveness flows like a great river that has no beginning and no end. It has its source with God and so goes back to God. Therefore, I say to you the ancient words, 'The

---

1. *Psalm 23.*

Lord is my shepherd, I shall not lack, he restoreth my soul', which had gone astray. Though it be of centuries ago, I shudder at my iniquities.

I, under the guise of religion, preached so loudly in my hypocrite's voice about God and the holy son Jesus Christ. Oh, yes, strident were my tones when I declared to all and sundry that I was a true son of God.

I held forth, letting the people think I had the secret ear of God and that only I knew how to worship God.

I let it be thought that I was a man of great and deep feeling! A man who had experienced contact with God in my innermost chamber. Therefore do I declare unto you, 'He restoreth my soul'.

It is nigh on four centuries ago that I betrayed my God, that I lost my soul. Yes, but I have been received back into the fold now and I endeavour to do what I can for man.

I left on the pages of history a foul chapter, a foul chapter.

Are you my friends? I wonder.

A foul chapter, bedevilled with my own pride, my arrogance and my bestiality. Oh, I do not mince words describing the beast I was, for it says in the holy book somewhere that the 'beast walks abroad'. Oh, ye gods of old, they were right! I was the beast and I changed the face of history, particularly in my native land, England.

I know today the tale of that land is a sorry one indeed! Violence abroad, violence within. The beast stalks again. Am I, with others of my ilk, responsible for this? Am I the cause, down the long years of the horror I left behind me, the cause and the effect of today?

I am my own judge. None other judged me when I emerged from the dark hells, which I entered when I left my earthly home. I had no way of gauging time in those dismal places, but it will do you good to know the one who sought me out of that hell was the one whose head fell at my command. That was my ministering angel.

I believed in a God of vengeance who I declaimed in the scriptures, "An eye for an eye and a tooth for a tooth".[2]

When this gentle victim of my iron-clad pride came and sought me out, I cowered away from him for I thought, he comes now to claim my life.

I, the wicked, wicked man, found love and mercy and compassion reaching down to me from the eyes of the man at whose feet I knelt like a craven coward. I was begging for my life!

So did I pass into spirit, with this assumption that God is a god of vengeance and it followed me into hell.

I come before you, arraigned before you if you care to judge me, to tell you that I learned in that moment that God is love.

Oh, how I betrayed that love.

I sought to flee my benefactor who had been my victim as he lifted me to my feet and I threw my hand across my eyes and I cried, "Poltroon that I am. Leave me be, leave me be. You have come but to taunt me."

He said, "Nay, I come but to befriend you and take you out of the darkness and into the light of mercy and the light of God."

Now I began my real hell. For I fled from him back into the dark place in which I

2. *Matthew 5 verse 38.*

had been incarcerated by my black thoughts. He never left me, he never ceased from his ministrations unto me and at last, the great shepherd opened wide his arms to me and said, "Come home my son."

Then, for the first time since that hateful day when I had seen his head roll, did I find relief in tears.

Oh, the blessed river of mercy that flowed through me with those tears wiping away all memory of my horrible deed. All memory of my viciousness and I stood, my soul restored.

Yea, I had come through the shadow of death only through the mercy of the man that I had destroyed. So does God work!

·I am here today to tell you that I seek out all over the world, men whose hearts are as beastly as mine own. I work unseen, unbeknown to them, to restore their soul that before it is too late, they too, may hear the summons, 'come home my son'.

I would doff my hat to you if I wore one. There is no need for me to hide beneath its broad brim any longer! My eyes are clear and they have seen the true glory of God. My heart and soul at long last are as clear as the river of mercy, which encompasses the earth from which all men may drink.

"I was a-thirst and thou didst give me to drink. I was a-hungered and thou didst feed me, for thou art my good shepherd and I do not lack".[3]

Thank you.

Angela on Oliver Cromwell and King Charles I

A man of great strength of character, great power. Great powers of persuasion! He had a great following but even as he caused the head of his victim King Charles I to roll, so his own was put upon a pike. Yes, he lost his head. Not by the axe, no, that would have been too merciful for him then. Do you know the physical head has never been returned to the physical body. Have you guessed his name? Yes, that was Cromwell.

So they come and they make their bow to you and give you a little of history trying to show you, all down the ages, of love that is God.

How in the end it finds them all, binds up their wounds, heals the broken heart and restores the soul. Wonderful, is it not?

We had some difficulty in getting him to speak as he was feeling deeply penitent. It is the first time that he has used an earth body and it brought back to him his past. He relived what he had done, guilty of many bad deeds ... but it is all well now. He has passed on now out of the room quite happy again. It was just the coming back.

It will surprise historians to know that King Charles I was deeply mystical and he would go into his innermost chamber and find God. Therefore he met his death as a gentleman and a king, as a true follower of Jesus. As the master would do, without fear.

3. *Mathew 25 verse 35.*

Do you know your history? Have you read that he was so brave and his kingly gesture that he made? Look up your history books![4]

There was a great welcome for him I believe when he came into spirit. I was not present, but he is a very great light indeed.

Now this man who spoke to you, you must not forget he had a brilliant brain and a brilliant insight into all minds, except God's!

He could look at a man and almost delineate his character in a moment! Almost knew his thoughts. He could have been a power for such good. Anyway, that is what he is doing now. He seeks out as he told you.

I thought I would just enlarge on that statement of his, for he was getting more and more overcome as he kept talking! With his strong powers, which have never diminished, don't think that he cannot tell from the auras of many how evil they are and with great distress to himself. Yes, indeed! He goes into that aura and tries to influence this man or that against doing just what he did. Not lopping off heads, but making the same mistakes that are going to rebound and rebound down through the centuries of time.

It is quite true what he said that he changed the face of English history. Quite true. For had he left that unhappy king to continue his allotted task … then the unhappy successor, he too a very brilliant man, but deep in his heart always resenting that his royal father had been so scurvily treated by Parliament and by this man.

Do you see? Do you see? Or do you!

4. *King Charles I was condemned to death on January 30, 1649, for refusing to recognise the court over a religious question. He conducted himself bravely and with dignity, praying on the scaffold and then indicating that he was ready to die.*

A great financial magnate, next in line for a knighthood
"Cold comfort for the materialist"

I greet you all. I am no prophet so don't look to me for the words of wisdom.

I come to you all tonight to make confession. They say confession is good for the soul. That is as it may be.

I am just an ordinary fellow indeed. I will imagine myself sitting at my desk addressing a board meeting …

I was known as a self-made man on the earth. Yes. I came from quite an ordinary English family. They are dammed good, the lot of them. Just that I was not from an aristocratic family, but a middle class … going our quite pleasant little way in the town in which we lived. I had an ordinary youth. I went to a good school but because I had, well, it's not boasting to say, I had a good brain, above the ordinary, I went on a scholarship to university and became known as a great financial magnate, then left the earth plane not so long ago. Therefore, I am able to speak in the manner in which I spoke on the earth as I have been earth bound.

Now, don't ask me who I was. I'd like to forget that as quickly as possible and try to find out who I am and who I'm going to be in the future!

Well, from ordinary beginnings I rose to a great position in the big city. Other financiers would come to me and ask, 'Give us your advice on this or that'.

Now in my household, we believed in God and Jesus Christ. I never queried, I accepted everything I was told by my mother. My father was a bit negligent. He was embarrassed when I asked him about God so it was left to my mother.

So I grew up without any blatantly wrong ideas of deity. But then deity was so remote to me, the idea of the divine never really penetrated into the recesses of my soul! I was a decent fellow. I didn't do more than my ordinary amount of cheating, nothing piffling, I went for things in a grand manner!

Now comes the tragedy of it. I got richer and richer and to use an earth expression, I was 'stinking rich'. The richer I got, the further and further away I went from what I knew of God, which was precious little, but it was always there. Right through my school days and bosky days I used to say my prayers, 'Our Father which art in heaven'.

Well, believe me, in the prison house, which I had built, I had turned the key on myself as I amassed this money. What a tragi-comedy! If only I had the power to climb upon Nelson's monument and with a loudspeaker say to all the rich ones, 'Lord of the earth, you damned fools, you come over here empty handed, for God's sake get rid of all your great masses of money which means nothing to you but the power it has brought you!' The doffing of the hat and the bending of the knee to your millions, giving you the entirely fallacious idea that you are God upon the earth. That by the wave of your hand you can destroy nations, you can destroy rivals. Man reels later on with the sense of power that money gives him.

Oh, I see it clearly now and I am sick at heart.

There was much stress laid on that word 'comfort'. Well, I follow humbly in our blessed and beautiful Angela's footsteps and say to you, believe me, there is no comfort in being the owner of millions of pounds.

At first, you are a mighty fine fellow that you and you alone, whether by fair means or foul, have achieved this power over man. Later on, for the sake of it all, you sign away lump sums for the charities that don't mean a thing to you! The joy of giving to the poor, the needy and the sick? No, you gave for the joy that your name will figure at the head of the list and you are next in line for a knighthood!

Oh, I have been in deep consultation here with a very advanced soul and I have made confession from beginning to end. It does me good to come here and hold your attention for a short while so that you can see the cold comfort for the grabber, cold comfort for the materialist and almost damnation for him. The chaos that moneyed power has brought about in our world today.

I am going to make amends. God hear me. I am almost on my knees to that faraway deity (not far away, only in man's mind) and I am going to say 'give me one more chance, only one, to make amends to those rivals I broke in my march towards the top'.

Lord knows when that chance will be, but give it to me.

Thank you. Goodnight.

Ella: God bless you.

Magnate: Thank you. I wish someone had said those words to me when I was on earth! When I look around and see the harmony, the peace and the comfort in this room, I could tear my hair out at the roots that I did not follow this way of light. Tell that to your world, they may know who I am.

Angela

Now, my beloved ones, till we meet again. That is but one of the vast concourse of souls that came over. He wanted to so we allowed him to come through. The centre point of what I came to tell you is that materialism rots away the foundation of family life and national life, because it is going away from God.

Sir Winston Churchill (1874–1965), British statesman, soldier and author
"Only I knew that we lay there like an ant just waiting for the boot of the conqueror to crush us!

As a reporter for London's *Daily Graphic*, he reported military events in Cuba as early as 1895. Later, he was sent by the *Morning Post* to cover the South African war where he was captured and then escaped Boer imprisonment. He served and fought in India, was elected to Parliament as a Conservative, then crossed to the Liberal Party. He led many expeditions during WWI, served in France, and helped negotiate the treaty that set up the Irish Free State. One of his failed initiatives was opposition to the Indian nationalist movement. As an immense public figure and truly great orator, his whole career was highlighted by his extraordinary vitality, imagination and boldness of character. He became Prime Minister during WWII and is remembered for maintaining British resistance to Germany and his stubborn refusal to make peace before Adolf Hitler was crushed. He was knighted in 1953 and awarded the Nobel Prize for literature and oratory.

Oh, oh, listening to the magnate, those are my sentiments!
What fools we are, what utter fools and what little thanks we get for what we do. We prostitute the ideals with which we start out shining as brightly as any Roman warrior's shield. Oh, how soon that shield is dulled and tarnished! If only I could illustrate for you all sitting here in your comfortable way of life what hell it is to be a public figure, a statesman, a politician and a leader. To quote Shakespeare, "Uneasy lies the head that wears the crown".

Well, that was all right in the time this other man was talking about, but in my time what uneasiness did the crown cause the king or queen? It caused me the uneasiness that lay heavy on *my* head, not theirs!

I was there to take the reins in my hands and guide the ship of state through the cascades and the waterfalls and the torrents and the rocks that beset out pathway. Oh, God! What a fool I was! Why in carnation didn't my inner sense say to me, for God's sake, get out of it all, find peace of mind?

I used to shed tears so easily, particularly in the last besotted years of my life and I'm shedding them now by the gallon!

My son, my thrice-unhappy daughter! For all my so-called brilliance of mind and capacities, I cannot comfort them. I cannot reach them. On one occasion when I did manage to, I called out to him and said, "I'm here to help you".

Do you know what he said to me, my flesh and blood? Looking at me with loathing, he said to me, "Get the hell out of here!"

Yes, the guns assured my departure from the world but no guns boomed to welcome me into this world in which I am of so little account.

Oh, I was wont to read my bible searching wisdom and guidance. I was rather like those petty gamblers who take a pin and stab it into a racing list of nags and hope to find a winner. Well, I used to do that with the bible. Childish, eh?

Sometimes I hit the mark! One day I was having such troubles, I sought help in the quietness of my study and I jabbed in the pin and found, irony of ironies, I found these words at the point of my pin, "Unto us a son is born".

The son that was born brought heartache to his mother and God knows my son did the same to his mother! So perhaps it was appropriate that I found those words.

I know, I know. You have guessed my identity. What have I got to hide? Look at me. a pitiful being.

[He then had a coughing spell, emanated through Tara. This occurred because of his coming into the earth conditions from which he left.]

I am not allowed to do that. Yes, if you had heard me cough you would know it was me all right. What have I got to show? Come, on, tell me. Don't pity me, let me look at my own faults full in the face, come on.

Nanette: You gave us courage during the war. All those wonderful broadcasts went into all the little homes of Britain. Great courage you gave us.

Churchill: Only I, my dear lady, knew how fallacious it was. Only I knew that we lay there like an ant just waiting for the boot of the conqueror to crush us!

It was not I that gave you that courage, it was the spirits of men that had been great men in history in Britain. Drake, being one of them, Alfred the Great, Arthur of Camelot. They came to the help of Britain and do you know why? Because Jesus walked that land. There the light shone for the first time in the western world. That is why it cannot disappear from the annals of history, because the holy child set foot there.

Now don't give me credit, I don't deserve it.

No. No. I'm telling the truth. I did not know the truth until I came here and I gave them the sign for victory. There was silence.

I had to learn I had nothing to do with it. It was the mighty spirits of the past, determined never to have that little place sullied and dragged down into the depths. No, the time will never come that Britain or the Isles are destroyed? No. But always the possibility is there that it will be covered by water and sink for a while, yes?

But that won't be in your time, so don't worry your heads over that!

I have to go now but it is helping me to talk, to expose my true self not only to myself.

Ella: Our love goes with you.

Churchill: You know I didn't rate love very highly in my earth life. I had experienced too little love. That elusive quality. As a child, an *enfant*, I was deprived of maternal and paternal love. As a father, I hold very little. My own fault. My own executioner I am. It was my wife, the only love I ever knew.

Yes. A sorry state! But I'll come round out of this post mortem depression. I suppose I was old and tired and half dotty when I left!

Good morning.

Angela speaks of Churchill

Well, you know it takes all kinds to make a world, just as it takes flour, sugar and butter to make a cake! So we try and serve you up a different meal spiritually each time we sit. At the same time we're considerate of your appetites. You will notice that I'm coming back to you, Guy.

Guy: That's a sore point!

[Guy was fairly rotund and Angela shares a joke with him.]

Angela: Yes, well we love to give you a varied meal! At the same time you are all helping these people at a time when it's never so nice to seek out unexplored crannies of your own soul and find they are covered with a mass of poison ivy.

But he is a doughty man. He will find himself soon. It's quite true that he did bear the burden of the crown. Yes and I think it was too much for him really, too long.

Now I came in for a moment to clear the vocal cords of Tara because he was very emotional. Thank you for that surge of love you gave him. It came as a great surprise because he was a man who as he truly says (and he wants me to repeat this) "knew very little love". Well, he had a kind of affection, an affectionate hold on the minds of the people, but they were too ready to forget him at times too. Don't forget nothing is as fallible as public affection! The hero of today can be the outcast of tomorrow. So it goes. That is what he has told me. He found that so, several times in his life. As you see it is always power, power, power!

You have two examples here today, you have Cromwell and you have this other human suffering through power and its aftermath and only they can clear away the wreckage. We stand by but they have to do it themselves.

Marina
"The pull of motherhood is very strong"

This is believed to be Princess Marina, the strikingly beautiful daughter of Prince Nicholas of Greece. She was married to the Duke of Kent in 1934, had three children, one of whom was Princess Alexandra. The Duke and Duchess of Kent were known for their annual appearances in the royal box at Wimbledon. He died before she did during WWII when his aircraft crashed into a Scottish hillside on August 25, 1942. She died 28 July 1972 in Cape Town.

I bid you all good ... it is evening?

Ella: Yes, it is evening here.

Speaker: I take the tacit kindness to let me speak although I have not asked your permission to do this. It is rather important for me at the moment to make contact, through this lady, with the earth once more because I have been told I am moving on now to a brighter place.

One is torn between husband and children so often on the earth and it was to my great amazement to find it was so on this side as well! I wanted to be with him and I wanted to be with them, for I was very close to my children after he died. I was all they had, their world. So it was when I found I had passed beyond the veil, which I knew all about when I was still in my earthly body.

Therefore, it was no great shattering experience to me when I found I had cast it off. I mean, my physical body. But there was the tie, this pulling. It is a central pulling of yourself towards those who are dear to you and whom you have just left so recently. Otherwise, there was no reason for me not to move on immediately to where my husband waited for me.

Well, you will understand what I am talking about.

I also came to give word of the bereavement that will come to the royal family quite soon. Yes, so when it does happen, I know you will not forget that I asked you if you could send your concerted thoughts of love to this particular member of my family.

By now I think you know, I am Marina.

Ella: Always so beautiful.

Marina: I don't know so much about the beautiful. I am just Marina now. No highness, no royal highness, nothing. Just Marina, torn between mother and wife.

I would ask for your own sakes not to mention this to anyone, please, for my sake as well. Please only after this death takes place, perhaps you can relate my coming here tonight.

Thank you very much for allowing me to come.

Please, no royalty, I am just a woman. A departed soul, glad for so many reasons to have left earth, which had lost much of its savour. I had thought immediately the reunion took place in spirit that I would be detached from the earth and go with him.

It is quite a different story, this pull. Motherhood is very strong.

I am going now. I do deeply appreciate being able to speak and have the courage to speak and give my name, on behalf of him too. One last commentary before I leave this body. It is rather a shock when you arrive on this side after being parted for many years from the man you married. Well, you have advanced in years, you know from your daily appearance in the mirror and you have aged and to find this extraordinary young man waiting for you! Quite a shock.

Angela

Just waiting for her to take herself off. He is waiting for her. Yes, she must go now.

There comes a time when that silver cord of motherhood must be broken, you see. Not broken, but set aside. She is a woman of powerful personality who can be of great use on our side, but she retired much into herself before she came to us and that is a habit that tends to grip one.

A royal came with a message for Michéle
"Love is the true ruler of mankind"

I have had special permission from the Master to come today. I was on the earth when to be royal was to be regal. There is a great difference between royal and regal. Many have failed in the latter!

We are old friends, Ella. I don't see any desire for you to curtsy! No one thought to offer the young queen a cushion when first she sat on the wooden throne!

We were tragedy ridden for many years with famine in the land and civil war.

My loved one Michéle. The deepest affection. I come down in centuries to claim my own ...

I was your mother so long ago and am ever with you in spirit. How I can recall your little dark head. This my yuletide gift from the Master. My tears of joy! You were always the favoured one, you the only female. Go your way in this life. Love is the true ruler of mankind.

I will have to say farewell. I shall not speak again, it is quite an effort. I am extremely tall and slender, rather what you call a tight fit in this body.

I will give your name to someone else to give you. To give it now would bring the tears. I would start a well of tears. Your mother of so long ago is with you and guiding your precious feet. The royal cloak is about you. The hand of memory plucked the strings of my heart, as the minstrels plucked the lyre as the queen held back her tears.

I did not rule, I reigned.

Even so, long ago I knew all men were equal in the sight of God.

I am grateful indeed that I have given voice after so long only because my little daughter has returned. My soul has followed the pathway of her soul.

Angela

Tragedy-ridden for many years. Famine in the land and civil war. Given at birth a tender heart. She supped with her subjects, wished to go into a convent after she lost her three children. Two golden boys and her dark haired child.

No monk or priest could help her or comfort her. One of the great unseen always here. She has a little kingdom and court of her own, a court of love from which go forth messengers to the lower planes. Many from the dark planes are brought to her in her queenly robes. They think she is queen of heaven.

No one disillusions them until they are acclimatised to the new life.

The king was but a shadow.

She elected to come on this day when you were here. If you could have seen her glory! The bands of colour, gold. And a choir of little angel boys were singing. There is always a great rejoicing when a reunion takes place.

Tara may complain of a headache for the great power of the queen affects the physical body. Indeed were you blessed!

If you could only see the cohorts of angels being gathered now that physical contact has been made. Not all mothers yearn for a child. It is unique in spirit. She is a wonderful, wonderful being. A woman of great saintliness with the gift of warm humanity. She made her mark on history, which is much revered on our side.

Great was her emotion at meeting you, you nestled so deeply in the heart of that great queen. You came at the tail end of the family. She did not survive you very long as life had lost all meaning for her.

Keep your mind clear and sweet, Michéle. I know the value of this and with your long history from down the centuries, you will reap the joy and happiness, which is due to you, a thousand fold.

Crowned once again, Michéle, could not escape the word Michael!

Pontius Pilatus (A.D. 26 – unknown), Roman prefect of Judea
"Much has been erased from the records"

He was supposedly a ruthless governor and was removed at the complaint of the Sumaritans among whom he engineered a massacre. His attempt to evade responsibility at the trial of Jesus was caused by his fear of the power of high priests and his difficult responsibility for the peace of Palestine. According to tradition, he committed suicide in Rome.

It is not correct to say I am a soul in travail. Ah me, I *was* a soul in travail and am since at peace with myself.

On my reluctant shoulders rested the peace of the land in travail at the moment, Jerusalem.

I was responsible entirely for maintaining the miserable conditions between my sternly controlled soldiery and the hatred-filled citizens of the mis-called 'Holy City'.

It was not really necessary for me to make the descent into hades again today, but this urge has been growing in my soul to let you good people know the clemency of the God I denied and defamed.

Oh, it is not as an act of repentance that I am here, far from this. I only come through to underline the message of Joshua the Master, 'All is love'[5].

I carry you back in thought to the time of his trial in which I participated and played so unmanly a part.

My name today on your little earth is still synonymous with cowardice and contempt and had he not released me from my self-made prison I would not have attempted this communion today.

I, Pontius Pilatus greet you.

Does it seem alien to me to say I greet in love? Now let me harken back to that fateful and pitiful last day.

I am still sometimes outraged by the misrepresentation and the false rumours concerning that bright (and it was a bright) day. You would think the sky would have been overcast, weeping at the folly of man, but it was not so, my friends. The sky was bright and the sun was shining. I said, "Behold this man". For I, with my arrogant Roman eye had glanced upon that man and seen that here indeed, was a man!

A man who had borne the scourging, the mishandling of my own guards and who stood there in his hour of triumph, to the outward eye a piteous beaten wreck of manhood. But never, my friends, have I seen a head held so high, or such dignity.

I looked at this man and it was to myself that I spoke, not to the rabble, when I said, "Behold the man".

I saw there was a supreme being. For that noble head looked at me and from eyes, my friends, never seen on earth before or since. There was for me, Pilatus, the tyrant, the bully, the procurator, call me what you will, there was only compassion

---

5. Paraphrase of 1 John 4 verse 16 and Galatians 5 verse 2.

and love. In his own manner he conveyed this to me and it seemed to me as though my heart suddenly stood still. He conveyed to me, his pity for me that I had to condemn him.

My friends, this was the first time in my turbulent life, that I had seen compassion and pity beaming at me from another human face. Would that the world knew my reaction to that divine being. You will readily understand that I could not recognise his divinity because my mind was cluttered with our own foolish gods. It behoves me to tell you I had no truck with the Roman or the Greek gods, but knew no better. Therefore you will understand that I did not see this man as divine, then. I only said to myself, "Behold the man".

Now do you see when I tell you the misrepresentation? I alone saw the supreme man. Do you follow me now? Not so the world.

Could I trace for you the dignity, the nobility of that tattered man. The stone of ages melted in my proud and arrogant Roman heart. I had no God to whom I could cry and say, 'Tell me, what I, Pilatus, can do to save this man from this unworthy rabble?'

Do you understand me, my friends?

Group: Very well, indeed.

P Pilatus: I could not bring myself to quench that unearthly light in those eyes. I could not bring myself to condemn to that shameful death, this noble being, who could with but one look convey to me his pity for me.

I, the strong god at whose very presence men trembled in fear of their property and their lives. I took the coward's way when I finally renounced him. I tried to shift from my shoulders this appalling responsibility of this man's death, but the wily Jew knew I was already in disfavour in Rome. I held my office merely because of my marriage to Claudia Procula, not by virtue of my ability, my courage as a Roman, no, by what you would call 'influence at court'!

But I was in disfavour and the Jew played upon this streak of cowardice in me.

Strange to think that the only truly noble being I ever encountered in my days on the earth was one of that race. I had for them nothing, but contempt. Nothing! There was nothing in them that was endearing to me. And there, before me, in what I now know was an archetype of man, stood a Jew, who looked upon me with love.

I must stress this particular facet of my life here. You must remember that every Jew I encountered looked at me with barely concealed hate, murder, revenge, clearly depicted on their countenances. But not this Jew. Oh, how troubled I was. How troubled and how amazed at myself that the ice in my heart had melted.

It will not surprise you, as it surprised me, that for the first and only time in this life of Pontius Pilatus, he knew love in his heart for another human being! For that look of love, so compelling, woke what is a seed in every being's heart – love in me.

Much has been erased from the records to suit this race. In my despair and my newly found love for this supreme man who stood there, I cried to him, "Tell me the truth about yourself". I did not say "What is the truth?". I was not concerned with truth at that moment, only insofar as it was connected with this supreme man. Do you follow me?

He, out of his compassion and pity for me, could not give me the answer to that.

Time was running out and even in that moment he thought of me. For had he told me of his mission, could I have denied his private audience with myself with love burgeoning in my own heart for him? I loved him as a brother, a totally new experience. I would have embraced this man in the face of the screaming mob. I would have held him to the heart that he had newly awakened in me.

But bound by the trammels of my office, I stood helpless.

I will tell you, it was my head that was lowered in shame at myself and in the horror of my fellow man demanding the life of this gentle, but oh so great man.

I wish to state to you, when my eyes and head were lowered, I could not meet the benevolence of that love. I could not endure it. It was making a coward out of me for I came face to face with myself in that moment of revelation.

I gazed upon those hands, my friends, I have seen men's hands when they are in agony of body, oh, too often for me to wish to recall and those hands are always clenched, but not this man's hands. I noticed in that moment how beautifully fashioned they were. They were clasped together in what I now know as an attitude of prayer for his tormentors.

I washed my hands of him but oh, my friends, the water turned to blood for me.

From that day onwards, I entered into my own private hell. A hell made darker for me and more bitter by the fact that my wife had known of this great man. She did not dare tell me that she was a secret follower of the man. She came to me in her extremity of pain and said, "I had a dream". It was no dream. She knew every movement that was going to take place to bring him to his end. In her adoration of him, she came to me, breaking an inflexible law of Rome and she dared this for that man.

When he was put upon that 'tree of shame', she came to me and confessed she worshipped him too and made clear to me then that God dwelt in this man.

Too late for tears, too late to cry out, 'Why did I not embrace you, my brother in God? Why did I not hold you to the heart you had called into life?'

Oh, my friends, please do not think I am a simpleton. No, you will not think that. You are too aware of God in man.

I must end my tale of Pontius Pilatus. One of brutality and arrogant cruelty.

Angela following speaks of Pilatus's testing time

He had such a burning desire … he was a-fire to set matters right concerning what he calls 'the records'.

I understand that at the beginning, after he passed over, the Master was there to console him and lift him up into the realm where he really was destined.

You know, after that day his entire nature changed and he too, found the teachings of Jesus. You will note history has very little more to record about him. That is not so. Records *were* kept of him and his doings, but the Jewish people suppressed them and burnt the records.

I would imagine that Tara is going to go head over heels when she hears that he has been! Not that she nurtures any feelings of distaste for him in her heart, I think it has been explained to her somewhere in all her different lives that she has led since then. She probably encountered him because he now works, you might say 'hand in glove' with the great ones in spirit.

You see, he was himself an extremely advanced soul who had taken on that incarnation to be there at the time of the Master's trial. He had been told before descending into the earth body that the Master would not truly die on the cross. When it came to that look of recognition that passed between them when they met again, remember, he spoke of that 'seed of love in his heart', it was in his soul, the recognition.

Well, can we say history would have changed had he …

But it was his testing time and Jesus knew this very well.

For when Pilatus hesitated, he could have saved him. But as he explained to you, his whole career was in jeopardy at the time and memory, soul memory, was not strong enough for him to bring about what would have been his crowning act. That is why he went into the terrible hell of remorse and self-reproach.

Nevertheless, knowing the Master, my dear ones, I can tell you this, he knew quite well what Pilatus was going to do and that is why he was filled with such compassion for him. He knew it was a test for him and he realised that he was going to fail. Not that it would affect him in our world of spirit because that rests with each man, his ability to pass a test.

Nobody condemns him, nobody judges him. After all, the great question to put to yourself is; what would I have done under those circumstances?

You see? It is very difficult for you to answer that question yourself because unless you have been put to the test you really can't say what you would do. After all, it's very easy for you to say, 'Oh, but I would have done differently'. But would you?

Therefore with his great clairvoyance, Jesus could clearly see that at the last minute he would falter, for it meant a break with his whole material world, also the disgrace. He was already having difficulties with the high priest and the *sanhedrin*[6] and Jesus understood all this.

6. The highest court of justice and the supreme council in ancient Jerusalem

Chapter 13: Geographical Movement and the Third World

Angela – A plan for third world countries
"And the old order passeth, gives way to the new"

I am no Florence Nightingale with the lamp. I'm only Angela hoping to bring a little light.

Hello Ella, are you feeling under the weather? Never mind, it will pass soon. Nora, Anna, Rennie, all's well? Looking ten years younger already.

Well, we stress over and over again using the Master's words, "Let not your hearts be troubled".[7]

It is inevitable. It is the plan and who are we, you and I, to query the working out of the plan? It is man who destroys the plan and it did not, for one moment, include warfare, disease or any of the horrors that man has perpetrated and brought about on this planet.

There was a plan for the 'third world' countries to come forward and take their place in the race of man. That is the root race at this moment on the earth planet.

They cannot be stepchildren any longer. They are God's children, just the same as you and I. There is no difference or differentiation in the divine plan. They must be brought forward.

With the progress of knowledge and light, the plan was that those peoples would come into their rightful place in a peaceful manner. But that the more highly civilised man becomes, the more material he becomes and when the material side takes over, the spiritual fades away into the background. Until at last in the inevitable march of things, the spiritual, being the only reality of life, comes uppermost again.

If you were to gaze out onto the planet as we do from our 'four listening posts',[8]

7. John 14 verse 1.
8. A higher group of minds who monitor the planets.

you would see a resurgence, a renaissance of spiritual energy going out from every land, continent, call it what you will. There comes news to us of more groups, more individuals seeking.

The church, I know, is in disfavour at the moment because I listen in, you see, to what goes on around Tara. I also receive, glean from her mind, her reaction when she reads her paper in the morning and at night and I know that the world is in disfavour with your church council.

There is a spirit of anarchy abroad. Yes, anarchy taking place in your church because it is breaking down the old established order. It is worn out, effete. Little or no comfort any more. You know the words, 'and the old order passeth that gives way to the new'. That is what it is.

No old order passes away without a last minute struggle and the struggle very often takes the form of what you have been told before, the dark forces! They stand at bay like an animal with its back against the wall. It shows its most vicious side in its fear of an oncoming annihilation. Do you follow?

Well, that is what is taking place all over the world.

Angela speaks about migration
"Justice is slow but deadly sure"

This was a conversation inspired by extensive news coverage in the early 1960's about the influx of Asians into the United Kingdom.

Nanette: Angela, there seems to be a very great migration of Asians into England these days. Is there some special significance in this?

Angela: Yes, indeed there is. This migration has been vast within the last ten years all over the world. Think of Tibet and what happened there. A mass movement of Chinese people. There is Asian movement into Africa and into my own land of England.

There is a reason for it all. Cast your mind back to the reign of a certain great queen[9] and think what she did to what you class as coloured people. Think it over.

She took over India, parts of Africa, the colonies and now England has opened her doors.

Nanette: You mean the chickens come home to roost?

Angela: Coming home to roost but they are full-grown cocks now! Nothing else but that. Nothing else … Britain has to bear the result of what her queen did. They will batten[10] on her now as she battened on all her conquered countries and built up her vast wealth, her great empire, which has gone away to nothing.

Now her chickens are coming home and they are going to batten on the English people and there is nothing you can do. They have to learn a lesson. Justice is slow but it is deadly sure.

I have heard Tara say, "The mills of God grind slowly but they grind exceedingly small".

Wherever that hand stretched out there followed disaster and death. Tara's own country is still rift in two on account of it. The greed. These are harsh words but true.

What did Spain do with the Incas? Killed off an entire nation. For greed. And where is Spain today?

You can't take away from people that which is theirs and hope not to suffer. It is the Law. Do you understand?

I suppose a great majority of people who are flooding into England are those who are the very ones who died because of England. That is how it works. If you go back in history you will note that national changes are always preceded by migratory movements.

For instance, the evolution of Pakistan, the influx of the British into Australia, New

9. *Queen Victoria.*
10. *An old Norse word meaning to prosper at another's expense.*

Zealand and Canada, we also see a cross section of foreigners flowing into Europe and the indigenous people continuing to go abroad.

We are, as you see, moving people to stop static conditions.

There has been almost no emigration from Russia or China, due to their static conditions. Their internal troubles are like a blocked artery. The lifeblood is not flowing as it should, thereby giving rise to internal arterial problems.

America, such corruption in that continent undreamed of in the settled communities of Russia or China. It was to this 'new world' that the migrants from England and Europe flocked some 300 years ago.[11] She was to be the life-blood of your planet. But alas, as you can see from their published word, the massive and diversified migration has created a country with mixed and questionable moral standards including those at the political helm. It will take time to form one nation based on acceptable cohesive ethics.

Africa is a virgin country with little movement in or out. But in time, the so-called 'yellow tide' will mingle with those of darker blood. When they arrive in Africa they will be fusing their diligence with the oft' time lethargy of some of the original population.

About South Africa, I am asked, 'Is South Africa ready to accept this new phase or era if you like?'

Firstly, you must bear in mind that what you call South Africa is a relatively small geographical area in world terms. We, on the other hand, look at areas as people areas, without political boundaries.

Yes, you are definitely changing and have been for a long time. The southern tip of Africa was sparsely populated 400 years ago. Look at it today, Khoisan, Chinese, Malayans, Indians, Europeans and a variety of black people who have migrated from Central Africa.

But in time, things will even out a new phase in history.

Since the time of this recording, there have been marked changes in South African history. The ANC (African National Congress) was unbanned in 1989 and Nelson Rolihlahla Mandela was released from prison in 1990. We ushered in our first democratic Government in 1994 with Mandela as the first so-called 'black president'. President Thabo Mbeki succeeded him in 1998.

This would indeed seem to be a new phase of history.

11. Various events led to the population of the new world. Among them, the potato famine. The Quakers left on the ship 'the Mayflower' to escape conforming to the Church of England.

Angela on poor communities
"The slums of the astral planes"

Rennie: Angela, can you tell me what happens to the poor communities who live in squalor? When they pass over, are they housed in better quarters?

Angela: Rennie, we get down a very … we won't say puzzling … but …we are not only interested in the white people here, we are interested in every colour because we are all God's children, all from one source.

Generation after generation, people from poor communities tend to reincarnate into the same conditions from the one they have left on the earth plane. Here and there and much more so in recent years, you get an emergent soul who thinks above his or her squalor. The others just accept it as their sort of pathway in life. They don't even ask why. I'm afraid there are many people who, well, just squalor in their squalor, if you know what I mean.

Take the Goths, the Huns, a tale of bloodshed and murder and yet today they produce the finest musicians, writers and people of culture!

They don't just change because they have shed their bodies.

But don't worry, it's all coming right. There are always guides of all cultures who have advanced in thought processes in spirit who go out to help them in what you might call the slums of the astral planes.

Rennie: And are they happy, Angela?

Angela: Perfectly happy! What is there to make them unhappy? Spiritual advancement is to do with mental processes. People must realise that this isn't such a terribly sacred subject as it is a scientific subject. In future, science will be allied to the spirit side of life.

Well, then, as we are rather fond of telling you, you have all eternity before you, so that a lifetime more or less in squalor is fleeting. It is explained that they must try and reincarnate in a part, or a community, where there is advancement, socially and physically.

But … and I'm sure this will quite horrify you … many don't want to! They are perfectly content to go back to the very same conditions and they don't take very long either! They go back very quickly.

There is no prolonged stay because of the yearning to go amongst these overcrowded conditions where they enjoyed the proximity. It made them feel a family, a great vast family living together. They share each other's pains, joys, fights, everything! They long for that again because they haven't yet developed sufficiently to see the glory that awaits man because they are young souls.

You will never get old souls going back there, unless they go back as messengers or harbingers of good news. Then you will see that they arise out of those conditions. They will arrive and become a leader of a particular group.

It all depends on each independent being. Nobody pushes them around if they want to come and live in conditions like that. It is their choice.

We must remember too, that as civilisations advance there are better housing conditions for poor people. As soon as that happens, right away, within the human being there is a subtle uplifting of the way of thought. Not for nothing was that old adage brought, 'Cleanliness is next to Godliness'. Did I answer that?

All: Yes, indeed, most interesting.

6

Psychic Sciences

The scientific study of celestial objects, of space and of the physical universe as a whole.

Angela gets down to the point regarding the earth's resources
"The great ones have this little blue planet under constant surveillance"

A beautiful dream went forth and that dream ended when the world was formed. The work was finished. The love that sent forth that dream ended in concrete form and was never withdrawn.

Never think for a moment that the great mind is concerned only with the planet earth. Every part of creation is important because there can never be an end to that which has no beginning.

Now don't ask me to tell you when it all began because I don't know. It is too profound for me. Until such time comes when I can sit at the feet of the Great Almighty and have it all explained to me, I must be content to be in the kindergarten class!

Looking to the future of this world, the great scientists (with the help from the great ones on our side) say there will be no noxious fumes anymore! Your vehicles will move by atomic power.

There will be no denuding mother earth of her vital forces, her oil, copper, gold and coal. You will draw it all from father sun and poor beautiful tired earth will be allowed to rest in peace, recuperate and replace all that has been taken out.

You are part of the earth and your earthly bodies mirror the earth, including the salts … mostly water. If the minerals are removed from your body, you fall to pieces, don't you?

Now, look what they are doing to the long-suffering mother earth! Going down into her very bowels and removing her life nutrients, which hold her together.

But as I have said to you before, God and the great ones have this little blue planet under constant surveillance. All will come right.

At the moment your own planet is almost in its death throes now, through man. I know because I am with Tara. Well, I know it from this side anyway, I don't have to be told by your newspapers, but I am with Tara before she goes into meditation and she always reads her newspaper in a great hurry because she deems the call is so strong and she is inquisitive to know what has been going on in the world. So I read through her brain and I see the despair of the scientists the world over about your atmosphere slowly dying, oxygen being withdrawn. Your planet is becoming dead through lack of water.

It is man's doing, nothing else.

They talk about the good old days, don't they? I know. I get around! I have to keep *au fait* with what goes on in the world otherwise I can't discuss it with you when we meet. I hear people talk scornfully of the older folk who remember 'the good old days'. In many respects they were, you know. It was a leisurely life and the pace was good. It may occasionally be the pace of the ox, but still the oxen always get to their destination in the end, you know!

Look at it all today. There is one beautiful word I got from 'you know who'.[1] (He is much kinder to me now, the man with the beard and the eyebrows that waggle, much kinder! He had to be cut down to size on our side, very gently, but he had to be pruned.) Well, he gave me this lovely word 'frenetic', this feverish race of man to destroy itself.

However, there is a great movement afoot and of course it will never really happen.

1. Angela had an ongoing discourse with George Bernard Shaw, see page 61.

Angela
"A new planet is coming into being"

I think it has been mentioned here before that a new planet is coming into being. It is difficult to compute time, but as far as I can gather, it will be in another thousand years.

Time comes in cycles, great cycles and there were six. It petered out on the seventh cycle when form began.

Your genesis is not an original manuscript The writing came down from Babylon and from Syria where the Jews were in captivity for so long and they learned it from the Assyrians who copied it from a still older document and that document copied from an older and another and another from *xyz* right up to *abc*! Now I can't tell you more because I'm not interested in it enough. I am much more interested in the world and the universe as you know it today.

I have a more or less rough idea how it all began but it's too fathomless for me. I'm just content to be here!

But there was a time when it was all written down on tablets, the tablets that came with the coming of Light.[2]

There has been a lag in the new planet

Now to continue, there has been a lag in the new planet, which is coming into being. Don't ask me why, I can't tell you and no one else can tell you, but the fact is, it is not proceeding up to time.

You have been told that the creation of this planet of ours has been too quick? Now this appearing of the other planet will have to come about because it has been falling between two stools! Their knowledge of the fact that this planet was created a trifle too quickly meant that they have had to try and cut down the speed of the new one. Do you see?

Imagine two cylinders rotating at different speeds. In an effort to balance them up they slowed it down, now they have slowed it down a little too much, with the result our planet is speeding up a little. So now they have to speed up the new planet to make the perfect pair.

The two are inter-related, as are all your planets of the solar system, but in the great cosmic plan, this planet that we are on (I'm not in it, I'm on it!) something has gone a little wrong. Nevertheless, everything comes right in time.

So, you are going to have a series of cataclysms

If your balloon is not moving fast enough you jettison your sand bags. So in the days to come, it is not calamitous, but something will have to go and from that essence will go power and strength to the other planet for her to speed up. You see how it works? You don't, I don't! I am only telling you what I have been told.

It has been said that God is a perfect geometrician and mathematician and He

2. *The Tablets came from the Queen of Atlantis. See Chloris page 140.*

never makes a mistake. No, there's no mistake. It will all come back. It will right itself in a perfect process, this little planet of water.

You know, it was never meant to be a watery planet. That is a miscalculation that will be put right. You will hear of land coming up and the displacing of water. You will have further catastrophes. I believe they are trying to divert this to uninhabited places if possible. I am talking now of the council chamber from whom this information has been passed down to me.

Cataclysms and heavy floods

Things are going to clear up but there are going to be cataclysms, make no mistake. There will be heavy floods all over the world.

You know, Europe, for instance, is in a filthy condition. If you could but see the etheric double of the whole continent, which has been ravaged by war, bloodthirsty war, rapine, theft and every horror that man can perpetrate. You would almost say, 'let the whole continent sink under the waters, God'. You see it! You see it!

Now America was chosen to lead the world in the great new continent and there was vast emigration of people over from the old continent.[3] They constantly brought with them their decadence. You see how it goes? Man will not listen until it is too late.

It is never my intention, as you know, to bring distress and depression. I only show you the finger post pointing the way.

My father[4] used to say, "the road to hell is easy". You know, Rennie, were there to be a group of really strong souls working for light and for goodness, it would catch on like an epidemic over the world. It's the same thing if you go to a playhouse and some one stands up and says 'fire' … Panic immediately!

Well, why not send out goodness. Godliness. Shout it from the hilltop, anywhere you like and watch it work!

So remember, I ask with all my heart and I'm not giving a lecture now, but when these things happen, do not think of them as catastrophes, see them as for the good of the whole. If you can forget the personal side and the peoples of your planet (and I know it is difficult, but I'm trying to give you a spiritual uplift) look ahead as you plan for the children of the future and know that it is good.

Know that it is for the ultimate good of your planet and your solar system and that we are all one family in the system of planets. Now you can work that one out!

You have heard of your planet spoken of as mother earth, that applies to every other planet in the solar system. They are the mothers of whatever walks, flies, creeps or crawls in their ether and on their soil. All that springs from the planet, the mother.

Therefore, you have the brotherhood of man and you have the sisterhood of your planets. You are part of a household.

Your little planet was upset but no harm was done. Before something can go pop, it is set right. Therefore the mother earth sacrifices a little of this to the other planet.

3. The old continent is Europe and England.
4. Referring to Mr Rossetti, father of Christina and Dante Gabriel.

Chapter 15: Geology

The science of the earth, including the composition, structure and origin of it's rocks.

Angela speaks of the land mass rising in Africa
"I can see an island there – Madagascar"

I should think of the land mass coming up from your own coast of Africa! Your western and eastern coasts but it will also be lower down than that, coming up where you live.

My scientist friend is giving me a mental map of Africa and I see it will be on your eastern side, I can see an island there, Madagascar. Well, it will be lower down than that and will come up close to where you live. It is coming up very rapidly indeed.

Tidal waves

Information is relayed to the scientist and others, from the 'four outposts of the world'[5] who keep an eye on the earth and he said, you will get two tidal waves here in this part of your world. It will be an indication of the swift coming up of the new land. Land usually takes (to use a word they use so often) eons of time.

However, there has been great activity in the underground part, below the earth's crust, a terrific outpouring of energy, atomic energy probably, from the earth's crust and that is pushing up the new land.

I think this has to be verified due to this action created by your planet going to the other planet. Don't forget, it's already there and now coming up very rapidly and the time will come (open your ears wide) when it will be almost a continent!

We get all the thoughts that come up and the talk, the everlasting talk that goes on and on and accomplishes nothing!

When we get word about the fear that the world is over populated, if only we

5. *The spirit environmentalists.*

could tell them to have faith in the Creator of the world.

The new land will create a land-locked sea like the Mediterranean. In time to come you will have very little shipping crossing the seas, it is already happening.

This comment by Angela was made at least 23 years ago. We already have fewer ships crossing the seas because the world has become air dominated.

Angela
Atlantis is rising again

At the moment, the world is in an octopus grip of fear and insecurity. You are harassed daily. I read it with Tara, 'population explosion'. I can't quite follow what that means but I have a very good idea because there is a plan.

I have told you about the fresh lands coming up.

Well, Atlantis is rising again! Very steadily. One of these days the hump is going to break through the water.[6]

That will be when you get the floods, but the fresh land must come up. No land is intended to lie forever at the bottom of the ocean, for what good is it there except as a sewerage farm for fish?

Am I being vulgar, Rennie? I don't think he heard me. Should I speak more loudly for you?

Rennie: No, no, please.

Angela: You didn't hear what I said.

Rennie: No, I didn't.

Angela: I said, "Why should all that rich land lie at the bottom of the ocean just to be a sewerage farm for fish?" And it is coming up well fertilised after the fish have used it as a sewerage farm. It will come up rich and fallow and provide food for all the exposed people you talk about!

You see, the planet isn't intended, never was and never will be intended, to be a watery planet. I told you that. But you must remember that to induce or bring about the building up of a planet, well, your mind would reel if I could tell you.

We have to know this, Rennie, we have to go to the halls of knowledge when we pass over, if we decide to return and try to tell mankind about the marvels of the universe.

Places that are considered to be from the lost city of Atlantis have been found on the coast of America. Pillars can be seen today submerged in the waters around Bimini, approximately fourty kilometres off Miami. Under sea pillars, stairways and places have also been found outside Gibraltar, including the pillars of Hercules.

Plato refers to Atlantis existing as an island in 20,000 B.C. He claims that the Atlantic Ocean extended from the Sargasso Sea to the Azores. He also wrote of three periods of destruction from 15,000 B.C. to 10,000 B.C. The inhabitants apparently spread to Europe and the Americas, which would explain some similarities.

There are many books on the subject, some of which are listed in the 'Further Reading' section on page 274.

6. *There have been many different underwater sites, we have no way of knowing if this is the land mass in Africa or a different land rising.*

Angela: I could rant and rave on, hour after hour, but I can't tire Tara. I can't hold the attention too long, but it's like that with all people that lecture, so if we can find someone like you, Rennie, who is willing to take over part of the burden and let all this flow through you, a shout of joy goes up from spirit for another victory.

Every man and woman is a potential medium, a potential channel because it is a God-given gift. The spirit within is the dominating factor, not the grey matter.

I have spoken of this before, so I am not going to beat that drum again tonight because we are not going to prolong this meeting, which we will do if I get into my stride! So now I am going to make way for somebody else.

Now Rennie, from next Thursday, I wish you to be placed at my right side so that I might give you power and those who stand behind and around Tara can give you power. Then we will place Tara's hand in yours and you will have the power going through you. In making that contact, we can then keep Tara under control, because if you go under we cannot hold Tara without speech. Do you see?

It's complicated but it's the truth. We can't sit in the body and say nothing. We can't play numb skulls and dumb skulls, we have to talk, otherwise the power dies down. So if we put you next to her, I will talk to whoever is speaking through you. I, or one of the others, through Tara, will encourage the newcomer or old comer to speak through you, so the way can be paved for the preparing sage to give out his or her gems of wisdom.

Once you hear it on the tape, Rennie, you will be full of confidence.

Rennie was not too disturbed by this news as he had understood many years previously that he had the gift of mediumship, although rarely used.

Nanette – The story of Rennie
"How he became a medium"

My parents had just returned to England from their last, long theatre tour of India and the Far East when World War II broke out. Bombing and burning of London began and my father, Rennie, being on the reserve of officers, joined the army.

He and my mother, Ella decided that we should move out of London to a safer area in the countryside. So the entire house of beautiful eastern furnishings and our personal belongings were put into storage for ten days. We had been away for three days looking for a country cottage to move into, when a telegram arrived informing us that the depository had been hit by an incendiary bomb and had burned for two days. Nothing could be saved.

However, we still had the clothes we stood up in and our lives. At ten years old, my first lesson in life came from my mother's reaction, "One must not put too much importance on material possessions".

For a while we resided in a suite and rooms in a grand old house. The owners were spiritualists and they held Sunday services, séances and healing circles. The latter were conducted by a Harley Street doctor who was also a deep trance medium whose guide worked through him.

My parents were invited to attend one of these sessions for the very first time in their lives. The evening went along in its usual serene way when suddenly my father started speaking in a foreign language. He had gone into a deep trance.

The doctor's healing guide then departed from the doctor, another soul entered him and walked over to where my father was sitting. They began speaking in the same totally unknown language.

The two souls held a very animated conversation for several minutes.

The healing guide later returned to apologise for the break in the proceedings explaining that these two people had once been monks at a Buddhist monastery in Tibet, a hundred years ago! This was the first time that they had come across each other in spirit since that time.

The meeting closed. Everyone was overjoyed in their responses:

"Oh, Rennie you are a natural born trance medium."

"How wonderful."

"You must 'sit' for us."

Rennie, who had quietly believed he was having a private little snooze, was shocked and appalled at the idea of a strange entity using his body and vowed never to go back to a meeting again!

Ella, of course, was thrilled to bits.

I should just mention that my father had a habit of reading at night before falling asleep. The book would flop down and my mother would lean over and switch off the light. Not long after the Tibetan episode, she was about to do just that when a voice from my father said in a soft Scottish accent, "Good evening little lady, my name is Scot Riddle. I met your husband when he was a wee boy and his father and I were brother doctors in Edinburgh".

Scot proceeded to instruct her on the way of spirit, life in the other dimension and how it all worked. He described Ella's mother's home in spirit and the old English type garden that she had created. Her piano that looked like glass and how the notes of music swirled in colour as she played.

He spoke too, of the family pets that had ended up with her, including Ella's naughty grey parrot that had a penchant for getting stuck in the cooking pots on the top shelf and then would screech for help ... "Ella, Ella, Ella!"

At the outset, Dr Riddle suggested, "We won't tell your husband about our little chats until his mind has become accustomed to the subject."

This was the start of a long friendship and many conversations over the years with the family, rather like fireside chats, with Ella's grandchildren, Michéle and Michael included. It was a year before Ella told Rennie about Dr Riddle!

By then he had read and learned much about these things, so he accepted it quite happily.

Although he never used them consciously, he never lost his psychic abilities.

At one of the next meetings with Tara's group, we did as Angela suggested and used Rennie as a channeller. Angela's methods of transference worked perfectly well and Rennie was often used after that.

Chapter 16: Egypt and Archaeology

The study of the material remains of the cultures of the past.

Sir Flinders Petrie (1853–1942), English archaeologist and noted Egyptologist
"There is going to be a discovery under the Egyptian sands"

Born in Charlton, he was Professor of Egyptology at the University College in London and excavated ancient remains in Britain, Egypt and Palestine. His most important excavations were at Memphis, but he made many other outstanding discoveries such as the sites of Greek settlements at Nancratis and Daphe; the tombs of the first Dynasty at Abydos; inscriptions of the earliest known Egyptian reference to Israel; and the ruins of the ten cities at Tel-el-Hesy (south of Jerusalem). He founded the Egyptian Research account, which later became the British School of Archaeology of Egypt. His writings include: *Methods and Aims in Archaeology, Seventy Years in Archaeology*, and he wrote the first three volumes and edited, *A History of Egypt*.

I don't think any of you know me. Good evening to you.

I was an archaeologist. My name was Petrie. Being in spirit, I can say without being accused of being vain or glorious that I achieved for myself quite a reputation for my work in archaeology. There are a few books … volumes bearing my name.

I dipped into the past as far as mere man can see and discovered so much knowledge that was lost to mankind. This searching was of great interest to me since I began my career, because when you dig up the past you uncover more and more of the history of mankind and find that he hardly changes! It evokes in a man's heart great surprises, when he suddenly opens up a house of 600 or 800 years ago, to find that man and his wife and family were living a family life very much like our own citizens of the earth. We live with perhaps more comfort, but the cohesion has gone.

I can tell you from my observations, since the time that men gathered a few rocks into a circle and put some clods of earth on it and called it 'home', that I gaze in horror at reports received in spirit. The breaking of family life and pulling down of the old ideals that make life worth living is heart-rending to me and to countless others.

Now I wish to tell you that when I passed into the life of spirit, my very first thought was that I shall look up all my old friends whose bones and goods and chattels I had dug up out of the desert!

By the way, can you hear me? I don't know how I am pitching it. I had a rather slow, monotonous voice and I remember eavesdropping one day when I heard a man say, "I wish to God he would put a bit of up and down into his way of speaking!" But one is born like that and unaware of such failings until some kind or unkindly person tells you!

Reincarnation

Well, to continue, it was not an easy task. I hardly ran into any of them from earth or from heaven, whatever you like to say.

It was then that I ran into the word reincarnation for the very first time. I had always been so busy digging up their history and their way of life that I had never given their souls a thought! So when that word reincarnation was spoken and that issue was raised, I was as great an ignoramus as the pharaoh who dug a spade into the desert to look for mead. I knew nothing.

Well, there is a place here called the hall of records,[7] there are many of them, one on each plane of spirit and you can, if you wish, go and look up your own past lives.

I have listened in on these meetings here and you might remember when it was told you that a pharaoh had ended up as a pork butcher in Cleveland, America, complete with blue striped apron! Well, that pharaoh was somebody I was instrumental in bringing to life and freeing from the earth. It was I who discovered that he had descended from his high estate to the chopping block in America! So there was one I had to tick off my list. I could not gather from his lips the truth about his life. Gone he was. Gone into the illusion of matter, the earth life again. Here I sit patiently for him to return so that I can assure myself that what I had discovered, what I felt and surmised to be truth, was indeed the truth!

Do believe me all of you, in every walk of life, in every mode of work and in every thought and word, the sublime importance of that word 'truth'. I cannot express it enough. For think, if God were not truth, if God slipped an inch to the right or the left, where would we be?

"And the word was with God and the word was God."[8]

Now to continue my little talk. One ticked off my list. Number two was a woman, a pharaoh's queen.

I delved like Adam in the Egyptian soil, not the Garden of Eden and found a very charming wife of a pharaoh. A pharaoh of great, perhaps undeserved, fame. Well, I

7. See Akashic Records page 228.
8. John 1 verse 1.

went through the book of records and you will never credit me when I tell you where that light of love ended up, as a teacher in a small midlands town in England! Very prim and proper.

So there we were.

The pendulum goes back and forth and forth and back. He, who is a king today, may in tomorrow's life be a beggar upon the streets. He, who was a jester and a fool, might become the wise man, a sage whose words roll off the tongue as wisdom in its purest form.

Now I do not propose to sit here and tell you why this should be, for whenever we came across something from the past, evidence of people's lives long ago, the precept in my life and work was always 'when' not 'why'.

Now that I am in spirit, I am equally interested in following them up and having my words verified, stamped and posted as being correct. I drew blank in the end with every case. I could not have a conversation with the butcher or the teacher. Now instead of waiting two thousand years for me to give them life, I have to wait for them to give me life and truth!

Ma'at – the Egyptian word for truth

I came to tell you that this thread, which I could trace, is their way of life. Their way of building their homes. If you enter their tombs, you will see written in hieroglyphics on the walls and will know how they lived.

They lived by the word, *ma'at* which is the Egyptian word for truth. *Ma'at* ruled their pharaohs and nobles. How they abide by that word, truth.

That is why, if these words could be broadcast to anyone who cares to listen, I would say to them, live by the word *ma'at,* which sufficed for thousands of years for the rulers of Egypt. The great architects of their marvellous temples.

A discovery under the Egyptian sands

I will tell you another thing – a prophecy – although for me it is not one, for here in spirit the future as well as the past is recorded.

There is going to be a discovery under the Egyptian sands that is going to make your world agog and agape and throw extraordinary light on to the past.[9] As you know, prophecies made in this circle have been accurate and true, is that not so?

This Dynasty of Pharaohs that will be discovered is going to give modern man a nasty jab under his jawbone and he will reel back in astonishment over this particular line!

It has been held in a secret place for the time was not right for this information to be given to mankind.

I do not know if any of you are familiar with the bible. It was a great comfort and

9. *The sessions happened from approximately 1967–1979. Since then, there have been discoveries such as a pharaonic ship (the solar boat), Nefertiti's tomb and the mummy of Queen Tiye with her silky blonde hair. American archaeologists were scheduled to photograph rooms discovered under the Great Pyramid of Giza in September 2002.*

consolation to me, not all of it though. I took what was good and left the rest.

Under the Egyptian stars at night I would sit under a lamp, which was almost obscured by the clouds of insects and moths that gathered about it and read Ecclesiastes, which was my favourite book. You will see there that there is a time for everything and the time for disclosure of what I told you, is not too far in the future.

You cannot break a Law of God. You cannot hasten time, nor can you draw it back. In what I might almost call monotonous regularity in following out of the prophesied pattern, nothing you can do about it … nothing. Not even God, who is all truth, could mar His perfection by commuting one of his own laws.

Could He, thereby be showing He was imperfect? Do you follow what I'm trying to tell you?

You see, the time is there for each and every happening of small or great moment on the earth. It may surprise you, it will surprise you to learn that in the realm of spirit the same inexorable Law holds good.

I declare, I have not added to your knowledge in any notable manner by my few words here tonight. I did not intend to spout great streaming, winged words. I came for a friendly chat like we all do. We have to get into your vibrations as you have to get into ours and when communication is well and truly established, we can come and then, my dears, impart to you the knowledge we are yearning to impart.

An Egyptian spirit
Glimpses of the Pharaoh Akhenaten's life

On this occasion, Rennie was being used as the channeller. An Egyptian spirit took my father into deep trance then proceeded to describe a lecture session that was going on in spirit to an assembly of people. The lecturer was telling them that on earth there was a great upsurge of interest in ancient Egypt and the worship of the 'one God'. The Egyptian was speaking much of Akhenaten, pronouncing the name 'Ahnaten', whom he said was very fond of children and animals.

Akhenaton, the pharaoh, used to play a game with his children who were given coloured sticks of green, blue and amber. They would throw them on the ground making a pattern like spokes of a wheel. At the centre was a hub, which was a ring of melon. It looked like a sun and rays, very pretty.

Akhenaten, they were told, made replicas of this pattern, which will be found amongst other discoveries. He had a habit of wearing rings of various stones on each of his fingers and a scarab on his thumb, which he would rotate if the children were naughty!

The pharaoh suffered with a throat illness, which made swallowing anything very painful. The court physician had a sacred camel slaughtered. Pieces of the flesh were pounded to a powder and mixed with goat's milk and water from a plant found in the desert. Akhenaten was then able to swallow and in time the illness was cured.

He also had great pain in his eyes, which caused severe headaches. The physician placed certain stones on the closed eyelids, which then took the pain away.

He suffered also with itching on the fingers and between the toes.

I am speaking to you in our own language, Aramaic,[10] but as each word is spoken it is translated, by two others, into the new earth language. This medium I'm speaking through has no knowledge of this. He is a very spiritual man indeed so I am able to use him, though he does not consciously respond to this gift, which is a gift from God.

I see wine is being passed round in beautifully shaped jars, so I say quite simply, *Inshalla*.

---

10. *Aramaic was the language spoken in Armana, which was between Egypt and Palestine.*

Angela speaks of Nefertiti, Queen of Egypt
"Nefertiti could produce no more children and there had to be a royal prince"

The guide, White Wing, came to Tara one day in her meditations dressed as a pharaoh. She expressed surprise at his typical headdress. He said it was Atlantean. The Egyptians wore a degraded form of Atlantean headwear, which indicated the rays of the sun. There is a pencil portrait that came through Tara's hand of White Wing wearing the headdress. (See page 245.) Tara was psychically connected to her Egyptian past and on this occassion I recall that a few days prior to this session she had phoned me and complained of a pain in her eye.

Tara never dreams, she goes too far away. She will not recall that three or four nights ago she lived through her incarnation as Nefertiti and on waking, complained of a bruised feeling in one of her eyes.

The court sculptor in the Armana period[11] who loved and respected her deeply, modelled the now famous head from memory after she left Cam. When art was passing into reality and becoming less stylised, the left eye is shown white.[12]

Nefertiti had been badly hurt. In fact, she was blinded in one eye when she was struck by a priest who, along with General Horemhabe,[13] was bitterly against the Akhenaten reform and had little patience with it.

It was Nefertiti who brought the light of knowledge of the 'one God' to the pharaoh. This developed into an obsession in him almost beyond reason. It brought about criticism from his queen when affairs of state and country were put at severe risk due to Akhenaten's constant pre-occupation in establishing the worship of the one God throughout Egypt.

Queen Tiye, Akhenaten's mother, and her daughter-in-law, Nefertiti, were the best of friends, although not at-one-ment over the question of spirit. Nefertiti and Akhenaten had six daughters and it was an extremely happy court.

Nefertiti could produce no more children but there had to be a royal prince. They adored their six daughters but one of them had to be married to produce a prince to carry on the solar line.

Meritaten was the eldest, a beautiful and talented artist, very withdrawn. She lived for sculpture and was very upset when she heard she would have to give up her studio to get married. She was furious when she became pregnant. (Akhenaten was not the father. It was not so complicated.[14]) Born in agony, the boy child died soon after.

Many years ago in this life, Tara's mother, Hilda, had an argument with a priest over her daughter's psychic work and he cursed her. In anger, the mother then hurled the curse back at him and soon Tara's mother developed cataracts in both eyes! Tara suspected psychically that he was once the priest in Egypt who had struck and blinded Nefertiti.

11. *Tel el Armana period approximately 3 000 B.C.*
12. *This bust is now in the Berlin Museum.*
13. *General Horemhabe ruled immediately after Ay who followed Akhenaten.*
14. *Some history books have recorded that there was incest in the court.*

The science of the mind

A seeker from New Zealand
"The personality of the human being goes hand-in-hand with the brain, not the soul mind"

This speaker was suspected to be Verity Taswell who was a well-known communicator in psychic circles.

I am eternal and eternally happy! That is why I am here and to have a little chat. I am, without boasting, an accomplished speaker through the lips of mediums.

I was a seeker myself on the earth plane and went from one land to another. I became a trance medium, of the type that was aware of what the guides were saying through me, due to the fact that I did not go far away. Therefore, I was not a full degree medium and never professional. I lived in New Zealand.

Hannah: You said you were a seeker on this earth. Now you are on the other side have you found what you were seeking?

Speaker: You never do, my friends. That is why I came to speak to you. There is a never-ending vista, one door opening to another, corridor upon corridor of learning and absorption, horizon after horizon open out for us. Our thirst is insatiable for our own mental horizons to be opened up to the full glory of God.

The human personality

I am going to talk about the human personality and the changes man goes through during his stay on earth in his body.

The personality of the human being goes hand-in-hand with the brain, not the soul mind. There is the 'overself' that comes with the soul to inhibit the spirit body in this particular incarnation. With each phase a new personality develops.

The sweet, docile child is built in the beginning of a pattern, which forms the human personality, not the personality of the spirit. After puberty where there is uncertainty and bewilderment, we grow into young men and womanhood, eager to find love and careers. Marriage may then take place, children are born and a new form of love comes into being with the first cry of the newborn child. In the next ten years or so, people's lives are moulded. In the middle age, yet a new personality develops. Who has not seen in the so-called 'twilight of life', the sweet woman become spiteful, demanding, possessive. On the other hand, some of those who wanted to rule everybody suddenly let go of the reins and are content to sit and watch the fires of life die down.

Finally they will cross the threshold.

Looking back through this whole cycle you see the joys, the happinesses, the tears, fears, successes and losses. Every day that this person has lived in the body, he or she has built up through the years, a part of the personality.

When we become aware that we are in the spirit world, we realise that during the years we have built a jigsaw puzzle. The pieces when put together form a picture. So it is with our lives, our personality. The personality in our earthly body and we are shown the records.

The Akashic Records

It is amazing when picture after picture flashes by that it all seems so unimportant. It amazed me!

I saw myself as a young woman crying over the loss of a love affair and at the time it put out the light of the sun for me. The things we grieve ourselves over, which have such an enormous importance at the time that we feel that when they befall us, we cannot get over that blow. But we do! Hope springs eternal in the human breast and God knows what would happen to us if it were not so.

William: If there was no hope, there would be no point in believing in a creator, would there? Why is it that the churches in general withhold the full information of Jesus and incorrect translations of the bible. Why is the truth not given to the people and why do the people have to live in ignorance?

Speaker: In the minds of the average priest or minister, you will find only theology preached as it was just before the Christ. The Sadducees who believed only in power. The Pharisees believed in the life of the spirit and the life hereafter. Now the power has gone into the tenets of the church. It was a wise man who said power corrupts.

Reincarnation

Charles: Is it not so, that man having free will can reincarnate if he wants to? Karma is not immutable.

Speaker: Man has free will in every department of his life, therefore people can incarnate if they so wish it. In God's world, there is nobody to condemn you, nor judge you, it is within yourself that you judge and condemn your actions.

In the spirit world, as a newcomer, you will find that those who have gone before you are only too eager and pleased to show you the way. One is naturally drawn to those one feels in harmony with, 'birds of a feather will flock together'.

Dr Alexander Cannon, M.D., psychiatrist and author
"The strongest instinct in man is survival and that is survival of the body - the temple of the soul"

No birth or death dates were available to us, but we believe that he lived around the late 19th, early 20th century.

Known books written by Dr Alexander Cannon are: *Invisible Influence, Science of Hypnotism, Powers that be, Shadow of Destiny* and *The Power of Karma*. He was a highly qualified physician and psychiatrist. Whilst travelling in Tibet, he developed a strong interest in magic and occultism. The mainstream medical society viewed him with suspicion. He employed mediums to help him diagnose the mentally il and believed that the treatment of hypnosis could be used positively, but that it had to be properly administered. His method included relaxation, music and affirmations. He is known to have taught in the Isle of Man, was a teetotaller and remained unmarried his whole life

When I was on the earth plane I would say, "Good evening ladies and gentlemen", right after I had speechified, stating knowledge and my sensible themes. I would catch their thoughts and quite distinctly hear them say, 'The man is mad. A raving lunatic!' That is what I got for my pains!

But there were many of them who were moved by the truth that came from me, because truth when it is shining truth, can move most deeply and forcefully. Truth cannot be denied. At the risk of being labelled blasphemous, what I gave them was the truth which came from the great mind of God.

I shy away from that word 'fame' in connection with a man in the medical profession. You find it strange? You like my bedside manner? That is good. Well, I can attend to you, in fact, better from the planes of spirit for our lives lay far apart when I was on earth.

Now after all that preamble let me get down to what I came to tell you.

It was when I burst into print that I found my niche. I shall call them euphemistically, 'my teachings', which then streamed out across the world and found a resting place in many hearts and minds who sometimes accidentally stumbled across the great truths of God but had no scientific evidence to prove it.

So when I put it all into words, there in black and white, it was verifications of their own findings! Great was the joy in the hearts of those readers of mine and how great was my joy at the telephone messages, requests for interviews, letters that came streaming across from every corner of the world.

I lowered my head almost in modesty, for quite frankly, I had never expected such an avalanche of letters, such a demand for more and more. So there was an interminable flow of knowledge on my side. Not easily acquired. No, no. Many long years of patient seeking, finding, accepting, rejecting, tabulating what I had found. Sometimes soaring high, sometimes depressed at the futility of my own human limitations.

How often did I not wish I could cast off my heavy body and leave it for those shining planes! But one must be philosophical and know, unless you are unbalanced in your mind, that you cannot seek the way out before God calls you home. Don't accuse me of sounding like a bishop, but when I say that, I truly mean you are called home.

I put pen to paper tapped from this flood of knowledge and let it stream out. Do you know the response was greater even with the second literary effort on my part?

By now, I felt I had a host of friends all over the world. You can take it from me, in a lifetime as a doctor, you make great friends with those patients of yours whom you have healed, but if you can number them on the fingers of your hands then you're lucky. But when you deal with spirit, hands are clasped across the ocean although they may never meet. Firm friendships exist until the day you die, linked by that wonderful love of God, which should bind the whole human race together.

Now I will tell you, I never published nor uttered in my public lectures a single fact that I was not sure was the truth. So ladies and gents, (you are a gentleman I'm glad to see), the aura is good and sweet and sound. I used to say 'sound as a nut', but nowadays nut means something quite different! So I will not call you a nut, especially as my speciality was people who were 'nuts'!

I came to tell you I have been a spectator in this circle since its inception and knew all about it before it started. The committee had worked on your instrument for years trying to draw her into our net. We wanted someone through whom we could give voice, because the spoken voice is much more powerful than the written word.

This lady was most interested in all my writings. She herself had persuaded many people because she recognised the truth of what I wrote. We thought she would rebel if she knew that I had spoken through her, for fear that something of her subconscious should come through because she had read my work over and over again. But then I modestly made my entrance.

Great ones have spoken here to you, a most unusual occurrence to use one being for so many voices projected through her. She is a rare type of medium and we can use her with the utmost confidence. Our connivance has been truly repaid.

Exactly as my books have gone forward and are even now being published, there is a great clamouring for my works, maybe because they are written by a famous doctor! If a doctor or a scientist is competent to talk about things of the spirit, it makes it respectable. A label that over there, my dear sir, had me chuckling inwardly many a time.

We know there will be spiritually starved people on the earth, avid for what we come to tell and we have tried to bring along people of every walk of life on the earth to give their words on life as it should be lived and as it should be died. We have succeeded I know. The record is all up here in one of our great halls of wisdom and I spent some hours there a short time ago before I came down to you tonight. I was quite amazed at the erudition and wisdom and lovingness that came through for you.

The establishment will slide to the ground, for it has been an edifice built on shifting sands and now it is sinking into those sands through the sheer weight of its own stupidity. No sane reasoning man can accept what ignorant scribes wrote down three thousand, two thousand years ago. Not with the march of time and the march of science. So much more has our brain developed, since then, for us to accept this as gospel truth.

Now I wish to speak of your bodies, not only as a medical man but as a knowledgeable inheritor of the heritage, which is mine by right as it is yours.

Look after your bodies. They are lent to you for a short or long period upon the earth plane. In pretty language, let us call them the 'temple of the soul'.

If you were religiously minded, you would not befoul a temple erected to worship God. So do not befoul the temple of your spirit or your soul. This spirit body and the physical body are so closely and intimately linked that if you abuse the physical body inevitably the spirit body suffers too. Not the soul, that is inviolate, indestructible. Of God, what more can I say?

No condition in spirit, no condition on earth can touch the soul, but not so the spirit body which comes to protect the soul when your mind is happy.

Your body knows no pain, but when you are depressed and fretting over trifles that seem like mountains to you, the body suffers, you feel weary, your heart may even miss beats because the rhythm, (oh, that great word) the rhythm of the body has been disturbed, because the rhythm of the mind is out of step.

I have to go now but try to remember when life seems cruel, dreary, tragic, or comical, any name you wish to dub it, it cannot last.

Be full of delight and joy. You can look back over the dark week and wonder why you wept, why you worried. The worry we created in our own minds by anticipating that worry, was far greater than the one that turned out to be, eventually. Is that not so? Yes. So therefore lift up those minds of yours and you will see that your feet lift up!

With this in mind, you will notice how the depressed man, or the melancholy man, drags his feet. Notice the buoyant man who has a sense of himself, confident. A healthy mind, in a healthy body. Watch him striding along without a thought seemingly of the morrow. But you see, when the morrow comes bringing grief, he is prepared because he is strong in his mind and so his body is strong. Oh, weep not for tomorrow, for what tomorrow may bring may never come!

Do you remember that old aphorism, 'laugh and the world laughs with you, weep and you weep alone?' I know hardly any old proverb that holds as good as that one!

Remember, I hate to remind you, I would prefer to forget it myself, but I am in a female body and speak as a man. I was a psychiatrist and saw the seamy side of life. Oh, the hell, the hell that people build up for themselves. It is incredible but alas, only too true.

Therefore, to end my little homily, try to look upon life as something to be lived with gusto, enjoyment. Remember each day, each day on your earth plane might be your last! So mysterious are the workings of God. Nobody knows when the call is coming. I am not being morbid, I am only trying to say live like that and think, 'this is my last day, let me live it to the full abundantly. Let me live it so'. You will see how different your life will be.

[He turned his head to one of the sitters]

My dear lady, you are suffering, I know, with some trouble.

Ella: Yes, I am.

Dr A Cannon: Do you know the deep and underlying cause of that is in your own mind?

Ella: Really?

Dr A Cannon: Yes, really! I have made a study of you. You are dear to my instrument. Let go of your worry.

Ella: I thought I had.

Dr A Cannon: No. You have not. You have not! Search your mind and you'll be surprised what little maggots come crawling out. Squash them, my dear lady, with a firm foot! Do not worry about your daughter. Is she not in our charge?

[Nanette was overseas at the time.]

Ella: Yes. I know this.

Dr A Cannon: How deeply do you know that? Well, ever and on there goes out a little feeler, I use your words, "I wonder how she is?"

Ella: Oh, well, yes.

Dr A Cannon: Yes! Then at once a little fear goes crawling down your skin and finds an outlet.

Ella: Really?

Dr A Cannon: Really.

Ella: Then it's nothing I touch or am allergic to, that brings out this rash?

Dr A Cannon: No, nothing you touch. It's what you touch with your mind. Now take that to your heart.

[There was a short silence.]

Annabel: I wonder if I could ask you about my aunt in Italy. I am very worried about her.

Dr A Cannon: Yes, I was anticipating your question so I was keeping quiet for you!

Annabel: Thank you. She has been suffering from something for so long and the doctors don't seem to be able to help.

Dr A Cannon: Well, it has had a grip on her for so long now that the soul is inclined to recede to rest, you know. But leave her to God that is all I can tell you. She would be ... a word that I would never use in my practice on earth, I shied away from certain words and positively leapt away from the word ... hopeless!

In my estimation of the life, I could not concede that any life that came from God could be documented and placed into a pigeonhole and labelled 'hopeless'. I laboured on until the end and kindly death took my patient away, or they departed into regions of darkness where naught could reach them. But I console myself that when death overtook them, there would be a little shining brother waiting for them to bring them back into the light again.

Annabel: I just wondered what could be the cause?

Dr A Cannon: There are so many causes. As I was telling the lady on my left what the mind can do, the mind is the most powerful vibration in the world. It is from the mind of men that the great wars spring and destroy half of humanity. It is from the mind that great and wonderful poetry comes and brings springtime into the hearts of man. It is from the mind of man that great music melody comes to bring joy and upliftment to man. It is the mind that can work out the most devilish plan for the downfall of nations of men. And it is mind that can conceive the most wonderful plans for the upliftment of man! The mind, the mind. Always the mind. It can make you a great being, to bring joy to the children of God, a ministering angel if you wish it. The question is of free will.

Believe me, in every soul that comes from God there are unimaginable potentialities for greatness, but it is left to man to decide whether he is going to be a knight or a rascal! Yes, my friend?

Annabel: Can you help her in any way?

Dr A Cannon: I see the picture at the moment as very dark. I'm linking up with her through you. I will do my best from my side, I promise you. I will bring my famous bedside manner to her in her sleep state. Perhaps we can persuade the lady in question that life is not so dark and dreary after all. Is there a thread of melancholia running through the family?

Annabel: I think there must have been.

Dr A Cannon: I get it, I get it. Never mind, I will do my best. Having not been in spirit long, my knowledge of these cases is still rapier sharp. (You'd think I was a military man the way I talk of rapiers and swords and I was quite the reverse, quite the reverse!)

Annabel: I do hope I can find some books of yours.

Dr A Cannon: They will come your way. I'll see to that. My mind is strong enough. Remember, I had with my mind to overcome and control diseased minds and bring them back into the light again. This is not done by brutality, it is done by patience and love of your work.

Nora: Are you Alexander Cannon?

Dr A Cannon: Would you excuse me, I would prefer to remain anonymous. I think it is better so.

Nora: Are there any books by ….?

Dr A Cannon: You were going to say 'by you'! My wit is still nimble, my dear lady!

Nora: There are several that I have not read.

Dr A Cannon: Then repair the damage at once, for your own sake! Yes, I am he. The roar of the cannon I try to disguise!

You must remember I had much experience in the domains of God before I left the earth plane. I practised meditation, taught to me by the Grand Lama of Tibet and so was I able to attain, what can I say, heights? And I did, in the shortest possible time. With a master like that and my own understanding of the power of the mind, you see, I did reach great heights very quickly. Then in reaching those heights, naturally I released myself into the planes of spirit. Oh, yes, I had wondrous adventures, but I thought, as I was writing for scientists, doctors and lay people in a semi-scientific manner, that I was writing for both sides of the fence. I thought that if I went into rhapsodies about the planes I had seen and the visitations I had made into spirit, I might find the science side of the fence turning a bit sceptical about that. 'Oh, he thinks he is in heaven, you know!' That sort of thing. I couldn't bear one word that would cast scorn or doubt on something as wonderful as the domains of God. But you can take it from me, it is there and so beautiful.

I was having a long talk with a really famous scientist who went over, as they say, a few years before myself and I said to him, "You know we have to be jolly careful not to paint these heavens in too glowing colours because we might create a human desire in the minds of man to give up the rather dreary earth life he knows and make speed and all haste for us!"

And he said, "Yes, I suppose there is that danger. But after all, you must not forget, Cannon, the strongest instinct in man is survival and that is survival of the body, otherwise man would have died out a million years ago." And that is true.

Most people would shrug it off and say, 'I have to be here'. But you see, there are no human words, even for so descriptive a pen as mine turned out to be, that could paint for you the unimaginable beauty and remember it *ad infinitum*. It never fails, it never satiates because you reach what you seek as it has happened to this instrument. If you can say, 'I can see nothing more beautiful', you will experience nothing grander than this.

God has a stocking full of surprises for you all and you just go on and on. Then remember, when our solar system has exhausted its glories for you, you pass out into galactic space.

I am no astronomer. I was an amateur and I cannot attempt one word to tell of that, so look ahead.

Reincarnation

Before I go, I come to that word reincarnation. For years I fought this word, I fought all that went with this word, what it intimated, I abhorred the idea!

Ella: Did you really?

Dr A Cannon: Certainly I did. I abhorred the idea of coming back into another body. God knows that I should be anything but myself! But *Powers that Be* (that is a book I have written) explains in no uncertain manner, in most forceful terms that it was the only just way for men and women upon the earth. I, being a veritable hound for justice, saw it and immediately the whole picture became clear.

How can we expect, when there is so much vastness ahead of us, to learn of this planet in one short life?

I think if I were to set you an examination paper and ask various questions about the earth, its past, its future, its composition, you would all fail completely. Yet you've all lived on the earth at various times but, as you get, let us say a surgeon, from the time he puts those magical words behind his name, the indication that he is now proficient or should be proficient in carving people up! He has a one-way mind! He operates all day when he is not sitting in his rooms listening to peoples' woes, comes home tired, he mulls over in his mind, 'Is this one going to recover? That one going to die? Will I lose my reputation as a surgeon if this one dies?' The squirrel runs round in the same old cage.

Let me set him a paper on the workings of nature, which we learn about as soon as we come over! Our ignorance is so appalling but there are these wonderful teachers who have willingly given up the fifth plane and the sixth plane to come down and teach us.

Now the better educated you are in this world, the more you pack into your brain, the easier you find it to learn over there. Quite natural is it not? Quite natural.

There are great changes ahead. The world is going to change mentally and spiritually. Long overdue. Please, please, if you ever feel a little depressed, send me a thought and I will give you a crack on the skull to let the little imp of depression escape. It is in your power to say, 'be gone' or, as Shakespeare said, "Go to". For my part, you can add 'hell' onto that. You were too polite to say it! Well, it was usage then.

Now my dear friends, it has been delightful for me, I so much regret we cannot talk again.

Annabel: But we have your books.

Dr A Cannon: You have my books and you may, each one of you who own one of my books, would you write on the flyleaf, 'Love from my dear friend Alexander Cannon?' I mean that. I must go now. May the love of an old doctor follow you through the days of your life still to be lived out on the earth plane.

God bless you.

Chapter 18: Medical Mysteries

The Science of diagnosing and treating illnesses.

The Aga Khan talks directly to the visiting doctor
"You came to this planet as a messenger of light"

Would everyone mind if I addressed myself solely to the young man for a short while?

⌐The group acknowledged this freely. We were happy to receive any information given to us.

We put into the mind of Tara those words about the Chinese aggression. Let me tell you what brought about that aggression.

At the time of the withdrawal of the British Raj, Hindu slew Moslem, likewise Sikh slew others. My own people broke their Law, "Though shalt not kill" and the dark forces held sway amongst the people of your land. Their very religious teachings, the vital words which bound them to their God, violated and destroyed and made a mockery of those very people of your land for whom human life was sacred and well over two million souls were projected into spirit.

They found themselves in the mists in spirit. Bewildered, bereft, huddled together, and hating each other, still swearing in their astral mind vengeance against those who had precipitated them into what should have been paradise.

From that collective mind, the peoples of India in their grief and torment in spirit went forth. The evil that brought the Chinese people onto the border of your land, your own people were to blame.

You have to learn many things, my young friend, on your way to God.

Now, I would speak on a personal matter pertaining to yourself. There is a change coming into your life. I am not given to prophesy but these words are given to me to be passed on to you. You will leave your present occupation and will settle down to find fame for yourself. You are a dedicated man. You have for your guide one of the greatest names in English medicine and I give it to you now with great joy indeed, Lord (no longer Lord) but his earthly name, Lord Lister.

I tell you this because we know you are devoid of spiritual and earthly pride. The very advancement of your soul forbids you to feel pride in your accomplishments or in your own soul. Therefore, it is right and proper that you should know whom your protector in spirit is. The great Lister, no Lord here, no Aga Khan, no late King of England, no Queen Victoria, no ruling Princes of India. What you are, my friend, is what you are in spirit, yes.

The Jewish prophet and master said, "As a man thinketh in his heart, so is he".[15]

When you come to our side and you are stripped of this earthly mask. Your etheric body, as they term it here, is identical with the physical body you use as a vehicle. The simulacra of every physical organ you had on earth and why not? Would you have the great mind cull you of this organ or that organ when you have been accustomed to the use thereof? It is all so orderly, beautiful and harmonious but it is what you are in your soul that is the yardstick of where you go and what you are in spirit.

Oh! If I could have done this on earth. Fifteen million odd subjects and not to one did I reveal the truth.

Angela addresses Dr Chakreverty

There is a great light about you. Yes indeed, the aura is beautiful and you must keep it so.

Dr C: It's very nice of you to say that. I am very average but I want to do more than that. Will I succeed?

Angela: The oriental gentleman has told you in no uncertain words you will also work with us for spirit. You have opened up yourself to your great master in medicine, and what he does for you. Open yourself up to that which has been told you from spirit and therefore your fulfilment in every sense of the word. You have sown many seeds of greatness, you now must reap the harvest. Is that not wonderful?

So greet each day with joy in your heart and lift up your eyes to the hills. Now you will understand, if you are as well versed as I think you are in your religion, that these are holy hills in spirit. Peaks of great beauty and that little understood word 'holy'.

Tara has been to one of them and felt the holiness emanating from that peak.

Now in the ancient days, long before the Old Testament, the truth was known by the ancient ones, "I shall lift up mine eyes to the hills from whence cometh my strength".[16]

It was not the hills of the material world. No, it was the hills known to those with their great inner knowledge of the mysteries and the imponderable things that pertain to God. If they can't absorb it they are then taken to the hills and told to lift up their spiritual eyes and from there they receive their strength.

15. *Proverbs 23 verse 7.*
16. *Psalms 1 verse 21.*

Therefore, my beloved friend, lift up your inner eye to the hills. Draw your strength from that. Let no man intimidate you, or hurt you. Arm yourself in light and holiness and none can assail you. Go upon the pathway destined for you from the moment you came to this planet as a messenger of light. Be happy in this knowledge.

Angela chats to Annabel about heart transplants
"Not everything is Karma. No, not so"

You asked me about Luke.[17]

Well, the Master Jesus is really the great physician because you know what Luke knew about medicine in those days was less than Tara knows now! His earth knowledge then was purely a reflection of the time in which he came. They lacked the knowledge of human anatomy and of blood that came centuries later after he was on earth.

They worked with herbs and potions and were able to set an arm or a leg fairly skilfully. They had that little knowledge, but I mean, what did they really know about the human body? Nothing.

Annabel: As we are talking medically, there is a little Italian girl who has just had valves placed in her heart. It seems with these operations the patients do not always live. Will she live only a little while?

Angela: I will find out for you. Tara's husband[18] on this side keeps himself informed of the new heart techniques from the medics who come over.

I was once asked if I thought it wrong and I said, "No, not at all", because the heart is just flesh and blood and the seat of the heart is not in the heart centre, it is above. Why be so sentimental about what is just a part of the rest of the body? You wouldn't make a song and dance about the liver or kidneys, would you now?

But I wouldn't advise anyone to tamper with the brain. That is quite a different kettle of fish. That has to do with the man's psyche. But the heart is an organ, it doesn't think or feel. When you say, I have a pain from heartache or grief, it is what is in the mind. This is what comes from ancient times when people knew that your life depended on the beating of your heart or the stopping of the heart and it was linked so with the emotions. However, the actual heart area has nothing to do with it, it is the mind that sends down the pain to the heart when you are deeply grief stricken.

It's not the pain that causes death, it is an ache. 'I have heartache'. It is a message going down from the mind attuned over aeons of time. But the heart registers sadness or gladness. It is all in the mind, linking up that heart shaped symbol in your valentine card!

But the grey matter in the brain is controlled by the mind and has all the imprint of the mind there in all the little cells. The thoughts and feelings, you can't transfer that to another body, then you are asking for trouble.

Annabel: We are very anxious about this little thing. Her father has come from Italy. She is looking well now and happy, but because it is this kind of operation she may not last long. Should it have been done?

17. *Saint Luke who was considered the Saint of healing.*
18. *Tara's late husband, Dr Koos Bosman, had passed over into spirit in the 1950's before the sessions started.*

Angela: Well, my love, if you were a parent and there was a wonderful doctor who could perform miracles and your child was in a state like that, would you not take that child to him and say, please help me? Even to prolong life for a while. The human heart hopes afresh all the time and there would be that thought, that prayer, that it would be permanent. So often these little ones come to prepare the way for a final help to mankind. They come for that and they come willingly.

So comfort yourself. Who knows, it might help mankind. The child was willing to make the sacrifice. It might be to her benefit if other little ones survive. Even an extra three or four years, are so precious to the parent. They would rather have the memory of the child looking well and bonny than a little frail and dying child.

Annabel: Well, I should still like to know if she will be all right, such a pretty little thing.

Angela: I will find out for you, but you put me in an awkward position as far as this is concerned for if I say this child will be called over to us and you say that, it is going to cause great distress.

Annabel: No, I would never say that. It's just I'm longing to know if she will be all right.

Angela: Do they know you were going to ask me?

Annabel: No, it is for me.

Angela: The thing is just to look ahead and wonder that if she continues to live, her beauty might not be a source of great sorrow to her. One doesn't know about these little lives that come over here unless one goes and reads the Akashic Records to see why it's all done. You must remember, I always stress, that not everything is karma. No, not so. There are people, I hear them, the slightest little thing goes wrong and they say, "It must be my karma". This is nonsense. It is the big, the great things that have happened in your past life. It is not the trivial little things that happen, it is the dramatic things that make such an impact on the soul that it never forgets.

You take Tara, for instance. All that she has been through. The grief and sorrow, physical pain, heartache. What terrible lives she must have led! Yet it is the exact reverse. It is circumstances. Often the people you come into contact with are working their karma off through you!

Say, if Tara and her husband had never met, all that sequence of events would never have taken place. Tara has told you that after the car accident, after they had put her leg into plaster of paris, she came out of the sleep state and found herself saying, "I have paid my debt, thank God".[19]

The knowledge came from the soul.

19. *This refers to the car accident that Tara had just had when Nanette and Tara first met and there was a fire in the ward where she was a patient.*

I don't know. She may have run someone over in her chariot past, ages ago, knocked him or her over and broken a leg! That is my reading of it. But if I were to go and look at Tara's Akashic Records, I'd be there for the next thousand years! I have heard Tara say, "I must have been cruel to somebody". But Tara can't be cruel, she never has been in any incarnation. She did not come with cruelty in her because she is not of this earth planet. So she does not take into her psyche or her soul, at any time, that which is part of the earth coarseness and cruelty.

Now did I answer that question? I'm not so sure now. I find it difficult to go into these highways and byways in life but I will do my best to find out about the child for you. But you know my love, in the trillions of souls that come over here, one little child that has been operated on will be difficult to track. You must give me her name and I will pass on the vibration to Tara's husband who is very much interested in helping wherever he can.

Annabel: Her name is Pamela.

Angela: That's a pretty name, Pamela. But you do appreciate that at the moment it is a closed subject to me, because you do see she has not come into Tara's orbit at all. I doubt if she has even read about it, so it is difficult for me to pick up that vibration.

Thank you for asking me. We will do our best.

Michéle and Angela discuss the possibilities of scientists freezing people with incurable diseases
"The silver cord connects the spiritual body to the physical body"

Michéle in her early teens at this point was interested in a discussion in newspapers and magazines about scientists freezing people with incurable diseases.

Michéle: Angela?

Angela: Yes, my love.

Michéle: You know about freezing people just after they have died? Do you know about that?

Angela: No, no!

Michéle: The scientists talk about freezing people with incurable diseases so that when there is a cure for them, they could de-freeze them. I was thinking that if they died, the spirit would go out and they couldn't freeze that in, they wouldn't be able to wake them up, would they?

Angela: Oh, no. Not if they were dead, love. The soul must go away from the body. It cannot stay, at the uttermost, longer than three days.

Michéle: And what if they freeze it just before it died?

Angela: Well now, I'll have to ask. It would be a very cruel thing to do to the intended victim, don't you think?

But there again, we have the great mind of God. Man in all his greatness and scientific glory, could never have thought out the silver cord.

The silver cord connects the spiritual body to the physical body, which is attached for about three days, never longer than that, because the power isn't strong enough after that, nor is it meant to be. It sends down enough electrical impulses of life, which come down through the silver cord exactly the same way that Tara goes out in her meditation. She is attached, everyone is. I use her as an example. You are attached by this cord from the back of your head to the back of your etheric body, or your spiritual body, which sounds swankier, doesn't it!

Well now, if that cord were severed, immediately putrefaction would take place, which would be most distressing for the relatives gathered round, you see? As it is, even in very hot weather, that power coming isn't sufficient to keep it all together for long, but it would be so much more nasty if the cord were severed. That is one reason why the cord does not break away for three days.

When that soul or spirit body is too shocked, especially in shock deaths or suicides, that soul can't gather itself together to move away peacefully and quietly as it should, as there is no cord.

So how they propose ... well, these people cannot know about the silver cord ...

But if a person were truly dead, the cord would go and no freezing could keep that soul there after it moved out of the body, with death as its object.

You must never think that death comes as an enemy. It comes as a great and wonderful friend to those whose bodies are tired and worn out. For those weary of life who do not want to live any more, death comes like a kindly angel. It comes like a ministering angel to those in agony of mind and body. Small children don't even know about it. So it is a dreadful thought that you call it the 'grim reaper'. It is the shining angel of death, if they only knew it.

Chapter 19: Physics

The science of dealing with the properties and interaction of matter and energy.

A scientist explains the process of dying
"When the silver cord is severed"

I wish with all my heart that people would have the damn decency to die in an orderly manner. Prepare themselves with knowledge.

I wish you could see from our side the earthly birth from the first contraction and see the wonderful orderliness of it. What a scientist is God. I look forward to the time when people will learn and have a new approach to the life in the spheres in a tranquil manner, thereby releasing those like us for other activities. But there is much evolutionary progress here, as on earth.

Organic substances that make up the physical body

The physical body is made up of organic substances, ingested by the earth food of the mother whilst building the body. It is composed of atoms, which are playing a mad whirligig, but an orderly gig, each following the other in a pattern, each a thinking member of the physical body.

The spiritual body dwells inside. It is inorganic matter, not of the earth. It is spiritual matter, inseparable from immortal matter.

The spiritual body sends out the signal to the master cell in the brain (organic matter), time's up! Then the marching orders are given.

When the majestic spiritual body receives the signal it knows it must prepare for the journey onwards to immortality, in an orderly withdrawal from the brain. From that moment begins the death of that human being.

Organic matter, by virtue of atoms of composition, becomes static and can no longer develop power to rejuvenate itself. Then come the molecules and atoms, which can go no further than that vibration.

So the first affected will be the eyes, hearing, memory, maybe a dragging arm or leg. It is then felt in the thinking, that slow sinking into nothingness will have an adverse effect on the spiritual composition of atoms. One failure after the other with the final emergence of living mineral from the dead body. Immediate separation does not take place, it lies just above the earth body.

You often hear people say, "How calm and youthful he looks". It is merely the reflection of the spirit body still attached by the lifeline, which has not been completely severed.

The soul composes itself so as not to experience any shock at the new conditions, which can last from five minutes to seven days depending on spiritual knowledge and understanding. Beyond that, organic matter cannot be held in perfection.

When the silver cord is severed, all association is broken between physical and spiritual bodies. Such is the compassion of God that the bereaved ones see only the peace and beauty of their beloved. For if there was immediate separation, the body would putrefy, which happens in sudden death as in the battlefields.

The so-called, death struggle, is merely organic mater reluctant to go into annihilation.

The soul does not suffer. Such a scientist is God. The wonderful orderliness of it all.

English physicist

"It was part of my life's work, this study of the relationship of the spirit of man with his physical body"

It was deduced by the message that came through Archbishop Cosmo Lang of Canterbury (page 101) that this was Professor Lodge. Sometimes this is how people came to us, the airwaves would be prepared beforehand.

Professor Oliver Lodge also known as Sir Oliver Lodge, F.R.S made valuable contributions to the development of the wireless and telegraphy. He conducted research on electrons, the ether and lightening. In 1902 he was knighted. He is author of many works including: *Ether and Reality, Electrons, Atoms and Rays, Life and Matter, Elementary Mechanics, Man and the Universe*. He was greatly interested in reconciling science and religion and an ardent believer in spiritualism and survival after death.

Good evening. I shall try to accomplish this. Anyway, have a jolly good shot at it. I will accept the verdict of my selective and selected audience.

I, in common with many who have been using this earthly instrument of late, have been given the most dire warning not to injure the instrument's vocal cords by impinging upon them our deeper masculine tones. I have far too great a respect for her physical organism. I understand it all so well, for it was part of my life's work.

My life's work, the study of the relationship of the spirit of man with his physical body. The inter-relationship of the spiritual world with your physical world.

I have passed on for a number of years now. To us of course, just a flash, but to you certainly a period of time noted and set down by my obituary in the *Sunday Times*.

Charles: May we know who you are?

Physicist: In a moment, my dear fellow, in a moment. Let me try to find my way into the enclaves of your heart before I tell you my name. You think me a little discourteous. This colleague of mine who calls himself "the scientist" said to me, "It has been your dubious pleasure to listen to him in this room."

All: Yes, indeed.

Physicist: Well, he has got a broad grin behind his beard when I call it a dubious pleasure! We must have our little fun, we had plenty on the earth plane. We are not dull, dreary fellows here, you know, indeed we're not. The things we had to stifle our laughter about on the earth, we can give full vent to here, because it is not malicious, it is merely the foibles and the follies of our fellow men.

Now I sound like that fellow Cosmo Lang! I must shut up and get on with my own work, which is to say, 'Cobbler, stick to your last'.

I am, mark you well my emphasis on those two words, *a physicist*. I will not say I was one! I would not insult your intelligence. No, my God, I still am. Therefore accept me as being present and correct and in my right mind when I say, "I am a physicist" and hope to be that for many a period of time for that was my training on earth by great good fortune and love of God.

[There was a short silence, and he then continued.]

Physicist: I beg your pardon, I remembered I was talking rather gustily!

Well, I was able to combine my scientific training with my yearning for spiritual truth. Now, I had a reputation and this I say in considered words, an unblemished record on earth, because it was my wont and absolute, unconquerable determination to arrive at the root of truth. The truth in everything that was important enough to merit my full attention.

Having been so thoroughly grounded in every branch of my special subject physics, I had a slight impediment with the two letters *s* and *c* in conjunction with each other and I find using the tongue in the physical body, they trip me up again, I find I am still prone to this little fault in my speech!

He had an impediment on earth, but now he does not still lisp through Tara, which is why he was having the difficulty.

Now I must get on.

In this grounding I was talking about, I laid myself a foundation that nothing could shake when it came to spiritual matters because I saw the perfect mathematical outline working out of this entire cosmos.

I was a man of many interests. Astronomy being one of my quite unpublicised sidelines. To appreciate the immensity of creation, my friends, look at the stars, the planets and the sun!

When it came to finding out what spirit consisted of, going into it with all the ardour and joy which I put into solving a scientific problem, I discovered that what I had thought was emptiness, a shadow, a dream, was in truth, reality. And the world on which my two broad feet were firmly planted … was the dream!

Gone were the old, solid, comfortable concepts of the world in which we lived. Microscopic our idea and knowledge of God! Totally wrong. Oh, so totally wrong.

Now, if you would like me to enlarge on this mighty subject I will be only too delighted to on our next meeting.

Next meeting: "The body dies but not the man"

Well, here I am. Known as the Professor on the earth plane. My speech is much as it was when I spoke from the podium, why shouldn't I speak like that here?

I am not here under false pretences, just a man shot of his damn earth body. Thank God for it. Walking about in freedom, freedom of thought, my friends. How marvellous to see it.

That old fellow Shakespeare, you know, I didn't care for him very much. Too much learning at school of Shakespeare plays, but he was dead right when he said, "Shuffle off your mortal coil".[20] A damn heavy coil it is too. It became so burdensome to me during the last years on earth. God knows I couldn't wait to get out of it! I had great pain, in case you think I'm a whining beggar, great pain.

Now I am going to give you a lecture on why you cannot die. That is one thing you must remember. One ineluctable fact of life. A man cannot die. His body, yes, but not the man, no.

A man's physical body is composed of atoms, right? Of organic matter. Now each little atom whirling in space inside the physical body is a little world of its own and my friends, I had to find this out only after I arrived in spirit, a thinking world.

Now that body of organic matter is like all organic matter, it can only progress to a certain degree of development, then remains static. In its static state, no more energy can come into it, so it begins to atrophy and it goes down the scale back to where it came from, right?

Now, at the time of conception, in that organic matter cell, there comes inorganic matter, spirit.

Cell by cell the bodies are formed, intertwined, interlaced most exquisitely, most beautifully. A perfect scientific job. Now inorganic matter, by virtue of its very (now I am stuck for a word) toxins of its base substance, will always go on drawing in fresh energy from the source. The never dying energy of the source. So it cannot die. It cannot go back into organic energy like the organic atom can, it can only go back to where it comes from. Therefore it cannot die.

Now the two go, you might say hand-in-glove through a man's life. The spiritual body encased in the physical body. Inorganic matter enclosed in organic matter. Deep within both, the thinking cell, which is the heart centre of the soul, invisible to man.

At a certain time in the life of the man or woman, it is usually estimated to be at the age of sixty, there comes a definite change in the cells. The organic matter with its thinking cell, realises the warning bell has sounded and, as one man to another, if we were at the bar, I would say to you, my friends, 'Time's up gents'!

Now immediately that signal is given, the organic body panics because in its thinking way it knows annihilation awaits. It goes back into the organic matter from which it came.

Well, the first signs will come. The eyes begin to dim, hearing becomes poor because the soul is beginning to withdraw from the vital centre of the soul seat. The spirit body is gradually withdrawing. It may start with paralysis left side, right side, a stroke, whatever you like to call it. The first signs come. The signal has gone from the brain, 'old man, you must be on your way'.

Now, let us take this hypothetical old man on to his bed. Death is waiting to beckon. You gaze with tears pouring down your cheeks when you should be rejoicing for the poor devil! You think it is the death agony, it is nothing of the sort. It is the death struggle.

[He chuckles here.]

20. This is a quote from Shakespeare's Hamlet.

It is the organic cells struggling to hold the inorganic body there to save themselves from annihilation. Don't forget, I told you they think!

Do you realise, that every little atom discernible to the most powerful microscope is a world, a universe in itself. Otherwise how then would you have a group of cells knowing they have to go into place to make the kidneys of a man's body, knowing what sex this body is going to be? This is too abstruse for me to go into here but I am merely giving you the pattern of thought of this atomic world you carry around inside your coat of skin.

Well, the withdrawal takes place beautifully, in a very orderly manner except for the dreadful misbehaviour of the organic cells now knowing that they've had it!

The others rejoice and withdraw in their beautifully ordered manner to be above the now silent body, which some poet so idiotically called, the cold clay.

You might have noticed, I don't know, but if you have seen the corpse of an older person a few hours after death, I have seen many and heard the remarks that people make saying, 'How young he looks, how young she looks, not a line on their faces.' Let me tell you why.

That inorganic perfected body is still connected to the dead, totally dead. Once the life force is gone, the organic matter is dead, dead, dead, but it is still connected on the smooth countenance of the spirit body by a sort of magnetic cord, poetically termed, the silver cord.

I have now finished with all organic and inorganic matter.

There lies a sleep, which comes upon such a soul as it withdraws, a period of unconsciousness, varying in individuals according to his or her intellectual power. So that placid countenance is reflected down what is known as the silver cord into the dead mask below and a semblance of youth appears.

Now, let me explain to you and illustrate the perfection of the divine mind, which has worked this all out to the minutest degree. The spirit body is held attached for a varying period, as I have said. The longest is three days. It cannot cling to the dead earth. It has now conquered the earth and it wishes to go.

Were it to part immediately and at once, the organic matter would be a stinking mass of putrification. Instant withdrawal of the life forces would cause the atoms to fall apart, giving further distress to the mourners.

I would point a parable to you from the bible which I didn't believe in very much and still don't, yet it does have some damn good sense if you read it properly. One prayer is, "Oh God, save us from sudden death".[21]

Now I have been on the battlefields in France and my friends and I have seen men with half their bodies blown away. Well, I can tell you that had those men died in a normal manner, they would not have become the mass of corruption that they were in four hours after death. So you see, when you break one of those beautiful and immutable Laws, you would destroy your brother and condemn him to not even a damn decent ending before we could even bury him.

Yes, that is why we come down to talk as we do. Have I made myself clear on the matter?

Of course I give you only a précis of the whole matter. Were I to go into full detail

21. *Paraphrase of Job 9 verse 23.*

I would have my blackboard here and chalk in my hand to illustrate and enlarge and you would be wiser people.

I thought I knew so much, my friends. Don't forget I was a scientist. But what I called myself when I had been on this side a year was the 'pseudo scientist' because that is what I was!

Death, this perfect rebirth. In birth, the child emerges from the organic body of the mother, in death, the newborn soul emerges from the organic body, which has been its vehicle for its present lifetime. All so perfect and beautiful.

Now, do you realise that because you are a race of purblind men who will not listen and will not seek the truth, you keep a veritable world of souls like this group that comes here from their own progression. They are willing to sacrifice themselves to help you and you and you, in the awful shambles that you make of this wonderful event called death.

I don't know if you have been told but just as the universe has its evolutionary surge upwards, the spirit world has these great souls (and I exclude myself from that term), who spend lifetime after lifetime ministering those coming up out of the mists. It should be such a beautiful end to a man's life.

This medium, Tara, as she is called in spirit, has experienced the first death already and had all her little filaments sundered. They could be likened to little mooring lines, which hold the spirit body to the physical.

The mind of man will become so attuned through the knowledge of his source and of God, that he will experience much more harmony of his body. So much so that many of his ailments will no longer occur. Even now you have on the earth ordinary men who have become sages, if you wish to call them that, who through the meditation process have conquered their earth bodies and do not suffer pain. In the years to come, when man is educated along these lines, it will not be at all unusual.

Death originally, was brought as a means of escape from the planet back to the source that was all. Not physical deaths as you know it now, no ... the two became one. The organic and the spiritualised were simply wafted away to celestial regions ... transmitted ... that is the word. With man, well you heard the story, I listened in, too, of how man fell from grace and discovered physical death.[22]

Hannah: Why were the earth scientists concerned that the astronauts were not contaminated after the moonwalk?

Physicist: Well, it is quite natural for those scientists, knowing that our planet is a seething mass of germs, to conclude that the other is a dead planet that too, could be a seething mass of germs. Do you think that there is no plan at the back of all this my dear lady?

Hannah: Yes, there must be.

Physicist: Yes well, do you think that in this world that they are all trying to save and

22. See Chloris under 'Philosophies of Life' section page 140.

nurse back to sanity and health, that they are likely to allow anything to be brought from another planet that could be detrimental to this planet and so make their job a damn sight harder? Give them credit for more sense my dear lady. No, have no fear on that point.

Hannah: I have no fear, only curiosity.

Physicist: Well, that was a manner of speech with me. I was at a meeting a short time ago and it was announced, I cannot recall which particular spirit was speaking at the time, but it was announced there that the world was due for many surprises in the not too distant future. I can add a rider to that and say, in the language of my students "And how!"

Well, I think I had better be on my way.

A friend of mine who used to be an editor of a newspaper down below had a favourite expression whenever we met, he used to say, "Well, Prof, how's tricks ..." (most ungrammatical) "how's tricks in the world of science?"

And I would say, "Well, how's tricks in the news world?" And that was our greeting over a quiet glass of beer.

Well, you know, when he came over the border about a fortnight ago, I said to him, "Well, how's tricks in the news world below?"

And he said, "Absolutely bloody well nothing."

That is the truth, that is what he said to me and he felt at home immediately.

I rather suspect that this might have been Maurice Barbanelle who was the editor of *Psychic News*.

7

Esoteric

Chapter 20: Akashic Records

A stranger comes to cleanse himself
"It is like looking at a film of your life"

I will tell you why I am here. It is not so long according to earth time that I came over to what is known as the world of spirit. I am not going into detailed account of my first years here, that interests only me, but you are aware of the proceedings when an unversed man like myself comes into spirit. Some of us are like the legion of the lost, not necessarily damned, but definitely lost. Sometimes through our own fault, other times unwitting and unwilling victims of our ignorance.

After wandering in the shades, or the mists, I was fetched by some kindly guide. I was taken from them for my own sake, not by my request, to a quiet place. I was then told I would be shown a throwback of this last life of mine on the earth.

I admit I was filled with trepidation at the thought because there were many episodes in my life I certainly wouldn't have liked my mater or pater to behold! But here I was being left alone.

Well, to get on with my story. I then started on this beautiful lesson in the art of living. It is perfectly true. It is like looking at a film of your life! Picture after picture floats before you. Some fill you with shock and surprise, even loathing. Well, it seems to be a law of compensation. There are ones that linger the longest before you where every little detail, I swear to you, is shown. Nothing is obliterated.

I will be quite frank. I had gone through my not-too-long life thinking I was quite a decent sort of man. But horror piled upon horror. Truly, when I realised how selfish, self indulgent and utterly careless I had been of other human beings, conditions of life, way of life and thought! I had never given the matter one moment of consideration.

I suppose my life was a pretty average sort of life that practically any man might live. You know, the usual sowing of wild oats when you are young and know everything. But I was appalled to see what came in the train of some of my deeds!

The things left undone that I should have done. I had to observe the tears of my mater when she heard of some peccadillo of mine which didn't seem too soul shaking to me at the time ... but to my mother! I witness her distress. It cut to the bone with her. It was the usual silly story of being involved with a married woman. I don't mind, I've got nothing to hide. I thought I was being a very gallant fellow indeed but I brought tragedy there. I had to look at that, mark, learn and inwardly digest. Not a nice experience.

So, it has not filled me with the desire to fly away back like the ladybird to my home and life on the earth plane. No. I mull it over and over in my mind and wonder how the deuce I ever came to be such a cad! But at the time, do please understand me, I had no notion of being a cad. I merely followed my inclination to satisfy a woman older than I.

Well, after that episode, I sent out a call and asked to be delivered out of this hall of judgement. It was too much for me. I regret the pain I caused my maternal parent. When we are out of our body here we suffer agony over an affair that we just lightly tossed aside.

I am not here to lecture you. I'm here to cleanse myself. I'm not going to come back and talk to you again. I'm just a guest who is allowed to get cleansed and it gives me a great amount of relief that I can talk this matter over with people of the earth plane.

Strange as it may seem to you, I feel you would be more understanding perhaps of that weakness of mine.

Angela speaks of the halls of learning
"It can be projected upon a great shining wall in moving pictures"

When you come over it will be a great delight, for those who are guides of this kind of work, to take you all to the Halls of Learning. There they have what we, in my time on earth, called, 'a magic lantern.'

Well, they have a very, very magic lantern.

We can go back to the beginning of time! It can be projected upon a wall, a great shining wall in moving pictures and you can see the beginning of your earth and all the aeons of time. All that is past and all that is happening on your earth at the moment. Then there is another. If you could see this building of shining, living alabaster. It portrays the future.

You are encompassed by a cloud of heavenly witnesses, never out of their sight or mind, for the expanded mind in spirit is able to cope with more than one thought or one picture at a time. It is no longer trammelled by the flesh, therefore the mind of the released person can hold within its lens (I am borrowing a word from your camera now) not one image, but many. Exactly as the camera can focus on the landscape and take it all in at once and keep the memory in the printed card.

Well, that is our mind. We can take in so much more.

The finite mind can only deal with one subject at a time and then not for too long because it wearies.

Remember we, the guardians, never weary, never grow tired of thinking of you, of looking after you. Our love never grows less, it increases. So please do not think that you walk alone, you are never alone, never.

Planet earth is a training ground. A nursery school, which is a peculiar simile to use, but it is so.

It will serve its purpose and will more or less close its doors and mankind will proceed *en masse* to other planets and other worlds.

It is a vast plan and it staggers me!

You know when I was at school, I was a complete duffer at mathematics. I cannot even do it now, I cannot. So when I go around pestering all the great ones with questions about how it is all being worked out, the great universal cosmic plan, well, you know, they just smile and shake their heads and turn away when they see me coming because they know whatever they tell me just sinks in so far!

I must go now, there is someone preparing to come and speak to you.

I love you, I love you, I love you!

Chapter 21: Psychic Gifts

Nanette
Spiritual terms

There is often an element of mystery that surrounds communication between spirit and the earth plane. Here are just three of the different ways in which it can occur.

Clairvoyance
The spirit or etheric eye of the clairvoyant person functions at a faster vibration than the physical eye and can therefore see people in their spirit forms. *The Oxford Dictionary* says: "Clear Sight. Alleged power of perceiving things beyond the natural range of light." They are able to transmit to their physical brains what they are seeing.

Clairaudience
The physical ear is no barrier to the spirit or etheric ear inside it, which is able to tune in to the faster vibrations of a spirit person speaking to them.

Channelling or trance mediumship
This is a deep unconsciousness in which a medium allows a spirit being to enter and use his or her body and vocal cords. The medium is unaware of what transpires during this state. If she or he is in deep trance then they will appear as if in a normal sleep state, but still attached as we all are by what is called the lifeline or, if you like, an etheric umbilical chord, the silver cord.

When a medium goes into trance, it is always our responsibility to ensure that she or he is protected from sudden loud noises such as door knocking, telephones ringing and particularly, from being touched without prior warning or prior permission from the spirit using the medium's body. These things can sometimes bring the medium back into the body far too quickly causing severe shock to the nervous system with a possible haemorrhage, nausea or even death being the result.

So, it is as well to know these things and the risks involved.

In the long distant past, mediums were treated with great care and respect as precious instruments of the great spirit. As Angela has told us of the first ancient séance and trance mediums, these people were called, the Comforters.

Angela speaks of the Comforters, the first trance mediums on earth
"A woman became the first trance subject on the Akashic Records"

Long before there were priests, people were conscious of a great mind overshadowing all. They appealed to this immense unnamed, this power, that held their known world in thraldom. Illiterate, they knew of it and felt a part of it and yearned to be able to appeal to the power to protect the crops, to save them from illness, drought and floods.

So man, with all his unrealised past of intellect, sent up a plea, day and night. At last came a day, which at first caused much consternation, when a woman became the first trance subject on the Akashic Records.

Can you imagine the fear when a male voice issued forth from this woman? The controlling spirit spoke with such authority that the whole assembly of people fell flat on their faces in adoration.

Every day, the woman was taken into trance and instructions were given through her, by the controlling guardian angel of that tribe. Instructions on where they should go and why. He gave advice on health and moral laws, and guidance on a new way of living.

In the course of time, the medium was worshipped night and day.

This nomadic tribe came across another tribe and after they had decided to team up they told them about the 'brother' who spoke through a woman. That night they held a séance.

The second tribe spoke a different dialect, but even so, the brother addressed this tribe in their own language and they in turn went down on their knees in adoration.

Thereafter, a man suddenly went into trance and spoke in a woman's voice! That is how the spirit world first contacted the human race, the newborn race.

Thousands of years passed by and man's mind had been transformed by the successive teachings. They formed villages and communities for the benefit of God.

They had their mediums in a place set apart from other people. They lived in majesty and authority and were greatly loved.

A changing over from veneration of the medium later became a veneration of God. Through a human house of the medium to advise and comfort those who went to her.

In time, mediums were known as 'Comforters'.

Jesus himself would often go into trance for his disciples.

Just before Jesus left Jerusalem after the 'death', he assembled them together and said, "I shall no longer be able to speak with you, but the Comforter will come".[1]

He knew that in those days there were many mediums in the city of Jerusalem.

1. *John 14 vs 16, 26.*

Dr Alexander Cannon
"You have within the centre of your brain a third eye"

We tell you that you have within the centre of your brain a third eye, single in its power, beautiful in purpose. Cultivate that eye that it may later serve you.

First dwell upon the fact that this single eye is there. Talk to it consciously, command that it function, make it show you pictures when you close your eyes at night, dwell on these pictures.

Develop the habit of watching them closely. Distinguish forms, scenes that will quickly come clear as the thought is focused on them. Hold them before you, night after night and think, 'I am not of my body, I am only *in* my body'.

Behold, I can go out and mingle with these objects seen with the higher senses. I can thus be in my body protecting it against persons who are evil. I can also perceive what is happening at a distance!

Angela on the suppression of psychic gifts
"Tara found relief in meditations"

Tara always spent a few moments on yoga breathing before sitting for trance conditions. Everybody has their own way of dealing with their psychic abilities. She found great relief in her meditations.

So glad your headache has gone, Ella.

Ella: Yes, thank you dear.

Angela: You know, it is an indisputable fact that those who are psychically endowed suffer at the base of the neck. For that is where the fount of life is situated.

Ella: But darling, I'm not psychic.

Angela: Go to the bottom of the class, Ella. Your psychic centres glow like lamps! You have never bothered to put your psychic powers into practice. You have hung on the words of others. Had you sought like Tara did, you could have risen to great heights in this.

There is a medical word, Tara uses it and also I know it, the medulla oblongata which is situated at the base of the brain and is the fount of life. For those who are tuned in to the life beyond this one, the real life, inevitably there is a clash between the life of the earth and the life that is awakened in this great psychic centre. Tara has suffered this all her life. Likewise her sister, Paddy, or Patricia, who is extremely psychic and who, like yourself, is not ready to take it up seriously. It comes very often from suppression of the psychic gift, which must have an outlet.

Tara resisting trance conditions for so long found relief in her meditations when she learned to leave her body. It is a psychic complaint.

Now remember to talk to yourself when the pain comes and say 'all is well' to the seat of the soul. Not flippantly. It is in the power of every human being to heal themselves from within because it is the mind that holds the pain there. The mind says, 'I have pain' and it holds it fast.

Ella: I do try to dismiss it.

Angela: Yes, but not quite the way it should be done. The obvious answer is deep meditation. How do you think Tara recovers so quickly?

Ella: It's amazing.

Angela: Do you remember how she took time and trouble to cure herself of the gluten in her lungs? It took three hours.

Normally, she is too lazy, you can tell her! She will say, "I have got a pain but I'll let it go". But she won't! You can tell her from me when she has pain again, to sit for that pain, not in ordinary meditation, but on the seat of the pain and let it go!

She should know! She does know, but it's a great effort. She has her pills handy and she just takes one and the pain goes but it comes back again.

But we are not here to scold Tara, she has had enough on her fork lately.

Nanette: Tara has been very concerned over one of her daughters.

Angela: Ah, yes, well it goes back a very long time. It may startle you to know that that daughter was once her mother and at one stage saved her life! Tara has never forgotten in her soul, but it has not been revealed to her conscious mind.

Nanette: Do you want her to hear this part of the tape?

Angela: Well, I don't think we ought to tell her that. It goes into the distant past. It has always been. Now we cannot tell a lie, can we? For they parted then for a long time. Perhaps one could say that it was an association of blood as well as spirit throughout most of their lives on earth.

But you know Tara, even though she has this wonderful sense of humour, it may feel a little odd to look at this daughter and think she was once her mama! No. I think we'll leave that out. She does suffer intensely when anything threatens this girl because of the deep dread in her soul that comes from the memory of the sacrifice made for the child by the mother so long ago.

Angela speaks of the clairvoyant eye
"The Shining Ones ... his or her vibrations will give off coloured light"

I have become clairvoyant now. That surprises you does it not? Yes, I had to learn.

We go to our schools here when we express a wish to come down to help mankind and we learn to be clairvoyant.

This is an alien body to me, to us.

There was a new visitor today, Natalie Tretchikoff.

I am still weighing you up a trifle, if you don't mind. I would be glad if you would let yourself flow out to me and accept me for what I am and let us be good friends and work together for the sake of man.

They have séances in spirit, you know. Only people with fast psychic minds can see an evolved spirit. The more spiritual the being, the more his or her vibrations will give off coloured light. We don't only range through the spectrum here, we have colour that is never seen upon the earth plane. The clairvoyant eye might tune in for a moment and observe that the colour pink or colour blue has a whole range of colour imperceptible to normal sight. A gamut of colour you could call it. After a while, sometimes almost at once, the spirit will come over, clad in his spiritual robe, which can be in the style of a Roman toga, or a Greek gown, or an Indian. They will favour something that relates to their own land.

They are very gorgeous these robes, you know Guy, they are awarded as they pass from one realm to another.

Charles, I am not excluding you, my dear one, I am just addressing myself to the newcomer so that she can become accustomed to my peculiar way.

So they are awarded with great jewels[2] as they pass from one realm to the other. You know Budrain, by virtue of what he has done in spirit to equate or expiate what he did on earth, has advanced beyond all recognition and is now a shining star in the hierarchy.

When Tara was in England, she may have told you, the medium with whom she was sitting found her eyes had to be protected when in trance from Budrain's light! The guide explained to Tara when she put a hand across the eyes of the instrument, she explained that if she did not do this, his light is so blinding she may be permanently injured in the optic nerve!

That, I know, was a great surprise to Tara who had not visualised that he was quite so advanced. Well, it's the tremendous work he does for the earth plane. They do not do it for reward or for advancing spiritually. It is utterly, utterly selfless and entails great sacrifice. Although he and others like him would scorn to use that word in regard to themselves. But the work is selfless.

So, as they advance spiritually, they advance in glory too and he is now a member of the hierarchy. That means he has joined the assembly of what is called in spirit, 'the shining ones'.

Now when Tara leaves the earth, he will withdraw and they will pass on and no

2. *See 'Living in the Spirit World' section, page 33.*

longer contact this plane, but the good that they leave behind will endure forever. You will see in the time to come the results of the great task that has been undertaken. To use Budrain's words, 'cohorts of the spirit!'

Great and famous names of the past have joined this band of warriors in spirit, Arthur of Camelot is there, his knights, Charlemagne. Should I give secrets away?

Well, the sails of the great galleons of the spiritual fleet are billowing out and the battle has been joined. Victory will be decisive and we will have peace on the earth for a thousand years.

When man reaches that stage in his progression physically, mentally and spiritually, which one might deem as near perfection as can be (alas, so that he does not become like the Atlanteans who destroyed themselves due to their utopian life) the circle will come back again and the dark forces will have gathered strength.

There is nothing we can do about that. But it will mean a further advancement of the planet earth that, as you know, has a limited life. It will not be here for always.

Angela explains how a foreign person is understood
"Ectoplasm for power. On our side it is mind talking to mind, telepathy"

Hello, Hello!

Someone wants to speak now but I can't let them because they just might peter out in the middle. As Tara has told you, in materialisation séances they suddenly vanish because the ectoplasm isn't there. Well, we use that same ectoplasm for power. You know, as we so often say, it is not ours to command. There are so many vital elements that go to make up the whole for a successful meeting.

Annabel: Is it difficult for a foreign person to speak through, say, an English medium?

Angela: He is coached, you know. On our side it is mind talking to mind, telepathy.

For instance, if I am talking to a Hindu, I don't know his language at all but he understands me instantly because I pass him a mental image and he passes it back to me. It's a bit difficult for you to understand, wait until you come to us!

But if they are going to speak through a medium, like Tara, or any medium, they are coached in the language that medium uses. We are fortunate that every now and then they can interject a few words, or a few phrases of language that Tara does not know.

As you can remember Ella, this has been done in the past. It was recorded in Nanette's home when ancient Egyptian was spoken.

This was a recording that happened at my house many years ago. It is not included here.

An enormous amount of preparatory work is done because you see a lot of people come and talk who have not got very good memories. Nor when they were on the earth plane did they have the gift of oratory, so, a sort of typewritten copy of what they want to say is prepared and it is inscribed on the tablets of their mind. So you start them off and they go on grinding away with what they want to say, which has been put there.

As long as no one asks them a question or interrupts them, they can say their full say, but if anyone interjects, it switches them off and then we have to rush like mad cockroaches to get them on that track again.

We do this because you cannot have a break. The moment you have a break, the thread is broken and the power lags. This power is the most delicate and beautifully adjusted quality of spirit. Now, power can be used for both good and evil, for it is equal. But here it is perfectly balanced like Libra. It is only good. However, if it is the slightest bit off, ballast is taken out of the one pan, it causes a bit of confusion and we rush to help.

Nanette tells the story of a sadhu
A psychic experience about vanishing people

I can remember my father relating an incident that occurred in Calcutta when a *sadhu* or holy man had placed himself at the foot of a tree in a busy thoroughfare. The authorities soon asked him to go somewhere else. He explained for reasons of his own that it was necessary for him to sit there for twenty days and that he could not move.

Thereupon the officers lifted him bodily into their van and locked the door. After driving him to the outskirts of the city, they stopped to unlock the door only to find he was no longer there! Driving back to the city they found him sitting calmly under his tree.

In spite of his gentle remonstrations they once more lifted him onto the van, locking the door carefully.

Again they made their way to the outskirts of the city ready to release the *sadhu*. On arrival the officers discovered for the second time that he had disappeared into thin air. Returning to the city the men found him in his usual position.

After a third attempt to remove the sadhu ending in the same result, they left him to his meditations.

As in the case of a yogi, adept in the practice of de-materialising the atoms of the body and re-assembling them elsewhere, bi-location has been used by many masters in the past. It is also used by spiritual healers of India today. *Satya sai Baba* is an example of a healer using this kind of practice, not uncommon in India

Angela talks to Brian about spirit guides
"You do have your guide, your special, who comes at the moment of conception"

I just came to say I love you.

My voice changed. The spiritualisation of this body has taken place and it makes it difficult for us. It's all right for a newcomer like the doctor to use her, but we having used this body for so long, have accustomed our vibrations to the earth vibration, now we can't tune in properly. But for the doctor it was easier, though it all sounds complicated I know.

Brian: May I ask a question before it's too late?

Angela: Yes. Ask me anything you like as long as you don't ask me to marry you! Well, you can always wait till you come over! Yes, my love, what is it?

Brian: I feel I have so many friends and I know them all by name, but there is one I don't know about and it's rather important. It's my guide. I don't know who he is, so I never call him by name.

Angela: Well, you do have your guide, your special, who comes at the moment of conception, did you know that? I'll find out his name for you, I'll do that. Now what is the name of the man with the feathered hat?

It was a spirit drawing of a man with a jaunty hat that we had with us at the session.

Brian: I know him, he is a helper. His name is Juan.

Angela: Juan. That's right. Well, you have there a strong, strong guide. He is more than a helper now, he has attached himself to you and his aura mingles, intermingles with yours.

You know people have many guides, the number depending a great deal on your spiritual development. The more developed, the more spirit guides they attract. Naturally, like attracts like, you see?

Each person born of man and woman has a special guide. What was it called in ancient time? The guardian angel that you have right through your life and it is the guardian angel who eases the spirit body out of the physical body at the time of death and loosens the cord that binds you. If you could open yourself up to your guardian angel and say, 'I know that you are with me and I open myself to you, know I am safe in your hands'.

Generally, they have to battle against so much, the door is always closed to them. They knock and knock and it's only sometimes in moments of extreme danger that they can get through to you. You might call it the still, small voice that says to you, 'Don't do that, don't go this way or don't go that way or don't go in a conveyance'.

There are many people who owe their lives to listening to their guardian angel by cancelling a trip at the last moment when disaster has overtaken whatever vehicle they were going to travel in! It's all so vast.

Brian: I know.

Angela: If you think for one moment of the trillions of people on earth and their thoughts that are visible. You know we can see thoughts. They take form and we see them. That is how we can read your thoughts when we sit here and when you are at home or wherever we happen to be with you. These thoughts come streaming up into the ether. Many people don't think of people at all! Only if they have passed on recently, but as the years pass, you know, the memory dies away.

Others are praying, others are thinking bad thoughts. All go up into the ether. It is all there when you think of anybody, when you send a request or simply a flight of love.

You know, every name that has ever been on the earth has its vibration taken with it by the person to whom it belonged. Therefore, if you say 'Mary Smith' and you think of your Mary Smith, that vibration threads its way through the network and finds its vibration there. It's Mary Smith.

You would never dream of praying to God without first saying his name. I mean, you don't just say, 'look after me', 'help my mother'. You say 'Dear God' or 'Jesus' or perhaps your own special master. A vibration like that is a trillion percent stronger than any other vibrations as you can imagine.

I will get the name for you. Did you not ask me about your guide before?

Brian: I did, a while ago.

Angela: You must forgive me, my love. You see I have so much to think of with all the work around Tara at this moment. I think you have asked me if you had an incarnation in India. I have really been so busy, cross my heart and hope to die! I have my allotted task, which I have to fulfil.

Brian: It struck me the other night that I send thoughts to the others but not the one who has been with me the longest!

Angela: Well, they like to be acknowledged, don't worry! You should see them glow with pleasure when they get a thought of love from any of you on earth, you wouldn't believe it! They get positively coy, some of them. So! Yes, they get your thoughts.

Chapter 22: Spirit Drawings

Angela
Spirit drawings

Before one of the sessions closed, Nora managed to ask Angela this question.

Nora: Angela, tomorrow I am having a drawing done by a lady who does spirit drawings. Is it possible that my guide could come through?

Angela: Well, I will do my best. It is exactly the same thing as a medium, you cannot call the spirits to come if they don't wish to. Now not for one moment would your guide not wish to come, that would be her most earnest desire, but there may be circumstances, vibrations, anything that might prevent that. You mustn't forget that this lady is exhausted. I was there when Tara met her and she is nearing her end too!

Now that is just between these four walls. But it may be difficult for someone as great as your guide to come to an exhausted atmosphere.

There was a highly respected psychic artist in Cape Town at the time called Rosa Parvin. She was able to see spirit people and paint them. Most of them were in pastel. Very beautiful.

Tara also did spirit drawings but of a different nature. Not of other people's guides but of people who would communicate with her in meditation. She would get a feeling or a message from the out of body spirit. On one such occasion she got a message saying, 'Pick up your pen'.

Tara did this. She was not an artist but the spirit guided her hand in the shape of a face. On completion of the pencil drawing she realised that the picture was of Jesus. He had no long hair, facial hair or beard as depicted by the media. Tara's earth mind then took over and being imbued with the earth image of him, she drew in the hair and beard. Thrilled beyond measure she and Doctor Bosman framed the etching and put it on their bedroom wall and went to bed.

That night she heard a loud crack on the glass and heard a voice saying, 'I had no beard or long hair'. Tara thought it was her imagination, replaced the picture the next day and rehung it. The following two nights the same thing occurred. She heard the glass crack and on the third night, it fell to the floor.

Three times it was replaced and three times she had heard the words, 'I wore no beard or long hair.'

The next day Tara rubbed out the added bits as best she could and left the picture as it had come through her hand. Thereafter the picture hung peacefully.

She had no more trouble after that.

During deep meditation Jesus explained to her that it was because of hygienic reasons and his close contact with the lice-ridden poor that he kept his hair cropped. He also chose his robe from the broad loom which needed no seams for the same reason.

Tara had a collection of spirit drawings that were left to me after she had passed on.

Paul

Judas

Luke

Thomas

Philip

James, son of Alpheus

James

Mark

Mary Magdelene

Mathew

Nathaniel

John the Baptist

Mother Mary

Hagrat Inayat Khan

Bartholomew

Joan of Arc

White Wing

Queen Tiye

Queen Guenevere

Madame De Pompadour

Babaji

Buddha

Rabbi Wentzel

Untitled

8

Returning to the Spirit World

Chapter 23: Meditation

Indian Sage – The ancient art of meditation
"Meditation, the going within"

I greet you one and all. I never used a body to give my teachings before, so you will forgive me if my voice is not used with the resonance I was wont to use while on earth in the Himalayas. You will forgive too, if I do not speak eloquently and I am a failure in a language that is not my own. But you, I know, will be patient with me when I tell you my work on the earth was God. God and God alone.

It is some five decades since I returned to the eternal home that is the inevitable end of every soul that has manifested itself in an earthly body for a given number of years. I numbered amongst my devotees, one or two Europeans and three from the Americas, so it is not quite alien to me to gaze upon peoples not of my nationality.

By now you will have gathered I was an Indian. I had my cave in the foothills of the Himalayas.

I come to you tonight to give unto you the rudiments of the ancient art. It is an art, my friends, that needs great practice and perseverance to reach maturity in meditation.

I feel at the moment, looking down on your earth, which is mine too, by virtue of my heritage in my last incarnations, that I must come and try to persuade you to follow the ancient way of light and being within, to God.

It is not right for me to dilate at this moment on the tragic state of the planet earth. It is apparent from every quarter, in every day that you live and in every, unhappy night. It is there that the darkness has descended upon man. This has been coming into being for centuries and centuries when man in his blindness has turned away from God. When this happens, all is lost.

Now, by the word meditation, 'the going within', it would give me the greatest happiness in the world if I could prevail upon you, even one of you, mayhap two or three, to enter into this blissful state. On attaining even the most rudimentary condition of meditation you would then be able to send out great forces of prayer and light to help your unfortunate fellow citizens of the world.

When I tell you, disciples or neophyte,[1] the beginner initiate into meditation, in my time as master would be told, go within. Forget self that expresses itself. Self, self, the word in deed, gesture and thought does not express the God within. All that man is revolves, depends and hangs upon that God within, resident in the soul of man.

Man in his human life, so occupied with petty pursuits. Oh, do not raise a thought against me here, these petty pursuits are the normal everyday life of the average man, the householder, the wage earner, the father and mother of the family. Ah yes, but in looking back, it looks petty because man's self was caught up in the daily life with never a thought of God.

Now, to find yourself, sit then in peace and quietness and look inward where dwells the light. Within every man is the power to find the light within himself.

The light, my friends, is your soul, which came from God and therefore being from God, must be light.

Do not say then, do not as will happen torment yourself with the question, 'If God is all light and all knowledge why does He permit earthquakes, tidal waves and all earthly happenings that bring such agony to man?'

My friends, the first factor in your meditation is to know that God is above all this. It will be like tearing the heart out of your bosom to know that God is not concerned with earthly affairs. The vastness of God can only be comprehended when you go within.

I can truly say to you, as the great sun rises in the dawn and pursues his pathway across the skies, the whole world is under his influence. Everything comes to life when the sun comes up, everything; the birds sing and waken to a new day, the flowers open in the vast panorama of earth when the sun comes up, the sun pursues its majestic course across the heavens, totally unaware of its influence on the earth and upon man. So it is with God.

Do not think God is not watchful, ever awake to the plight of His created beings. Oh, no. He is fully aware but has given to you all your free will, so you can progress. You can only go on using your free will by finding out your mistakes and correcting them, by pursuing ever the light of knowledge, by education of the mind on earth, the mind of the soul, educated by God.

I go too deep into the imponderable verities here. Do I make it clear? Am not being too obtuse?

All: No, no.

Indian Sage: I can go on my way. I am using a western brain to manifest myself though. My influence is still greatly felt in my native land and if you think it strange that I have good usage of the English tongue, mayhap it will comfort you if I explain that I was educated at an English grammar school in India. My teachers were of

---

1. *This is an ancient word that comes down to us from Egypt.*

Scottish descent and I am regretful I bear little trace of the accent that was theirs peculiarly. I could not twist my tongue to follow them. This is merely to tell you I speak now in my almost normal tone as when I discoursed on earth.

To go into the innermost recesses of the soul, the first thing to do is to forget self.

Now my friends, I come to the most difficult in the way to God, for meditation is first, second and last through an opened heart and an open mind. We close our hearts and minds upon the earth to the verity of God. We hedge, we hide behind the barriers man has placed between himself and the great and divine mind that created all. Whether it be a stone on the wayside for you, do not be absorbed in self. It is the self in man who says, 'I hate', 'I love', 'I will', 'I won't'. That is self that rules you. When you come to the end of a short life or a long life governed by that I, I, I, what have you left? What have you to lean upon when the veil begins to lift and your fading eyes look down on the long dark valley? Nought. For your comfort, nought.

Therefore, while there is still time, go inward and search for God. Take it from me, a humble sage, that if the search for God be selfless, that is, not seeking yourself but your God, you will be rewarded beyond even what my enlightened words can convey to you. The delight, the dropping away of the feeling of frustrations, the feeling of futility, the resentment against your lot in life, the jealousies that pour into man, making him look with eyes of dislike and distrust upon those superior to him in position. And it reaches to a pitch of, 'Why was I born? What am I? Am I then just a being of flesh and bones and skin who cries to the eternal and receives no response?'

From our vantage point in spirit, we gaze down in profound pity upon all the votive candles that are lit to the Virgin Mary and to her son. We gaze down upon the hypocrisy of the sacrifice of monies given to your churches in the hopes of buying an easy passage into Heaven. These avail you nought.

So, I take you on my way. My way, followed by all the aspirants who seek God, "I am the way, the truth and the light".[2] In other words, I am the soul of man, that is the light that cometh with every man when he is born into what my teacher would call, 'this veil of tears'.

If there is but one who would, to my artless and selfless request, sit in meditation to help mankind in his hour of need, for daily, hourly, minutely there goes up the cry from myriads and myriads of sinking and frightened souls, 'God help us ... we are lost!'

Now you have a saying on the earth, 'Greater sacrifice hath no man than to lay down his life for his friend'.

That is fallacious my friends. There is no need to lay down your life for a friend. There is a much more beautiful and rewarding way. Give up your heart to save a friend. By a friend, I mean the whole world, for we should all be friends in God.

So those who wish to follow this old man, hearken then what I have said to you. Take out of your daily lives a quarter of an hour each day. God asks very little of you but love. Go quietly by yourself, sit you down in a comfortable chair, there is no need to sit in discomfort. It is better to relax and be comfortable so that you may sit and listen within. Listen to the soul, the light that comes from God, the mind of God within. It will whisper to you a few notes of its siren song, until at last it will burst into a paean of praise for all creation.

2. John 14 vs 6.

Be patient. I abjure you all, so let me ask of you, a bare fifteen minutes a day when you can spare it.

Is it not sad that I say, when you can spare it, for it is God who gave you life. This is not the little life on earth sojourn alone, but the eternal life that goes on and on into glory unimagined by you, until you have found god in all creation.

Now, in the dim light of the sanctuary of your soul, a little light will say unto God, 'I thank you for my life'. You go into silence, not to ask for anything but to give thanks and you will find the self sinking away with all its earthly sorrows, its yearnings, for it knows not what is grief, is pain. These all will sink down into the deep well of selflessness and you will find Godliness taking its place. From the moment you become conscious of your Father's presence, you will change.

You will find your attitude to people, to problems, to things that give you stress and strain, all fall away into this well of peace. You will progress from there strongly then, into the light and knowledge, to know that you have learned to be.

Now you will progress and then will come with a great rush like a tidal river into the soul, the knowing of God.

So now my pupils, you will have learned 'to be' and learn then 'to know'. Two great gifts from God, who else?

When you return and give an account of your stewardship on the earth plane, for we are all our brothers' keepers, all of us. Make no mistake, each action, each word spoken in anger, jealousy, against your fellow being, it will all be taken into account and only you will suffer, nobody else.

So let me hand you the key to the door that will open up the realm of God to you. Prayers, all prayer must come from the very foundation of yourself, from the very bowels of man, 'the being', not 'the self' of man.

There will be a fragrance attaching itself to you, in the knowing of God. Men will turn to you in sympathy for the gentleness that comes from you. For who can be wrathful when knowing of the gentle God within your heart. From there will be the flowing out into the great God-self, so immersed, so lost and yet so gloriously found. At long last you can say, 'I come to you as a little child, for all that is self has gone and is lost forever'.

It was thirty years before I lost my own self.

I must go now. We have a limited time each of us. Already I feel the backward pull of those in spirit saying to me, you must come back.

I speak slowly as I did upon the earth. For when one is being initiated into a new way of thought and if one who broaches the subject speaks fact, it is difficult when the mind is trying to grasp a new concept of life, to rush in a panic of words that tumble one after each other out of the speaker's lips. Is that not so?

Thank you.

Angela following the Sage

Hello, hello! I nearly went to sleep waiting!

He is a wonderful man and it would be impertinence for me to try and tell you how I see the picture from my point of view. He has to be of use. Not in the personal manner. These great masters are never personal, as we understand it. He comes with the view to uplift all mankind. Do you see?

He is not only going to speak through Tara, but all over the world where people sit in circles like this. Oh, yes, he will speak through different mediums, you will probably read about him because he was extremely well loved and revered when he was a teacher.

A 'master' they call him.

Now what he really means is this, it's all very wonderful for all to come as faithfully and lovingly as you have for the past years, but that, in the cosmic view, is not enough.

You see? You must go out, as I interpret it in my way of thought. He wants you to go out into yourselves to find the truth. You'll be going out into us!

You have been given many leads, so many pathways. Dispense with the crutch we could become for you. You have much good material on which to work. What you have received here and all of it, is truth. Every single word that has been spoken, all truth.

Now as he said, you don't start as an initiate. No. You have the knowledge. So many that start have none at all. If you look back, you will see the pieces falling into place and the pattern will assume a proper place in your daily lives.

Well, he came here now because as you know, Tara is not going to be with you much longer and we don't want to leave you just like that!

Tara was ill and we all knew that her days on earth were numbered. She knew it too. Deep in her soul, she knew that her mission on earth was over.

We will still be with you and as you know perfectly well, you can go into the silence if you want to. You don't have to go into the silence to contact us because the links are so strong that have been forged between us over the years.

There will be times when you will miss the personal contact through Tara, so we give you this 'jewel in the heart of the lotus', which is not only an eastern way of thought, it is prevalent in spirit because its meaning is very beautiful. As was explained to you, it was the heart of God. Not only for his sake, who was kind enough to leave his nirvana up there to come down to man and help man in the appalling days that lie ahead for us.

I am not putting my oar in here on my own, I am no savant, no sage, just Angela. But do that. Try and find a little peace, absolute relaxation. Just a few deep breaths, not like Tara does because that takes a while to learn how to do that and I don't want to burden you. Just take a few breaths and fold your hands on top of each other like a cup. The Holy Grail, if you like. Relax and don't force your mind to think, let God think for you. The God that is within. If you do that faithfully, but not with the thought that I must do this, no forcing, rather discard it than force it, just sit and think, 'I wish to do this, I desire to do it, it is good, it is sweet'. This will bring you peace.

After a while you find that you can't do without that daily conversation because you can speak then to God in your mind and it is infinitely sweet.

I have spoken to many people who have practised meditation and there wasn't one, there isn't one, who hasn't said to me, "I derived from it the greatest joy the human heart could ever conceive". Because you are only being honest with yourself and no longer through a glass, darkly. You will see yourself as you really are, not as you fancy yourself to be!

You will be in for a shock, I'm quite sure. But all that must drain away out of you so that the real true self can come through as sweet and clean and crystalline as it was when it came from God.

We come to help mankind to live a sweeter life, a kinder life. In yourselves there has developed more understanding, a more tolerant side. We can see it in you.

The sage will, I think, come once or twice more, but he has given you the foundation to work on and then the knowledge you will get from the awakened you will come from yourself. Do you see?

Charles: Angela, when you sit in meditation, is it enough just to sit and give thanks to God?

Angela: Well, what did the sage say? You can't go on saying thank you then it becomes static. Yes, that is stagnation! So each morning you can murmur a word or two of thanks, even if something not so good happened because there is a purpose to it all. Just sit quietly, called by some people, 'going into the silence'. It is in the working of your own soul, the mind of God working in you. It's nothing else but that. All, all, all is God.

Annabel: Can you give us a small example of what you just said?

Angela: What do you mean, what I've just said?

Annabel: A little example of meditation when you sit.

Angela: Well, it would take up too much time, but I will try and answer briefly. You know the sage told you to get away from self. Now by that 'self' he meant the physical you and the physical mind. The physical eye that sees the physical doesn't look beyond into the eternal and the spiritual, the things seen and unseen. I speak of the world in general. Few look beyond the seen into the unseen. Why? I did when I was on earth and my passage into God's realm was made so much easier for me.

I practised meditation too, but not quite on the eastern lines, more or less on my own. I knew many very clever people in my life on earth, I came into contact with great minds that thought very intellectually, so you could almost say I approached my meditation through an intellectual viewpoint. That is good, too …

Of course in the east, they approach it first and foremost through the spiritual. What they call the causal or the mental side. They approach it straight away by reaching out to contact God.

In India they are much more natural and normal in approaching God than we are. Yes, we do not speak about our love or our faith in God in our ordinary lives, we sort of hide it. Speaking for myself, I live for the Master Jesus because I see what he is. I see how great and wonderful a being he is, although I know the others are equally great and marvellous. But for me, he is the epitome of everything in a soul that is glorious and majestic and beautiful. You see?

In my days upon the earth, I could speak freely and openly without any embarrassment about loving Jesus Christ, but very few people do today. They shy away from the subject of saying, I believe in Jesus Christ. They might mumble it when they go to church on a Sunday, but how many come out with it as I do now? To me there is no other light as greatly scintillating as he because I fixed my mind on him as I would a great star. He was to me a great star. This great being who had come down to earth to help mankind.

Having used him as a focal point, he became alive to me and through contacting him I felt close to him. After years this was. I was then able to approach, the hitherto to me, unapproachable Godhead. He led me there by his way, which is light.

You know one of his names is Lana. Speak to Lana, 'Help me in this' and your call will be answered.

You have these great beings that come. They don't come just for their own edification, they come to edify those on earth. It is up to you to take their teachings right down into the innermost chambers of your soul and follow them. Live this way and be so much happier.

So, Annabel, do that if you wish. Call upon the Christ and say, 'I know you'. You have passed the first stage of the initiation already. You know, you know! Now use that knowledge as the cornerstone of your building that you are going to erect to God as your temple, each one of you.

Your body is the living temple. Look after it, do not despise it. Keep it healthy because it is the temple in which you dwell. Not for nothing is the earth called 'mother'. Mother earth lent you this body so that you could use it as a vehicle to express yourself in whatever form you chose to come, but you can still go outward into the cosmic world, upward into the great realms of spirit. You don't have to confine yourself into this little daily life. Look beyond it and you will find it ceases to hurt.

Nora: When you say upwards, I was visualising going inward to get upward to God.

Angela: It is a double entry and exit. You go in to get out, as this great man said. This is the key if you wish to use it to open the door.

Nora: Well, I try meditating every morning. I think I speak to God. I am used to saying the 'Our Father' prayer so I feel at home. Am I sort of going to the top step and missing the bottom step?

Angela: Not at all. You know the sage was telling me that some of the masters in India and Tibet and elsewhere, say that what they call 'self realisation' can come to one man almost overnight! If the first time he approaches that great awakening of self-realisation it comes to him like a lightening stroke, it is because in other lives he has been pursuing this pathway. So he came prepared to receive complete mastership. But others will sit in meditation, sometimes cutting themselves off from all contact with life outside while they are preparing themselves for admittance for full realisation.

It is really realising what you are and what God is. What life is all about.

It might take thirty years!

The great Buddha wandered for forty years until he found enlightenment. Have you thought what that word means? Enlightenment. He was called 'the enlightened one' but it took him forty years.

Joan: Good gracious.

Angela: Yes. Well … the Master Jesus, where do you think he was between the ages of twelve and thirty, when he started his ministry on the earth? The bible is very quiet about that but we know he went and practised his meditation and so he burst fully blossomed on that world. He knew his great power because with self-realisation, you are spirit. A spirit of God who gave you dominion over the whole earth, you can use those spiritual powers. His miracles were not supernatural, they were natural! We all have that power but we don't use it. "Seek and ye shall find, knock and it shall be opened unto you".[3] He was telling you of his own experiences then. Once you know the power, you are God within, 'I am that I am'.

When the 'I am' that appeared to Moses lit up the whole world so that he thought the bush was on fire, he asked who it was and the answer came, "I am". Well, you are that 'I am'. It comes from God incorporated into that word 'Om' which they send out on their breath.

Nora: The Aquarian Gospel, is that a teaching one can follow and believe?

Angela: You know, Nora, you have your reasoning power that comes from God and nobody else. In the words of the Master, 'Separate the wheat from the chaff'. Go through that in your mind. It is the way of light. In your enlightenment you will be able to say 'I know that that is the truth' and you will accept it so gladly. When you have been enlightened you will know what is the truth and you will grasp it and hold it fast against your heart.

When the Master Jesus instructed his disciples in meditation, he took them into the silence and taught them that when the self has gone, then comes the spirit. The Holy Ghost, the Holy Spirit, the Comforter.

It's all quite simple really, but when one approaches this subject of meditation it seems so vast, doesn't it? You feel like a child with your feet stuck on the earth! But for every cry that goes up from this planet, there are forty or fifty beings ready to help.

Rennie: I would like to ask you, Angela, what do you mean when you say, 'find the truth'. What is the truth? The truth of what?

Angela: The truth about your life on the earth plane.

Rennie: We know that we are on the earth plane.

Angela: Well, what do you know beyond that?

Rennie: May I ask another question? The word meditation as opposed to sincere prayer?

3. *Mathew 7 verse 7.*

Angela: Quite different.

Rennie: Why?

Angela: Because you don't go within yourself with prayer.

Rennie: But you should do.

Angela: You should do, but you don't!

Rennie: Oh, I think so.

Angela: Are you alluding to yourself?

Rennie: Yes. And my prayers have always been answered, so therefore I must have gone within myself.

Angela: Yes. Within yourself but that is not meditation.

Rennie: I don't see the …

Angela: Well, let me try and tell you. You send out prayer for help, don't you?

Rennie: Yes.

Angela: Yes. And what did the Sage just say to you? Do not light a candle asking for help. He said, "I thank you, God".

Rennie: Then the prayer is a misnomer?

Angela: Not at all. Why should it be?

Rennie: Then you don't ask for help.

Angela: But you *do* ask for help.

Rennie: You just said – Don't ask for help.

Angela: I said to you, 'Do you ask for help?' And you said, 'I do'. The sage said it was not necessary to ask.

Rennie: I don't see this point at all.

Angela: Do you pray every day for a quarter of an hour? Could you sustain that prayer?

Rennie: There are many things that I pray for, not only for myself but other people as well.

Angela: No, my love, don't beg my question. I'm asking you if you set out every day of your life, could you kneel down and give yourself up to sustained prayer?

Rennie: I give myself up to this every night and every morning.

Angela: What do you pray for?

Rennie: For every body. For my family, for myself, I ask God to help me to be good.

Angela: But you have lost the point, you see?

Rennie: I don't see. Because I mean to say it's been all right for all of my many years and prayers have been answered.

Angela: You are now being asked by this great man to pray for the world Rennie, not just the family circle.

Rennie: No, I'm not, Angela. I pray for the terrible state this world is in at the present time and all mankind. In my small way and in all due respect, I'm only an amateur. I don't know. I was brought up by religious people myself and it's always held me in good stead.

Angela: You don't have to do it if you don't want to. The sage doesn't say give up prayer. He has one salient prayer with which he starts, that one note of thankfulness to God.

Rennie: So you thank him when you pray.

Angela: You don't, you ask!

Rennie: You ask and you thank God.

Angela: You don't until you get it! But I'm not talking of you. Now listen to me, Rennie, wait until he comes again, I'm not putting you all into meditation. He doesn't force you into it, he doesn't even really ask you, he just suggests you go into meditation to contact God and help this whole planet.
   Do you pray for the coloured people in this country?

Rennie: Yes, I do Angela. I certainly do. And for the *Bantu*[4] and every mortal soul.

Angela: Well, you are just as good a man as I thought you were!

---

4. *Literally translated it means 'people' in Zulu and Xhosa. During the apartheid years it became a derogatory word for people of colour. Rennie might not have been aware of this at the time.*

[Everyone dissolved into laughter]

Angela: He wasn't alluding to you, my love, but how many people really do pray sincerely every day?

Rennie: Quite a lot of us.

Angela: As I said right at the beginning of the sittings that there would be the opening up of a way of thought.

Rennie: I admire him. I'm only talking from my own standpoint.

Angela: Rennie, just go your own way. You are probably contributing every bit as much to mankind and to God as anybody who sits meditating, in your own way. But this man is trying to help one to find oneself, as it is only in finding self that you find peace. For in finding self you forget self and remember only God. You heard him saying, "I hope I am not being to obtuse".

Rennie: He certainly said that.

Angela: Yes, he said "I hope I am not speaking too deeply". You must remember these were the lives on which he worked for all the years upon the earth and he will follow his way of thought to try and explain it.

Nora: Once I heard this described like ringing up on the telephone. You open and then you listen, then you put through your message and you know that you will get the answer if you listen.

Angela: Quite right. As the sage said, you must pray from your very bowels and from the foundations of your whole soul, you must pray. Effort must be put into it when you pray.

Rennie: Or meditate.

Angela: Or meditate. Meditation is not prayer per se. I suppose it looks a tremendous subject to concentrate on but you only have the words of Jesus who said, "Unless I come as a little child I cannot enter the Kingdom of Heaven".[5] You see, so many of his teachings are bound up with eastern thought. Not from the west. No.

Rennie: A child, must one teach a child to pray or meditate?

Angela: Whichever your way or inclination falls, Rennie. In the east they start meditating at the age of four. I would think you would call that a child. A child comes with much knowledge in its soul of the realms it has left behind.

5. *Matthew 18 verse 3.*

Rennie: So I understand.

Angela: Yes. It's only the passing of the years and the conflicts in life that will make these memories die away and fade into the limbo almost.

Rennie: And those men who have meditated, do they do anything else in their lives?

Angela: Yes. They pass their teaching to a great concourse of people of influence all over the world.

Rennie: They have no other vocation?

Angela: No. What better vocation is there than giving yourself to God in that manner?

Rennie: I appreciate that, but what about the everyday man who has a job to do each day? Can you ally that in a smaller way?

Angela: In a smaller way, yes. Live by that Godly manner and love, for love begets love and hate begets anger. Therefore you have Jesus saying, 'Turn the other cheek'[6]. He didn't mean turn the cheek to get slapped a second time! He meant walk away, turn the cheek and walk away. If you start an argument, anger feeds on anger and cruel things are said. There is much more to life. These great beings want the best for you, but as the great guide Budrain says, "We do not come cap in hand, we come to give, to teach, to help".

We are not divine beings, we are human beings who, by virtue of having passed on some time ago and learnt a little more, we try and come and help those we love. But if you don't want to accept us, we just pass on. The proof of the pudding is in the eating, you know, we have proved for ourselves that man is a triune – being body, spirit and soul.

We have proved to ourselves that our bodies die and our spirits, our souls go on to God. We know it. We know it. We only come down to tell you the same things. If you like it, take it to heart, if you don't like it, discard it. You have all eternity to learn.

Annabel: Very briefly, I just wondered whether it would explain it in a nutshell like this – when you pray you *send out*, when you meditate, you *receive in*. Does that put it correctly?

Angela: Quite right. Yes, the great ray of light is coming into you, you are opening up. Now when you are sending out in prayer you are not, in the manner of speaking of the sage, receiving light, you have to wait to see if your prayer is answered. But if you go into the silence and offer yourself up to God – not 'grant me this' and 'grant me that' – you just say, 'I give myself up to God'. Simple as that!

6. *Paraphrase to Matthew 5 verse 39 and Luke 6 verse 29.*

Then there will be no anger on the earth, no more stamping on other people's ideals but a leading up to a friendship, a brotherhood of man, because every living being on the earth, who ever was and ever will be, comes from the one source, which is God. And by the immutable Law must return to him. Must return.

Therefore, it is utterly wrong and depressing to one's own sense of nearness of God, to speak of black blood, coloured blood or any other. It is all the vital source that comes from God. It is your vitality. Draw any blood from any living being and you will find it is the same colour red. So you break the Law of the Almighty God who gave you 'being' on this earth by defaming the creation, by speaking of the agony of man.

I am quite exhausted!

The sage spoke beautifully, didn't he? Anyway, I think that the time has run out.

So ponder his words and remember he stressed, "Every man has his free will, do as you will".

Lana and Tara in transcendental meditation
"I was taken by Lana to Vietnam"

Tara recorded this piece into a tape recorder. It would have occurred around the time of the war in Vietnam.

I was taken by Lana to Vietnam. Straight to a battlefield. Alighted on a winding track through the jungle, we could see wheel tracks gouged out in the muddy surface. I saw that the tracks were half filled with muddy water. The sky was overcast and seemed to indicate more rain. I noticed my feet seemed to feel the gritty muddy surface and I smelled gun smoke and saw black clouds of smoke rolling above the treetops. I could smell death ... awful.

I turned to Lana but he had gone. In his space stood a tall hooded figure, the hood well over the face, which I never saw. Quite impossible to describe the majesty of this tall being.

Before I could ask where Lana was, he took me by the elbow and gently propelled me along the muddy winding track between the trees. I remember the desolation, the loneliness, the death and the muffled sound of guns.

Almost at once, we came to a bend in the road and there on the edge, close to a puddle of water, lay a naked baby of about ten or eleven months. It was on its back, with hands flung up and spread out. My heart lurched sickeningly and I knew the baby was on the point of dying, all alone and in such heartbreaking nakedness. I felt tears running out of my eyes.

We stopped next to the tiny baby and then the 'being' with me bent over it. If I could express ... I can't ... the compassion of him and the love, which seemed to stream out of him over the baby. He spoke for the first time, with ineffable tenderness, in that desolation of death, loneliness and the lowering sky. These words were said, "Come to me my beloved child ... come to me."

He held his hands above the child and to my utter amazement, I saw the spirit form of the baby rise slowly from the body. The face was peaceful, so different from the open-mouthed glazed eyes of the body on the ground. He gently received the little form in his cradled hands and passed it gently to another helper (unseen by me) and it vanished from my sight.

Again he took my elbow and further on we came across an old man walking ahead of us. His stick-like legs were bowed under a huge burden across his back and he supported himself on a staff as he struggled on. He wore a battered conical straw hat and was clothed in rags.

As we approached him he staggered and fell backwards, his load slightly cushioning his fall. Never can I describe the hopeless look of that tired old body as it lay there, its incredible wrinkled old face and toothless mouth sagging open, frothing at the corners. He shuddered once and twice, then lay still.

At once we were next to him and again the 'being' next to me bent over in that indescribably compassionate manner. He spread his hands out over the old man and waited a while, then I heard that same unforgettable voice saying, "Come to me my beloved child ... come to me."

A short time passed, how long it is impossible to say. Then I watched as the spirit form detached itself and floated upwards to be received by those ministering hands. The wondrous relief that was expressed by the newly released spirit, the thankfulness that it was all over … the intolerable burden of poverty, old age and weariness.

The same procedure followed, he was handed on to another unseen helper.

Suddenly I was alone. Having witnessed the amazing miracle of old and young being released into a life that would be so much happier than the one left behind. It all seemed so gloriously simple. The transition, alike for the baby and the old man. The loving waiting hands and the passing into a spirit world.

I burst into tears of joy and wonderment and was at once back in my body in my room.

Chapter 24: Evolving in Spirit

An astronomer
"Man's radiant body"

Sometimes when the spirits wanted to have an urgent meeting they would contact Tara psychically, as was the case with this piece.

If I had not already arrived to speak of the radiant body today, the whole affair would have been called off in a manner that you would not be able to comprehend. It is already imprinted on the etheric that the words must be given forth. So here I am giving forth, or holding forth, you can take your choice.

Angela has introduced me as an astrologer. She has made a small mistake. Not then did I work with magic, I was an astronomer. In comparison with your great astronomers of today, I was a child playing with pebbles on the seashore. But my study was the stars and I contributed a little bit to man's knowledge of circumnavigating the globe by the stars.

Now don't ferret out who I was, my dear brother Charles, what little hair you have will fall out in that effort!

[Charles laughs]

In one life, I delved into the arcane. I did not advance very far. Who can? It can only be a mastermind in charge of all who can solve what He himself brought into being.

You must allow me to explain to you that when I say, He I am merely using the habitual expression or pronoun. Take your choice in describing the cosmic mind, the great eternal, the allness.

Forget a personal God for your own happiness. Do not think of the deity as someone in your own image. You will then flounder like little children in the dark. Take the wider view. Take the truth and only that.

I will make it as simple and short as possible.

There never was a time when man was not. That is a big pill for you to swallow, my dear lady and I cannot gild it. If you choke on the dose I give you, I take full blame but I must give what I know to be the absolute, irrefutable truth.

I myself, despite my past lives, am a child with my feet in the shallows of a shoreless sea of wisdom and knowledge, endeavouring to give to you the knowledge I have gleaned through arduous investigations and arduous experience. Therefore, accept me for what I am.

There will be seen on the horizon that another horizon beckons and so on for all eternity. So never was there a time when man was not and man is spirit. So you say God was always, therefore man is always.

Now, you know light was brought to your planet from an older brother of your system. That light that came was the radiant body of man's spiritual body. It had not yet attained what you call heaven. It had its purpose to fulfil on that planet.

You were told quite correctly there was no physical death.[7] Man did not have to die because when he had completed his cycle of experience and life on that planet, in his upward climb towards the stars and towards God, he was released then and simply mounted, if you like, into a higher sphere of experience and knowledge gained.

Well, a band of martyrs, as I call them, came down and they, in the course of the passing of time, took upon themselves their earth body. Oh, that was a long process, but it was finished in the end. The story was concluded and the radiant body, and it is indeed a radiant body, was imprisoned in a body of flesh.

Now there are very few, if any, who would call flesh radiant. You might apply that word to somebody who is radiantly beautiful but then you are only looking at the face. You are misusing the name radiant, for her beauty will fade, but never the radiance of the body, the radiant body, for it comes from God.

Now the radiant body encased in flesh has to work its way back out of the mire. This is not derogatory of the flesh for the only thing that it can do is to die out of this wilful body it took upon itself. It must die to escape, therefore do not mourn for one who dies.

We know this might sound callous when a loved one goes, but try and think of it as one of your band, the brotherhood of man, escaping from a long purgatory of pain and grief and frustration. That is part of the average man or woman on the earth, because he left his God and dimmed his radiance.

I shall continue to the time when he leaves his body. He escapes and I will take the average citizen who goes immediately on his flight. (We will not talk about the dwarfed and benighted souls and unhappy fallen ones who have to grope amongst the mists and the dark passages to find their way back to the light.)

He may pat himself on his back and think that he has led an orderly life on earth but it is when he comes into the first band of light, I talk now of the etheric band, the sphere, the plane, call it what you will, that he arrives in a place approximating

7. See Chloris page 140.

earth.

This place is suitable for his breathing apparatus, his seeing and his feeling apparatus. For the time that he chooses to remain there, shall we say, like an orderly decent citizen, he thinks all will be beautiful. It is only when he is brought face to face with himself and he looks back and he sees that no matter how decent and orderly he has been, he has not added one iota of light to his radiant body. He has gone his own humdrum way on the planet and has never lifted his soul to God. Never stretched out, reached out for the shining truth that would bring to the inner body within the flesh, the power to shine again and be beautiful.

Were you to take a highly spiritual being on the earth plane, let's call him John, we place him into a chamber into which we could flash what we call the 'violet light', you would see his body gleaming in its pristine glory through his solid body of flesh.

Were we to then take another person, who had never reached out to God and put him in the same chamber, you would merely see a dark blur. His body would be so obscured it would be unable to give forth its light.

Now we shall follow our friend we called John who is on the etheric plane.

How long his journey will be is entirely up to him. He may wonder why he does not see any angelic beings. Certainly there will be many people who have been there perhaps two or three hundred years and are beginning to learn of the lure of the horizons. They may begin to glow a little more brightly than our John.

Inevitably will come the yearning to know more and he will cry out, 'I must go on!' This is the first nibble at the wondrous bait, the exquisite beauty and the fields of learning that lie open to him. Instantly there is a guide from the plane above, a shining being, but a dull lamp compared with the great beacons of light further up.

He takes our John under his wing and instructs him in the spiritual side.

The great halls of learning

He will take him to the great halls of learning and he opens up the intellect for it must go hand in hand in spirit. You cannot be all spiritual and intellectually a bonehead. You cannot be all intellect and little spirit. There must be always one balancing the other in the reach for perfection.

Well, let us imagine that John stays there for another hundred years. Time is nothing, it is a tick of the clock. A thousand earth years and you are not conscious of it. During this time, the great guide, now joined by two or three other dedicated people (I will not call them artists for they have at least escaped the flesh by now) come there to uplift people like John, so that once more the radiant body can be regained to be man at his fullest! Man as near the Godhead as the radiant body can ever be, until it leaves your solar system and goes out into the vast unknown.

The second death

Well, the time comes when he has graduated from this plane of light, and then comes, what is rather peculiarly called by vast groups of people, 'the second death' which John has to undergo.

Now would you mind if I crossed my arms since this was my habitual way of standing when I delivered my lectures and once again there is the desire to follow the old habit. You will forgive me. I hope I can succeed! Yes, the old comfortable position is there. I used to call this my prop. I prop myself on my arms!

[Tara changed positions and sat with her arms crossed.]

Now he is not escaping from the physical body and I have not been able to fathom why it is called, death. He is merely going onwards but there is no physical darkness to escape from. He would not need to escape from this band of light where he had been so happy. Ah, but that is the radiant body, the memory he passes into. Shall I call it a sleep? I beg your pardon, a state of sleep, that from which he emerges having cast away the astral body, which has been concealing his light so well.

You must not forget the earth body is the cover for the astral body, which is the cover or protection for the spirit body.

Now he has cast aside, not escaped from, cast aside his astral body and he emerges very much brighter in his radiant body.

But, oh, oh, oh, our pilgrim has a long, long way to journey. So don't think, when I say that he is brighter that he has accomplished a miracle! No, the way back to God is in slow, but sure stages.

Were he suddenly to find himself a great blazing light, he would be dismayed and immediately seek re-entry, never denied to him, into the last plane of being. Do you see? Can you understand it? His mind would not be able to cope with the situation if he saw that his radiant body was fully restored. You see, it goes by degrees.

Am I making myself clear? It is appallingly difficult for me to talk through a female mind and a female body.

The fourth plane

Well, now he is up in another plane. We call it now the fourth plane, where greater opportunities are open to John.

Yes, he begins his training for the time when, like a tadpole, he will swim out into space, galactic space … there to find the task allotted to him by the great mind in charge of the entire universe. Worlds and worlds and worlds.

I could go on saying that word for a year of your time and I still would not encompass the number of worlds and universes John is going to enter when he leaves your little solar system. My little solar system too. For I have not yet got myself beyond the fifth plane, you see.

Let me go on slowly. He now begins his training and what a vast and intensive training this is, for here the soul is going to hold in the palm of his hand for aeons to come (that word that is much favoured here and it expresses time sufficiently well for me to use it) the destiny of evolving planets and evolving solar systems.

We want to perfect worlds like your planet earth. A tremendous statement to make, is it not? For you will want to say, 'all is well with the best possible world'. But in the eternal mind, it is evolving still into perfection and the time taken has been too long. Therefore, from errors, John will learn a quicker and more perfect way to evolve from the little planet that he will be given, or the big planet, depending on his progression.

This is very vast, I know, for you to digest, but I came to tell you about this. Now that I hear my voice again going out upon the ether, I am just wondering if I am not making it too highbrow or too lowbrow. I have the thoughts that I have to control. Thoughts that I have to herd like sheep into my own mind and I have to work with the subconscious mind of this lady and it is all very confusing. So you must forgive me if I am not putting it across concisely and with clarity!

Well, he will finish his period there of intense training but also intensive pleasure and intense joy. You name it. It is what John will experience as his soul begins its high function and his body glows with radiance.

By this time his spiritual eye will become fully accustomed to the glowing bodies about him. A great many of them from the earth plane have long since passed into the fifth plane but have elected, from their vast learning and experience, to tutor the younger souls coming up the ladder.

Now comes again the time when John could so easily think, 'I must return to earth. Take on another heavy body. I cannot keep all this beauty to myself, all this knowledge and love. I must share it with the people of the earth,' whose existence by now he has almost forgotten.

He may find he has to decide whether to go back or follow the great urge to continue upwards. Realising too, that he would never be able to return to tell them. So he goes to his masters and asks them, "What can I do? What must I do? Tell me!"

He has arrived at the crossroads, which face nearly everyone when they arrive at that stage of progression.

The guides, the brothers, you should see them! They, by this time have their minds and their thoughts so completely under control that they know how to hold back their own mind and influence nobody else.

The inevitable reply to his question is, "Go into retreat and face yourself and see what you feel about it."

So John does that for a period of time. Delving deep now, very deep into the soul, showing its God divinity more strongly now than ever.

In some cases, even those from so lofty and divine a sphere as the fourth plane, will feel the need to return to the earth for a while. Our John decides to go on to the causal plane or the mental plane. Losing now, all the earth vibrations. His sojourn on this most beautiful of all planes can extend to three thousand earth years or longer.

The fifth plane – Causal or mental plane

Now the soul comes into its own. John is beginning to get a pulse beat of the great heart of the universe. He can go down to the other planes for a short while if he so desires. However, the time comes when he goes into the Christ sphere. He is now wholly ... spirit ... light. Wholly God-like.

To see these great beings, you would have to be on that plane yourself or they would be totally invisible to the vibrations on the plane below.

I do not want you to think of these people as formless beings. No. How could we live in a formless universe? Such tarradiddle for people to think we become formless in spirit. No, there is a definite form. There they are in the position to influence your whole solar system. For in each planet there is a Christ sphere and they communicate with each other by mind. They do not visit and consult with each other.

When there is a desperate call from John's little earth (and when, my friends, does it not come, hourly or by the minute) he can descend by stages in exactly the same way in which he came up, by dimming his light, his radiant body, but not in the same period of time, because the call is urgent. Until at last, he can for a limited time, come down and speak through a body of a man or woman, like this woman Tara.

Then he must go back to the more comfortable vibrations commensurate to his own. Or, he can reincarnate on earth and became say a Jesus, a Gautama Buddha, a Mohamed, a Zoroaster or a Krishna.

The sixth and seventh planes

He then goes back and remains in the Christ sphere until the time comes when he takes the plunge. This is a plunge. He detaches himself completely and utterly for all time from that which is his familiar place and goes out into the universe in his full radiance, not even discernible to those left behind. He becomes God, the super mind, the super soul, he can no longer return to function on his earth plane or on the others right up to the Christ sphere. He has closed the door on his long climb and has achieved his glory.

Now he goes on to join the great race of elder brothers.

I will try and make you understand about those who control the universe under the name God. Never ever is the mind closed to the call for help from one of the babes of the universe. The call has gone forth from your planet. So rest assured that the elder brothers will not neglect your call and that you are looked after.

As soon as the mind and the spirit respond to the call of the soul, the memory, which is part of the spark in the spirit body, the sooner you will know God.

I hope you have enjoyed my little talk.

Angela's comments after the radiant body

He came from the first stages of the fifth plane.

When we announced that he was coming, he had only arrived half way, that is why the meeting had to be held today. For as when a car reaches the top of the hill and the car is going full speed, well ...

He was geared in his vibration surrounding the soul. It's not one little spirit body, not *one* vibration, don't ever think that, it's a group of vibrations, each one geared to come down. So he had to use Tara before he could go back again. Now he goes back.

I hope you are grateful to him for coming, for when the call is of purity as it is from our little circle here, it goes out to the whole world so that the reply comes from the higher ones.

The purer the call, the purer the mind that sends out the desire for knowledge. Instantly, like seeking like, you get the great ones. These vibrations that you send, asking for guidance, they will pass right through the vibrations until they reach a vibration which is commensurate with their own purity of thought.

You see, he is able to use Tara because her body is etherealised. But when you get these mediums on the earth plane, very worthy souls, whose bodies are dense and their minds are dense, if a visitor from one of the higher planes wishes to tell the earth something, you will get confusion because the clear mind cannot get what he wants to say through a mind whose radiant body can never be bright.

Now this man was of the greatest nobility in every incarnation. I went to look! I went to peep and read the records in our great halls. Oh, we run them in a very orderly manner. I glanced back at the last four lives and they have been impeccable.

He has been spoken of here already. 'Star of the morning' call it that.

Angela
"We do not call it death, we call it rebirth"

Man cannot die. His body dies, as have the many other bodies he has used since he first appeared on the earth planet. You cannot destroy the spirit, the soul.

You see, the spirit body – exactly as the physical body was developed by man to protect the spiritual body in which he first came and functioned on the earth plane in spirit form – is the guardian of the soul body. Man has many bodies, many layers that he has to strip off when he leaves the earth to come to us. We do not call it death, we call it rebirth.

He has to strip off his etheric body, his astral body, his emotional body until finally there emerges the perfect flame of the spirit body. Which, in our places of dwelling, our lands, our homes, our terrains, are as solid to us as you are to each other.

We are not wisps or wraiths drifting aimlessly about, we are colonies of extremely hard working but extremely happy people with our own homes, our hobbies, our gardens, our universities and libraries. As I have told you before, to turn to one page of the book of life and learn all there is to learn could take a thousand years. I have told you that.

So you see, that is the great plan of the Creator, that man never reaches saturation point. If he did become satiated, he would stagnate and there is no place for that in the great universe, not your little solar system.

You'll have to discard the insularity of that thought when you come over to spirit. You'll have to throw it into the trash can that is a minute spot in the great ocean of space! One should never allow the void to frighten one, for what appears to the physical eye as a void is but an illusion. It is filled with great, vibrant, wonderful pulsating worlds, all of them shaped the same way as your earth, globular, because that is the way it came.

That is the 'plan'. All of your cells are circular. That which is visible to us or to you, everything is circular in spirit, too.

You will be enraptured when you come over to us by the colours, the beauty. You know that God is good, God is purity, God is beauty and perpetual youth, perpetual strength and perpetual love.

Now what better ingredients could you have for a cake of life, or a slice of the cake, than a life that is free of travail, free of jealousy and covetousness. For what you want, you can have.

You have to work for it, you can't just stretch out your hand and take it, or you too would become static. You will find you are veritable infants even after many incarnations until you attach yourself to your over soul and find out who you have been in the past. You'll arrive strangers in a strange land. How thrilling and exciting and wonderful it is.

Here and there you will see, glimpse, a familiar place or haunt, or a familiar face, for you will have been permitted to come here in your sleep state. You see, your physical body is attached by the lifeline so you can't go too far. It can stretch a great distance, but if you go too far, it breaks off and then you are what is known as dead, physically dead. Your body, the life force is withdrawn and it goes back into the spirit body which then finds its place. Well, it's all so orderly.

Lana ending the sittings
"I come to close the ceremony"

Angela: Remember, that Jesus, Buddha, Krishna and Mohammed are working with great souls to unite all people. One day they will be united as one. One pathway to the one Father, God.

Lana: We are sad indeed that this has come to an end. Of course, we knew, even before they commenced that the sittings would be limited and we availed ourselves of every opportunity to hold one because they were so important. Even to the extent of bringing Tara when she was not feeling so well, or Ella when she was not feeling so well. All duly noted. Duly recorded in the great book of blessing!

I speak now in as near an imitation of the earth voice as is possible for me.

I come …

Charles Orfang: It's Lana!

Lana: Oh thank you my friend. Bless you. You knew me, you knew me. I come to close the ceremony. To close what has been a centre of great joy and help and, oh, such love.

It is deeply regrettable that we could not continue for at least another six months, but when we saw a short while ago what was expected to happen, we had to speed things regarding Tara and the closing of the circles.

You have done inestimable good. You have sent out boundless love. Call upon me day or night and know the response will be instantaneous.

Remember too, in view of the onerous work, that when I place myself at the head of my celestial armies, I still will find time to hold you fast in the shelter of my heart. For I am truly your 'good shepherd' and I truly, will lead you by 'the still waters' and make you to 'lie down in green pastures'.

So let the light of your countenance shine like a great jewel in the darkness of the world, so that when you pass by even those who know you not, they will feel that surely God was with me for a moment.

Chapter 25: The End of an Era

Nanette
Tara believed that her work should be shared

Lana spoke at the last recorded session at Narrow Waters in Bishop's Court. Shortly afterwards, my husband's tour of duty ended and we left for England, but the group continued at Tara's home for a further eight years. I returned often to visit my family and the group, until eventually residing permanently in Cape Town.

The time came when Tara no longer had the power to sustain trance conditions due to her failing health and energies. Many a time in the last years, she would place my hands on her stomach to relieve the discomfort. Her illness did not seem ominous at the time, but later proved to be cancer. Those of us who lived in her vicinity went to visit her every day. Joan often bringing home-made treats and Nora always ready to lend a hand in various comforting ways. There was always much laughter and chatter even in her pain. Often she would relate to us the people that she had conversed with during her meditations. These astral journeys were duly recorded with myself as the scribe!

I am certain Tara knew when she would die.

In the summer of 1979, Annabel and I visited one evening, followed by her daughter, Billie and her sister, Paddy. An unusual quietness descended on the room and with great serenity, Tara gave us her blessing. During the night she passed peacefully into spirit.

There was a quiet family funeral to mark her passing.

Recalling our happy friendship with Tara in Cape Town, the conversations that we had with amazing people who spoke through her, it all seemed so very natural and tangible, the marvel of it was sometimes almost taken for granted. Tara had often spoken to me of her wish that the messages and spiritual portraits should be shared with everyone. There was a bond of trust between us that they did not come only for us, and would one day be put out into the world.

As a youth, I recall using terms such as reincarnation, vibrations, spirits and karma and was considered a wee bit eccentric! But now such words are commonplace allowing people to explore these concepts and widen their understanding. Finding their way into film scripts, television programmes and new-age groups. The new generation children will surely bring new wisdom and greater compassion to this planet.

Since the time of these sessions, many of the group have moved on but continue to embrace spiritual paths in their own private ways.

Several of our group have begun new lives in spirit themselves. My parents, my first husband, Ronny Maxwell, Nora, Charles Orfang, Charles Adams and his mother, whom I never met. All of them have made contact through psychic mediums to show their love and continued interest in us. Confirming once again that we can share with all those who grieve, the comforting knowledge that partings are only for a little while.

I once read a marvellous phrase, 'God is my adventure' and I think for sixty years ever since, this has been my journey. As the much loved and revered teacher, *Bhagavan Sri Sathya Sai Baba*, reminds us so beautifully:

"There is only one caste
The caste of humanity.
There is only one Law
The Law of work and duty.
There is only one language
The language of heart.
There is only one religion
The religion of love."

I share the dream for a peaceful world, with one pathway to God.

The Essenes

Gospel of the Essenes by Edmond Bordeaux Szekely. C.N. Daniel Co. Lltd. England.
Essene Communions with the infinite:
   The Essene Science of Life.
   The Essenes by Josephus and his Contemporaries
The Essene Gospel of Peace – Books 1– 4
          Book One – *The Essene Gospel of Peace.*
          Book Two – *The Unknown Books of the Essenes.*
          Book Three – *Lost Souls of the Essene Brotherhood.*
          Book Four – *The Teachings of the Elect.*
All above books written by Edmond Bordeaux Szekely. Published by International
Biogenic Society.

The Albergensis

Albergensis Crusade by J Sumttion.
The Medieval World by Friederich Heer, Europe 1100–1350 N.A.L.
Albergensis Crusade by J Sumttion.
The Massacre of Montselur by Alden Bourg.
A Foot in Both Worlds by A Guirdham.

Jesus' Secret Life in India

History of India by J H Wheeler, University Press – Cambridge.
Jesus Lived in India (His unknown life before and after the crucifixion) by Holger Kersten,
Element Books Ltd, Dorset, England.
Ancient India by Prof Rapson.
The Lost Tribes by George Moore.
Jesus in Heaven on Earth by Al-Haj Khwaja – Nazir Ahmad.
The Unknown Life of Jesus Christ by Heyina Loranger.
Jesus in India (His escape and journey to India) by Hazrat Mirza Ghuam-Ahmad of
Qadian.
Kashmir by Sir Francis Younghusband (British Ambassador to the court of the
Maharaja of Kashmir).
The Apocryphal Actae Thomas: the Acts of Thomas.
General History of the Mogal Empire by the Jesuit Father Catrou.
Jesus died in Kashmir by Andreas Faber-Kaiser. Abacus edition 1978 History /
Religion. Published by Sphere Books Ltd. London.
The Mystical Life of Jesus by H. Spenser Lewis, PhD F.R.C.

Jesus and Joseph in England

Glastonbury Legends by R F Treharne.
Glastonbury Legends by J Robinson Armitage.

Ancient Egypt
Egypt of the Pharoahs by Sir Alan Gardiner.
Ancient Egyptian Religion by J. Cerny.

Atlantis
Atlantis by Edgar Cayce.
Atlantis the Anteduluvian World (Illustrated) by Ignatius Donnelly.
(The revised edition published by Gramcy Publishers, New York)

Books about the Afterlife/Spirit
Autobiography of a Yogi by Yogananda.
Man of Miracles by *Satya Saibaba.*
From the Turret by Richelieu.
Psychic Research Behind the Iron Curtain.
On the Edge of the Etheric by Arthur Findley (Pchychic Press Ltd.)
The Unfolding Universe by Arthur Findley.
Testimony of Light by Helen Greaves (Spearman Ltd.)
Invisible Influence by Dr Alexander Cannon.
Science of Hypnotism by Dr Alexander Cannon.
Powers that Be by Dr Alexander Cannon.
Shadow of Destiny by Dr Alexander Cannon.
The power of Karma by Dr Alexander Cannon.

History
The Age of Reason by Harold Niefson. (Panther History)
Medieval History by RH Davies.

Reference Books
The *Concise Oxford Dictionary* – 9th Edition.
The *Word Power Dictionary* 1996.
The *Chambers Biographical Dictionary* – 5th Edition.
The *Columbia Encyclopedia* – 5th Edition.

Nanette Adams

At the age of ten Nanette's early introduction into spirit communication was through the general interest of both her parents in the paranormal and her father's natural mediumship. As a teenager she was allowed to observe psychic phenomena of various descriptions in Britain and other ancient countries, particularly in India, the land of her birth. By the age of twenty, being satiated by phenomena, she needed different food for thought and became a theosophist and eagerly studied its tenets; the belief in the brotherhood of man; comparative religions and reincarnation.

These ancient teachings became like a golden thread that weaved through all the joys and vicissitudes of her life, which was as varied as her Scottish background. This included many great travellers, medical doctors, musicians, engineers and artists. With both parents having careers in British theatre, she too, followed their footsteps and became an actress, starting in repertory at the Lyceum in Edinburgh. Shakespeare was a special love.

Their home was an eighty foot boat moored at Tag's Island on the River Thames near Hampton Court. They lived aboard for nearly four years after losing everything they possessed in the London blitz. There were many in their position who felt that it was not the right time to furnish yet another home on land and boats don't require much in this way. Nanette enjoyed "messing around in boats" and found it a very friendly way of life.

When World War II ended, Nanette and her father joined the Combined Services Entertainment Unit (CSE) and the family was posted to Port Said in Egypt. They organised shows for the allied troops in the Middle East and she was lucky enough to be in a play that was sent to Palestine, then still untouched by the modern world. Two years later, she followed the sun to a new life in Cape Town, in radio and South African theatre, where she married an advertising film executive, Ronny Maxwell, and lived in a dream house. She had two talented children who grew up to become third generation thespians! They too, learned as she did, to understand the wider view concerning spirit.

Many years later, Nanette married the British Consul, Charles Adams.

After years of travelling abroad, Nanette finally returned to South Africa where she currently resides.